BY STEVEN RINELLA

THE COMPLETE GUIDE TO HUNTING, BUTCHERING, AND COOKING WILD GAME

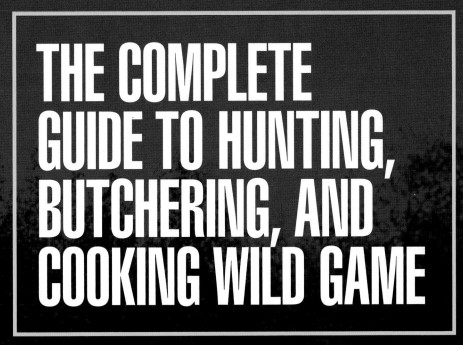

THE COMPLETE GUIDE TO HUNTING, BUTCHERING, AND COOKING WILD GAME

VOLUME 1: BIG GAME

STEVEN RINELLA

 SPIEGEL & GRAU   NEW YORK

A Spiegel & Grau Trade Paperback Original

Copyright © 2015 by Steven Rinella and Zero Point Zero Production, Inc.

Published in the United States by Spiegel & Grau, an imprint of Random House,
a division of Penguin Random House LLC, New York.

SPIEGEL & GRAU and the HOUSE colophon are registered trademarks of Penguin Random House LLC.

Library of Congress Cataloging-in-Publication Data
Rinella, Steven.
The complete guide to hunting, butchering, and cooking big game / Steven Rinella.
volumes cm
"A Spiegel & Grau trade paperback original."
Includes index.
Contents: volume 1. Big game
ISBN 978-0-8129-9406-3—ISBN 978-0-8129-9407-0 (ebook)
1. Hunting—United States—Equipment and supplies.   2. Hunting—United States.
3. Big game hunting—United States.   4. Game and game-birds, Dressing of.
5. Cooking (Game)   I. Title.
SK273.R56 2014
799.2—dc23
2014013333

Printed in the United States of America on acid-free paper

www.spiegelandgrau.com

9 8 7 6 5

Book design by Christopher M. Zucker

This book is dedicated to all of those hunters, and there are many, who fight for the conservation of wild animals and wild places.

CONTENTS

INTRODUCTION

T he Complete Guide to Hunting, Butchering, and Cooking Wild Game is meant for any hunter or soon-to-be hunter who is looking to forge a more intimate and adventurous relationship with the natural world through the process of acquiring and preparing wild meat. In today's world, in which we measure the difficulty of a task by counting how many clicks on a computer it requires, engaging in such a time-consuming and ancient activity is certain to strike some folks as being backward or even downright barbaric. Why would anyone choose to kill an animal when you could just buy it, already killed and packaged, from a grocery store? But since you've already made it past the cover of this book, I'll assume that you're free of the misguided notion that we can escape the ugly realities of our existence by turning our heads in another direction. Instead, you've probably already achieved what I consider to be a completely honest and enlightened perspective on meat: if you're gonna eat it, shoot it.

If so, you've come to the right place. Within these pages you will find a trove of hunting know-how that will educate, inspire, challenge, and even dare you to become a better hunter. This information is divided into five primary sections. Section 1 offers a comprehensive overview of equipment and apparel for the versatile big game hunter. Section 2 covers everything from identifying potential hunting areas and preseason scouting to specific hunting strategies and thoughts on proper shot placement. Section 3 gives insightful and relevant biological descriptions of fourteen North American big game species, along with detailed information about hunting each animal across a variety of landscapes using both firearms and archery equipment. Skinning and butchering big game, both in the field and at home, are covered in Section 4. Finally, Section 5 introduces you to a couple dozen big game recipes that capture the nose-to-tail spirit of the hunter who appreciates adventurous foods as well as classic wild game preparations.

The organization of this guidebook will help you navigate it without much hassle, but to get the full value you need to study the whole thing. Hunting knowledge is not always easily compartmentalized, and many crucial pieces of information will be encountered in places where you might not expect to find them. For instance, you might be disappointed that some specialized piece of hunting equipment is missing from Section 1: Gear. If so, you'll probably find that it's covered in detail in a later section where its purpose and use are explained in a better context. You will also find that many pages offer tips and tricks about specific aspects of hunting that can easily be borrowed and applied to another area. For instance, the buffalo passage in the Species section includes advice on handling large animal carcasses that might be relevant to a hunter of moose, elk, or bear. Likewise, there is information about wind direction and thermals in the Tactics and Strategies section that

would be important for a hunter whose personal interests might lead him directly and exclusively to the whitetail deer chapter. So make sure to take your time with this book; every page has something valuable to offer.

Some readers might wonder why so many pages in this book address subjects that might feel somewhat arcane. This is not a mistake or oversight; rather, it was my intention in crafting this book to give thorough treatment to those vitally important pieces of knowledge and opinion that have been missing from the greater body of instructional hunting material. But this book also addresses basic information, placing it in its proper, comprehensive setting, so that you'll come away with a better working knowledge of its meaning and importance.

I'd like to clarify that this book is not the product of a single author. While I've been hunting my entire life and have pursued and eaten many dozens of species across several continents over the span of thirty-plus years, I still don't know half of what I hope to learn about hunting by the time I die. I suppose it's unorthodox for a guidebook to include an admission of the author's limitations, but I want to be extremely clear about the fact that this book is the result of not only my own experiences but also the experiences of dozens of other hunters I've known through correspondence and personal interaction through the course of my life. You will meet many of these hunters by name within the pages of this book; others, you will meet only through the transmission of ideas that they've shared with me.

Finally, I should point out an unfortunate truth: no amount of words, photos, and illustrations can teach you how to become an effective and versatile big game hunter. As with every worthwhile pursuit, expertise as a hunter can only be achieved through real-world field experience. In fact, you'll need some amount of field experience in order to fully understand the resource that you're holding in your hands. Once you've gone into the woods and made a few mistakes, you'll return to this book with an enhanced appreciation for what it can do for you. Then, the next time you go into the woods, you'll be all the more deadly.

But don't make the mistake of thinking that hunting success is measured only in meat, hides, and horns. The benefits of the hunting lifestyle are much too complex and beautiful to be so narrowly defined. A true hunter recognizes that experiences are the ultimate hunting trophies; he takes pride in walking the ancient and noble pathway that was laid down by his forebearers; and even when he returns from a hunt cold, wet, and empty-handed, he does so with a full heart.

THE COMPLETE GUIDE TO HUNTING, BUTCHERING, AND COOKING WILD GAME

SECTION 1

GEAR

Gear is like booze. As you get older, you realize that quality is more important than quantity. I'd rather own one reliable, straight-shooting rifle than an arsenal of cheaply built guns. But a painful fact about high-quality hunting gear is that it tends to come at a high price. When you're considering your gear budget, it's important to step back and take a wide-angle look at your spending habits. I was once hunting elk in Montana when a guy pulled up to a trailhead in a shiny new $40,000 pickup in order to study a distant mountainside through a pair of $20 binoculars that would do little more than impair his natural vision. Of course, there's no way of knowing if that guy actually owned that truck, but you get my point: a serious hunter would have sacrificed the status car in order to afford a set of hard-core binoculars that could tear the mountainside to shreds.

That said, it's certainly true that gear does not make the man (or woman). If you don't have the discipline and drive to become a good hunter, no amount of high-dollar equipment is going to make up for that. But my theory on gear is that the hunter should be the weakest link on a hunt. I expect my gear to outperform me, so I have only myself to blame for my hunting failures. If I bail on a hunt early, it better be because I couldn't hack it, not because the sole of my boot peeled off or my rifle scope started making rattling noises after getting dinged on a rock.

When it comes to selecting hunting gear, I've found that personal recommendations from experienced hunters are far more valuable than any insights you might glean from reading descriptions about a product in catalogs. When a hunter tells me that he's been using a piece of gear for three seasons and has logged dozens of days in the field with it, I start to listen. In fact, most of the gear that you'll encounter in the following pages came to my attention in just that way: as recommendations from folks I trust. I then put the items through my own series of tests. The opinions that you'll be reading in this section come from decades of serious hunting, years that have been punctuated with many moments of great triumph—and many more moments of misery and frustration.

THE RIFLE

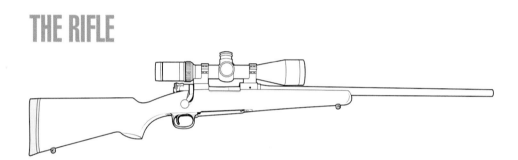

Don't be intimidated by anyone's experience, including mine. There have been and still are a few good writers with vast experience in the firearms field. There are also plenty of plain old fools writing about guns and shooting and plenty of younger fools, as well. Gun writers, especially those who have to produce a regular column, love controversy. That column becomes a beast that must be fed every month, so the columnist is always hungry for something to write about and controversial ideas generate reader interest and response. Perhaps it is understandable if they sometimes go overboard. Just don't go overboard with them.

—CHUCK HAWKS

Hunters take the subject of rifles so seriously that arguments about calibers can literally end friendships. People are willing to go to blows in defense of their favorite gun's reputation, and I suppose it's for good reason. Your rifle is one of your most important pieces of big game hunting gear. If you lack faith in your rifle's ability to shoot straight and true, it becomes hard to perform all the necessary work that goes into a successful hunt. While there are many styles of rifles on the market, including a rapidly increasing array of AR-format

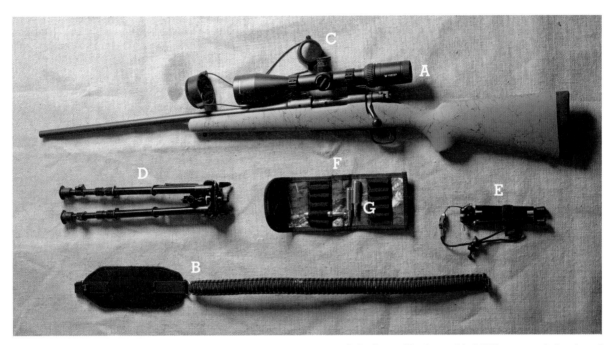

This is a superb all-purpose big game hunting rifle. It's a Weaver custom rifle built on a Winchester Model 70 action and chambered in .270 WSM.

ADDITIONAL COMPONENTS:

A: Vortex HS LR 4–16×50 rifle scope (see "Choosing a Rifle Scope" on page 8). **B:** Handmade sling with neoprene shoulder pad and braided paracord strap. An average hunting rifle weighs approximately 9 pounds. Carrying that amount of weight all day can be annoying and exhausting. Do not skimp on slings. The cheap ones fall apart. This type of sling gives you emergency access to over 100 feet of 550-pound test cord. **C:** Vortex scope cover. An essential but often overlooked piece of gear. Scopes are expensive, and you don't want the lens to get scratched. Plus it's difficult or even impossible to aim when your lens is obscured by snow or excessive moisture. Neoprene "scope socks" are another good bet because they're inexpensive, are long-lasting, and provide a bit of protection against impacts to the scope body. Rubber "bikini-style" scope covers are great at keeping out moisture but tend to fall apart. Same with flip-cap scope covers. If you're sitting in a blind, these are fine, but hard-core backpack hunters often find that flip caps are easy to demolish. **D:** Heavy-duty Harris bipod. Perfect for long-range shooting from a prone position, but hardly essential in areas where long-range shots are not likely. This type of bipod can be folded forward, so it's out of the way when not in use. The downside is that it is a tad heavy and tends to get hung up when you're hiking through thick brush. **E:** Snipe-pod bipod. A lightweight detachable bipod that can be worn on your belt and quickly attached to the rifle before shooting. Downside is that it's not as stable as the Harris bipod. **F:** Folding ammo wallet. Keeps ammo organized and prevents the annoying rattle of loose cartridges in your pack or pocket. **G:** .270 WSM cartridges loaded with Barnes 129-grain LRX bullet.

NOT SHOWN, BUT STILL NECESSARY:

Muzzle cover: A rifle muzzle that is plugged with mud or snow is very dangerous, as the barrel could potentially rupture when you fire it. Cover your muzzle to prevent the intrusion of mud, snow, dust, or moisture into your barrel by using a piece of tape or, better, a heavy-duty small-size latex finger cot. Using a muzzle cover has been proven not to affect point of impact, as the gases moving ahead of the bullet blow off whatever cover is on your muzzle.

Gun sock: The Solo Hunter Gun Cover. Keeps your firearm protected from snow and mud while in the field and still allows for immediate access.

Travel case: A good travel case protects from dings and scratches that might be incurred during travel. Besides cosmetics, this ensures that your scope doesn't get knocked out of zero. Hard-sided cases, such as those from Pelican or Boyt, come with a protective foam insert that can be cut to accommodate your specific firearm. Airlines require such hard-sided cases and mandate that the case be locked.

weapons, the tried-and-true bolt-action rifle is still the standard go-to weapon for serious big game hunters. Properly tuned and outfitted, and with a disciplined and well-practiced shooter, a high-caliber bolt-action rifle topped with a variable-power scope can meet 95 percent of the big game hunting challenges that this continent has to offer. For maximum versatility and ease of finding ammunition, stick to common, time-proven big game calibers such as .270, 7 mm Rem Mag, .30-06, .308 Winchester, and .300 Win Mag (plus the short magnum versions of these same calibers).

These might seem a tad heavy for a North Carolina whitetail deer hunter, and some might be a tad light for an Alaska hunter who's itching to tangle with a coastal brown bear. But they are all superb guns for a generalist hunter who wants to be ready for anything without having to burn up his paychecks on an arsenal of weapons. After all, the North Carolina hunter might eventually run into one of that state's 500-pound black bears, and the Alaska hunter might get tired of trimming around fist-sized exit holes blown through his game meat by a mule-kicking elephant gun.

An assortment of big game hunting calibers. This selection is meant to serve as a general guideline for cartridge selection and will certainly not conform to the opinion of every expert. The light-side cartridges might be suitable for hunters who are strictly after whitetails. Middle-ground selections are good for generalist big game hunters. Heavy-side calibers are suitable for hunters with an appetite for really big game such as moose and grizzly.

AS PICTURED LEFT TO RIGHT:
The light side: .243 Winchester, .25-06 Remington. **The middle ground:** .270 Winchester, .308 Winchester, .30-06 Springfield, 7 mm Remington Magnum, .300 Winchester Magnum. **The heavy side:** .338 Winchester Magnum, .338 Remington Ultra magnum, .375 Holland & Holland magnum.

CARTRIDGE NOMENCLATURE

Cartridge nomenclature is some very tricky business and manages to baffle the majority of firearm owners. The American system is particularly vexing, though the majority of American cartridges do provide the caliber (the diameter of the rifle bore) first in the name. For example, a .30-06 is a .30-caliber round, meaning that the bore diameter is 0.3 inch. The remainder of a cartridge's name isn't so formulaic. In the case of the .30-06, for example, the name comes from the fact that it's a .30-caliber round that was first designed in 1906. The .300 Savage is another .30-caliber round, though "Savage" comes from the name of a rifle manufacturer. Adding to the confusion is the fact that so-called .30-caliber rounds actually measure 0.308 inch. Thus, a cartridge called the .308 Winchester is in fact the same caliber as a .30-06; like the .300 Savage, it carries the name of a rifle manufacturer.

Things are a little clearer with cartridges that were developed in the days of black powder, as the name carries the caliber and the original grain weight of the charge. A designation such as .45-70 would have indicated a .45-caliber bullet with a 70-grain charge of black powder. Sometimes you'll see an additional number on the end. For instance, a .45-70-405 would be a .45-caliber bullet weighing 405 grains and charged by 70 grains of black powder.

The European stuff is simple, which should be expected from a continent that embraces the metric system. A 7.62×39 is a 7.62 mm bullet with a case length of 39 mm. Across a wide variety of European cartridges, there is little or no variation in their system.

And then there are the "wildcat" cartridges, which find their genesis as experimental cartridges designed by tinkerers and ammunition manufacturers who blended available cartridges to make Franken-ammo. For instance, the 7 mm-08 comes from loading a 7 mm bullet into a .308 Winchester casing in a process known as "necking down" (reducing the neck of the case to accommodate a smaller bullet). Some of these wildcat experiments were successful in filling gaps between standard cartridges and are now produced by major ammunition companies.

CHOOSING A RIFLE SCOPE

The one thing to remember when considering the price and quality of a rifle scope (yes, there is a direct correlation) is this: better scopes buy you time. That is, a high-quality scope will function better in low light conditions than a cheaply built scope, allowing you to shoot effectively earlier in the morning and later in the evening. Staring through scopes while you're inside your favorite big-box sporting goods store will rarely show you the differences that you're paying for.

For a great do-it-all rifle scope, get a good-quality 3–9×40 mm scope with adjustable parallax from a reputable manufacturer such as Leupold, Nikon, or Vortex. Plan on paying at least $350. Never buy a scope that doesn't carry a warranty. There are many alternatives to the 3–9×40. For close-range shooting, say out to 200 yards, a 2–8×30 mm is all the scope you need. The smaller magnification allows for a huge field of view, making getting on target a breeze. When hunting in the West or anywhere else that requires longer-range shooting, a scope with a 50 mm objective and a top end magnification of 16× or even 24× will help pull those critters in close for exact bullet placement. The 50 mm objective lens also draws in more light, buying you time during low light conditions.

COMMON RETICLE TYPES

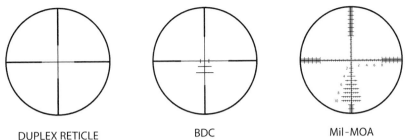

DUPLEX RETICLE   BDC   Mil-MOA

Duplex reticle: The most common reticle, suitable for virtually all hunting applications. It is clean and simple. BDC (bullet drop compensation) reticle: Each hash mark below the crosshair equates to a predetermined holdover for a specific cartridge and bullet at a certain distance. Mil or MOA reticle: Used for long-range shooting applications where precise holds for windage and elevation are crucial.

WHAT THE HELL IS PARALLAX?

Imagine an old-fashioned speedometer in a car, where the needle sits in front of a fixed circular face printed with numbers. Now picture that speedometer when viewed from the passenger's seat. From there, it's hard to get an accurate reading on the needle's position. While this isn't a perfect analogy, it helps explain a vexing problem that many people have with rifle scopes. Scopes with a fixed focus (that is, any scope without an adjustable objective or an adjustable parallax knob) are prefocused at the factory. Typically, fixed-focus scopes meant for center-fire cartridges are focused at 100 yards; fixed-focus scopes meant for air rifles or rim-fire cartridges are focused at 50 yards. This doesn't mean that these scopes are out of focus when looking at objects at other distances—your eye does the work of correcting the focus. It could mean, however, that you're looking at the crosshairs from the passenger seat. In other words, it might seem that the crosshairs drift around on the target with slight movements of your head. To correct this, make sure that your fixed-focus scope roughly corresponds with the distances that you're most likely to be shooting at. With a .22, that's probably going to be a 50-yard focus, and with center-fires, 100 yards. But if you're going to get serious about shooting accurately at longer ranges, you'll want a scope with parallax adjustment.

MUZZLE LOADERS

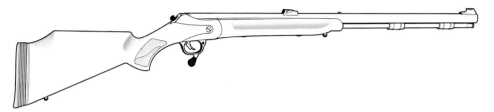

If you love to hunt, get a muzzle loader. Many states offer extended muzzle loader hunting seasons that provide low-competition opportunities to enjoy the woods without the crowds. But before you start comparing performance and price of new muzzle loaders, check your state's regulations on hunting with one. The legal requirements of each state are different, and some are so stringent that they might choose your new muzzle loader for you. Some

This hunter, Dan Doty, killed a great-tasting whitetail buck with his muzzle loader on public land in North Dakota.

states have special flintlock-only seasons, which restrict hunters to the most primitive of muzzle loaders. Other states don't allow scopes on muzzle loaders, while some have minimum caliber requirements. There are even restrictions on which type of bullets and powder you can use. It's essential that you carefully study your state's hunting regulations before diving into the world of black powder.

When you do begin shopping for a muzzle loader, be prepared to spend $300–$500 for a quality midpriced rifle. Since you will end up cleaning a muzzle loader often—in fact, some guys clean after every shot—buy one with a removable breech plug. Black powder is still used by many hunters, but black-powder substitutes such as Hodgdon Triple Seven make for easier cleaning. The 28-inch barrels are fairly common—these are long, heavy, and quite accurate. The .50-caliber is the most common muzzle loading rifle, and it is accepted in all states. Bullets and accessories for .50-caliber rifles are widely available.

Because some states allow scoped muzzle loaders and others do not, it's handy to have a rifle with a rail that can accept both open sights and a scope. A muzzle loader does not need too powerful a scope, due to the limited shooting range. (A 150-yard shot is considered long by many muzzle loader hunters.) A fixed 4× scope works great. Many of the current muzzle loaders on the market come with open sights fitted with fiber-optic wires that increase your ability to shoot in low light conditions. These are great at closer ranges, but they can begin to obscure your image of the target when shooting past 100 yards. For those who want to shoot at longer distances in areas that prohibit the use of scopes on muzzle loaders, try using a peep sight. Many hunters consider these to be an ideal compromise between open sights and a scope.

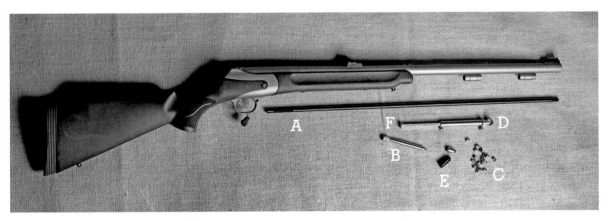

An all-purpose big game muzzle loader, the .50-caliber T/C Triumph with some essential accessories.
A: Ramrod. **B:** Cleaning jag. **C:** Winchester primers. **D:** Hodgdon propellant. **E:** 250-grain T/C Shock Wave .50-caliber sabots. **F:** Powder measurer.

COMMON TYPES OF OPEN SIGHTS

PARTRIDGE PEEP V-NOTCH BEAD

A few common styles of open sights. When shooting with open sights, it's best to visually set the target (in this case, a gray dot) on top of the sight post.

SLUG GUNS

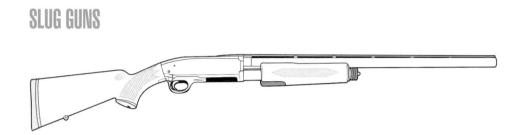

The most common reason to use a slug gun (a shotgun equipped for shooting solid projectiles) is because you are hunting in an area where high-powered rifles are not allowed. Shotgun-only zones are found all across the Midwest, including states such as Michigan, Indiana, Iowa, Illinois, and many others. Many folks speculate as to why these areas are deemed shotgun only, but safety is the common explanation given by government agencies. Shotgun slugs don't fly as far as bullets fired from high-powered rifles and are therefore safer for use in areas with high densities of people, cars, and buildings.

There are a few different ways to get set up with a good slug gun. The easiest and cheapest version of a slug gun is to take your existing "do-all" smoothbore shotgun (like a Browning BPS or Remington 870) and screw in an open choke that's wide enough to accommodate a slug. There are several downfalls to this method, the greatest being accuracy. Shotguns firing slugs from standard open chokes have an effective range of only about 50 yards. Adding a scope to such a rig will do little to help, as the effective range of the firearm hardly warrants a magnified image. Open sights work just fine.

A better option is to buy a rifled slug barrel for your "do-all" shotgun. When deer season rolls around, just throw on your rifled slug barrel and you're in business. *Rifling* is a term for the spiraled grooves cut into the bore of a rifle barrel. These grooves cause the bullet to

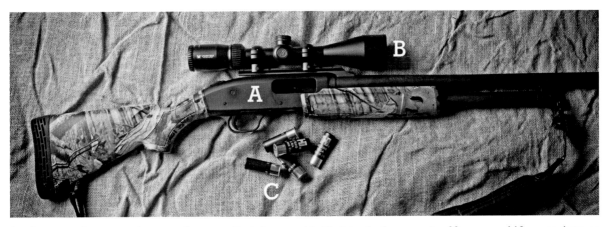

An all-purpose slug gun can be as simple or complicated as you wish. Most standard pump-action 20-gauge and 12-gauge shotguns including the Remington 870 and the Browning BPS can be converted into an effective slug gun with only minimal expense. Pictured here: **A:** Mossberg FLEX 12-gauge shotgun chambered for 2¾-inch and 3-inch shells and fitted with a rifled barrel. **B:** Vortex Crossfire II. **C:** Hornady SST 300-grain saboted slugs.

spin, which stabilizes the bullet and gives it both better accuracy and longer range.

The above method works quite well, but there's still a drawback. On convertible shotgun systems, the interface between the action and the barrel is not as tight and therefore accuracy can suffer. That—plus a few other reasons—is why many serious slug gun hunters choose the pricier yet more effective option of buying a shotgun manufactured specifically for shooting slugs. This gun will come with a rifled barrel tapped for scope mounts and a crisp-feeling trigger. Many such ready-made slug guns perform more like a rifle than a shotgun, with effective ranges in excess of 200 yards. (Hint: The Savage model 220F is an exceptional slug gun. It retails for around $500.)

A NOTE ON SLUGS

Use conventional slugs when shooting a smoothbore shotgun. These slugs are cut with spiraled grooves, which mimics the effect that a rifled barrel has on a bullet. Rifled slug barrels are meant to be used with "saboted" slugs—basically a slug that's wrapped in a plastic cup that makes contact with the rifled barrel and throws the slug into a spin. The sabot also helps to seal the barrel, minimizing the loss of barrel pressure, which might otherwise escape around the edges of the slug. This increases muzzle velocity and range.

A stable rest and proper form are important when zeroing your rifle.

GETTING ZEROED

There are many ways to sight in, or "zero," a scoped firearm. Here's the most basic:

1. Fire three shots at the bull's-eye of a large paper target. (A piece of duct tape measuring 1 inch by 1 inch stuck to a large sheet of white paper makes a usable target.)

2. Mentally average the center of your three shots, and measure the horizontal and vertical distances that separate that point from the bull's-eye. Remove the turret caps on your scope and make the necessary adjustments. Moving the turret in the "up" direction, as depicted on the turret, moves the bullet's point of impact in the corresponding direction. Same with the left or right arrows on the turret that control horizontal movement. (Most scopes are adjustable in increments

of ¼ MOA. See page 16 for an explanation of MOA.)

3. Shoot another three shots. You should notice that the center of your three-shot group has moved toward the bull's-eye—and, hopefully, has hit it. If the bullet's point of impact hasn't moved according to your adjustments, repeat step 2. If you still have problems, you're likely dealing with an accuracy issue that could come from user error, equipment malfunction, or both. If the center of the group has gotten closer but is still not on the bull's-eye, measure the new distances and adjust the scope turrets again. Repeat as necessary.

4. Once your bullet is hitting dead center, fire a series of three rounds to make sure that the gun is grouping well. At 100 yards, you should at least be able to fit three rounds inside a

3-inch circle when shooting from a proper rest. If you plan on shooting out to 300 yards, you should at least be able to group three rounds inside a 2-inch circle at that 100-yard distance. If you're going to shoot past 300 yards . . . well, you'd better shoot enough to know what you're doing.

If you're having trouble getting this kind of accuracy out of your firearm, it's time to revisit both the shooter and the rifle. Start by asking yourself the following questions. If the answer to any of these is yes, try to remedy the situation. If you still can't figure out the problem, it might be time for a visit to the gunsmith or a marksmanship clinic.

1. Are you flinching in anticipation of the firearm's noise and kick? (A flinching shooter will never shoot consistently.)
2. Is your form improper? Are you jerking the trigger rather than squeezing it? Are you putting unnecessary torque on the grip or your forearm in an effort to hold the rifle on target?

Are you altering the position of your cheek on the stock from one shot to the next?
3. Is your shooting rest unstable? Does the rifle feel wobbly while you're aiming?

Once you've ruled out shooter error, ask a few questions about your rifle.

1. Is the bore of your rifle excessively dirty? (A dirty barrel causes erratic shooting. See "Routine Rifle Cleaning" on page 17.)
2. Is your scope damaged? Is there a loose reticle? Is the scope's body badly dinged or dented? Did it take a serious blow?
3. Is your scope poorly mounted? Are the rings or mounts loose or improperly installed? Do you feel any wiggle or turning when you put pressure on the scope or try to spin it?
4. Does the rifle shoot equally poorly with different ammo? (Often a rifle might shoot horribly with one type of ammo and then shoot much better with another type. Experiment with different brands of ammo as well as different bullet weights.)

THE ONE SHOT ZEROING TECHNIQUE

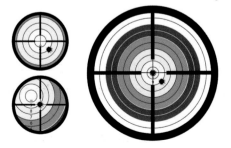

Another zeroing method is known as the one-shot technique. Here's how it works.
A: Top left: Fire a shot at the target. In this illustration, the bullet has hit low and right. **B:** Lower left: Position the rifle so that it's aiming at the bull's-eye, and then hold it securely while a friend adjusts the turrets so that the crosshairs move over to the bullet hole. At this point the rifle should be sighted in. **C:** Right: Shoot a second round to make sure you're zeroed.

UNDERSTANDING MOA

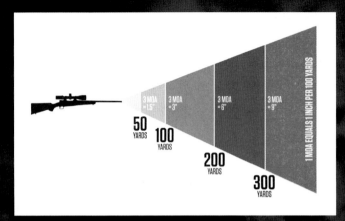

MOA, or minute of angle, is a term often used in discussions about shooting and rifle accuracy. To understand MOA, imagine a 360-degree circle with a dot in the center. Now take one of those degrees and divide it into 60 parts, so you've got 1/60th of a degree. That's one MOA, also known as an arc minute. At a distance of 100 yards from the center of the circle, an MOA will subtend approximately 1 inch. At 200 yards, it will subtend 2 inches. At 400 yards, 4 inches. If your rifle is off by 4 inches, or four MOA, at 100 yards, it'll be off by 16 inches at 400 yards. When you see a rifle that's advertised as shooting sub-MOA groups, the seller is claiming that the rifle is accurate enough to fire several rounds into a circle smaller than 1 inch at a distance of 100 yards. If you're capable of shooting sub-MOA groups— a goal that every hunter should strive for—you and your rifle are both doing something right.

TIPS FOR GUN CARE IN THE FIELD

1. Keep an oiled lint-free cloth in your gun case at all times and use it to wipe down your weapon after it has been exposed to moisture.

2. Never leave a wet firearm inside a case any longer than an hour or two.

3. Carry lens wipes and a lens brush for cleaning your rifle scope.

4. Always bring along a BoreSnake or similar product to clear any mud or snow that might get packed into the bore (which shouldn't happen, since you're supposed to keep your muzzle capped with tape or latex finger cots).

ROUTINE RIFLE CLEANING

After every trip to the rifle range or your hunting grounds, you should thoroughly dry your firearm and wipe down the bolt as well as the exterior metal portions with a lightly oiled rag. As far as cleaning the bore (the inside of the barrel) of your rifle, there are many different opinions on how often it should be done. However, the basic answer is that you should clean your firearm before the bore becomes so fouled that it has an adverse affect on accuracy. Dirty barrels are probably the number one reason that otherwise good shooting rifles turn bad. Depending on your gun, that could happen every ten shots or every hundred shots. If you want to be on the safe side, clean your rifle after every trip to the range, assuming that you shoot a couple dozen rounds. Some shooters claim that overcleaning/brushing can harm the bore of a rifle, though no part of the cleaning procedure exerts as much force on the barrel as a bullet that's traveling close to 3,000 feet per second. It is not necessary to clean your firearm after a hunting trip unless you did a lot of shooting or you got debris such as sand or mud (or worse, saltwater) down into the barrel.

Getting a barrel truly clean requires a few tools and products that are widely available, plus a lot of work.

- Gun cradle or vise. By securing the rifle in a vise or cradle, you have a solid work surface and two free hands. (Most cradles also offer a convenient place to store your cleaners and tools.)
- Coated cleaning rod. Coated cleaning rods have a protective surface that will not damage the bore of the rifle. The best cleaning rods also have free-spinning handles that allow the rod to turn with the barrel's rifling.
- Nylon or brass brush for loosening powder residue.
- Brass jag, used for holding and pushing cleaning patches through the barrel. Parker Hale–style jags are an excellent choice.
- Cleaning patches made from 100 percent cotton or cotton blend material.
- Bore guide. Essential for keeping the rod true and preventing cleaning products from dripping back into the action.
- A powder solvent such as Hoppe's No. 9.
- Copper solvent such as Sweet's 7.62.
- Lightweight gun oil such as Rem Oil.

Here's the procedure:

1. Using a cleaning rod and jag, run a few solvent-soaked patches through the bore. Follow these with a dry patch, then alternate between solvent-soaked patches and dry patches until the patches are coming out clean. This may take twenty or more repetitions on a really dirty rifle. **2.** On approximately every fifth cleaning, follow step 1 by using a copper solvent. Copper solvents should be used in strict accordance with the manufacturer's specifications.

3. Run a patch that's been lightly oiled with Rem Oil through the barrel. For long-term storage, the barrel is now done. If you're heading out to the range or on a hunt, run one last dry patch through the bore to remove excess oil. **4.** Spray the bolt with the powder solvent and wipe with a paper towel or rag. A toothbrush works great to loosen any caked-on crud.

ARCHERY EQUIPMENT

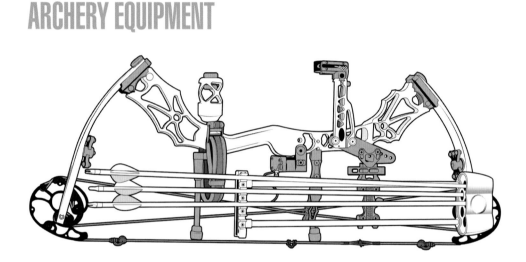

The closest thing that the hunting world has to a rivalry is the ever-present tension between die-hard firearm hunters and archery purists. The firearm folks will say that archery purists are sanctimonious blowhards who injure a lot of animals that are never recovered, while archery purists say that firearm hunters are afraid of a challenge and use technology as a crutch to make up for their lack of skill. Obviously, each extreme is way off. Just as pants and shorts both have their place in a person's wardrobe, firearms and bows each have their own particular role in the arsenal of a versatile hunter who's looking to maximize the amount of wild meat on his dinner table.

From a purely pragmatic standpoint, two of the most compelling reasons to take up bowhunting are to enjoy extended hunting seasons and to gain access to weapons-restricted hunting areas. In Michigan, for instance, you can typically hunt whitetails with a bow for a total of ten weeks per year. On the same patch of ground, you're allowed to hunt whitetails for only two weeks with a rifle or shotgun and another ten days with a muzzle loader. (If you choose, you can use your bow during the rifle and muzzle loader seasons as well.) As for weapons-restricted areas, a bow gives you access to land that might otherwise be completely closed to gun hunters. Such areas are particularly prevalent in suburban landscapes, where an errant slug or bullet might easily take out someone's window, or worse. Think of such places as the greater Washington, D.C., area and much of New York's Long Island.

But even rural and predominantly wilderness states have weapons-restricted hunting areas. In Missoula, Montana, there's an archery-only whitetail hunt where you can kill up to five does during a season that lasts over four months. These deer permits are not available to rifle hunters, and much of the land is outright closed to firearm hunting because of proximity to residential areas. Oddly enough, there's an archery-only duck hunt on a coastal refuge in the vicinity of Anchorage, Alaska. That alone should you make you a believer in archery equipment!

Archery equipment and rifles both have their places in the arsenal of a well-rounded hunter.

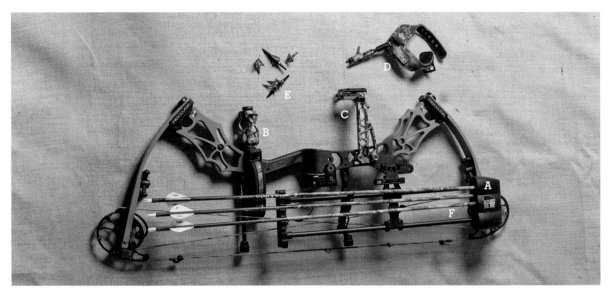

An Athens Recluse set at a draw weight of 70 pounds. This rig is a versatile hunting tool that can handle a wide variety of species under ever-shifting sets of circumstances—be it belly-crawling into a herd of javelina, sitting in a makeshift ground blind for elk, or perched high in a tree for whitetail deer.

ADDITIONAL COMPONENTS:

A: Quiver. Find one that holds your arrows securely and doesn't add too much bulk to your bow. For tree stand hunting, some folks prefer a quick-detach model, so only the bow and nocked arrow are in hand while waiting on ambush. This particular quiver is made by Tight Spot. It's an excellent choice. **B:** Stabilizer. As the name implies, this device stabilizes the bow as you shoot. Also absorbs some of the shock from firing the bow. This model is made by Action Archery. **C:** Sights. Go with simple, tough setups that can withstand being banged and dropped. Don't overcrowd the sight with too many pins, which can impair your sight picture. This sight, the Schaffer Opposition, is an excellent choice. **D:** Mechanical release. A mechanical release helps the shooter achieve consistent string releases, which lead to greater accuracy and tighter groups. Scott manufactures excellent mechanical releases. **E:** 100-grain, 4-blade Bloodshot broadheads; 100-grain, 3-blade Thunderhead broadheads (see page 23). **F:** Maxima Carbon Express Hunter arrows.

JANIS PUTELIS, A MONTANA-BASED HUNTER, WEIGHS IN ON ARCHERY PREPARATION

"As I prepare for archery hunting season, I'll shoot more practice arrows in a month than I'll shoot bullets in two years of practicing with my big game rifle. Mastery of archery requires constant repetition and focus, so that the process of shooting becomes involuntary—something that you do without even thinking about it.

"First, my gear must be honed. When getting my

gear in order, I rely heavily on the expertise of my favorite archery pro shops. They help me with making necessary tweaks to my rig, and with replacing any worn or damaged parts such as D-loops, peep sights, or frayed strings. If I must change or tweak my bow or accessories, I do so with ample time left to become intimate with the change. A lot of effort goes into getting a bow shot on a big game animal. In Colorado, a good hunter might put in nine or ten days just to earn a shot at a bull elk. That means that if you only hunt for a week every season, you might only get a shot every two years. I would hate to squander that rare opportunity due to lack of familiarity with my gear.

"Since arrow loss and breakage are unavoidable, I'll start with two dozen fresh arrows in the spring so that I don't need to add new arrows to my quiver as the months of practice wear on. (It makes no sense to practice with one bow and arrow setup all summer and then switch components just before the season.) I mark each arrow with a number or letter to identify it. As I practice throughout the spring and summer, I notice that some of the arrows fly more consistently than others. This is caused by many factors, including arrow straightness, fletching alignment, field point or broadhead alignment, and weight differences. (It's worth trying to re-fletch a faulty arrow or realign the point, but if the arrow is still bad after those tweaks are made, I set it aside for use on stumps or small game.) It does not pay to even practice with such an arrow, because it will degrade your confidence and disrupt your focus.

"Eventually, I separate my two dozen arrows into three groups: (1) arrows with poor consistency, (2) arrows with average consistency, and (3) arrows with exceptional consistency. This third group of arrows is the one that I'll be using for big game hunting. I like to have made this selection at least sixty days prior to the season, at which point I'm ready to start practicing with broadheads. This is important because broadheads tend to fly differently than practice tips or field points. Adjustments to the arrows themselves (fletching and insert alignment) might be made, or more commonly the sight pins will be moved to accommodate any point-of-impact changes. The use of mechanical broadheads can alleviate some of these adjustments, as the slimmer profile of the mechanicals lets them fly like a field point. However, I personally prefer the fixed-blade broadheads for big game hunting because I believe that simpler is better when it comes to arrows and heads.

"Over the spring and early summer, I'll be building my muscles and perfecting my form by shooting many arrows a day. This might be as many as six to ten arrows between each visit to the target to retrieve my shots. (I don't like shooting many more than that at a time, as I lose a little bit of focus once I've passed this threshold.) But as the summer progresses and I start practicing with broadheads, I begin shooting only two or three arrows at a time. This lets me concentrate on those few shots only, maintaining concentrated focus for each one. Then, as I walk to my target to retrieve the arrows, I clear my mind and reset it for another three-shot round.

"When there's only a month left before the season starts, I treat each practice shot as if it were the one that's going to kill an animal. I visualize the animal standing there. I visualize picking a spot and drawing my bow while the animal's head is facing away. I hold my bow at full draw and visualize the animal walking out from behind a tree. And finally, I visualize the arrow hitting its mark and penetrating deep into the vitals. The more I visualize all this during practice, the calmer I'll be when the moment arrives.

"I don't take 80-yard shots at animals, but I practice at that range often. The amount of mental focus and muscle control required to tightly group arrows—even in a 24-inch circle!—at 80 yards is tremendous. If I can easily connect on a target at 80 yards, I'll have a much easier time connecting on an animal at 30 yards.

"I practice at quartering-away angles, shooting through tight lanes, from sitting and kneeling positions, and any other scenario that I can think of to prepare me for a difficult shot in the field. I'll do fifty jumping jacks prior to shooting an arrow to simulate the physical excitement that comes from a real hunt, or I'll run a 100-yard dash to mimic a rapid heart rate from ascending a hill. I'll hold my bow at full draw for two minutes prior to releasing the arrow, a very common scenario encountered on a hunt. I invite friends over for a casual competition. We pin small balloons to the target and see who can pop the most, each taking one shot per turn. By throwing a dollar into the pot, we all focus a little more. It's a great way to add a little pressure.

"A mistake I've often made is ceasing to practice once the hunting season starts. I'm a well-oiled machine on day one of the season, but I'll get rusty if I fail to practice for a week. I make sure to keep an archery target in the truck, and I'll always fire a few arrows before entering the woods for a hunt. Besides keeping me in shooting form, this also lets me test my shooting with all my hunting gear on. This ensures that a face mask or a range finder holster won't interfere with my shot."

ARROW AND BROADHEAD BASICS

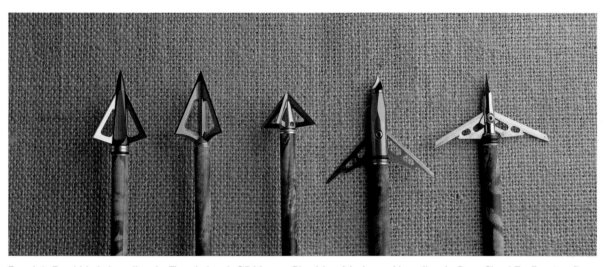

From left: Fixed-blade broadheads: Thunderhead, G5 Montec, Bloodshot. Mechanical broadheads: Rage Chisel Tip Extreme, Rage Hypodermic.

There are two main types of broadheads used by hunters: fixed-blade and mechanical. Fixed-blade broadheads have blades that are rigid and immovable; the blades of a mechanical broadhead open upon impact with the target. Mechanical heads generally fly better because they are more streamlined but have less penetration because some of the energy is lost in opening the blades. Mechanical blades are also prone to a variety of failures. If you abide by the "Keep it simple, stupid" mantra, the fixed-blade broadhead is for you—particularly when hunting large, hard-to-penetrate animals such as elk.

When it comes to opinions about arrows, there are two crowds: those who like arrows that are heavy and slow, and those who like arrows that are light and fast. Both arrows and broadheads are weighed in grains, an ancient measurement that came from the average mass of a cereal seed. There are 437.5 grains in one ounce. Most arrows are labeled with a "grains per inch" (gpi) value. Manufacturers typically build arrows weighing from 7 gpi to 12 gpi. Broadheads come as light as 85 grains and as heavy as 300 grains or more. The light and fast crowd will shoot an arrow averaging about 350 grains total weight. The lighter arrow increases speed and makes a flatter trajectory. This could be advantageous when shooting a whitetail deer, a species known for "jumping the string," or reacting so swiftly to the sound of the bow that they've already moved by the time the arrow reaches them. But when hunting larger and slower game, consider a heavier arrow weighing around 600 grains or more (broadhead included). The heavier arrow reduces noise and provides enough kinetic energy for deep penetration. This results in higher incidence of exit wounds on large-sized big game, which allows more blood loss for a quicker death as well as a better blood trail.

CARRY AN IN-FIELD BOW MAINTENANCE KIT

To overcome all but the most tragic bow equipment breaks, losses, and other accidents, carry these essentials: (1) a spare release, (2) Allen keys that fit your sight, (3) a multi-tool for general wrenching, and (4) superglue.

THIS COW ELK WAS HIT WITH A MECHANICAL BROADHEAD AT 40 YARDS. PENETRATION WAS POOR, THOUGH THERE WAS AMPLE BLOOD LOSS FROM THE ENTRANCE WOUND.

REMI WARREN, A MONTANA AND NEVADA HUNTER, WEIGHS IN ON HIS LOVE FOR LOW-TECH ARCHERY EQUIPMENT

"No modern hunter took up traditional bowhunting because it was the most effective way to hunt. It is about something different. It's about the joy in the experience. It's the rush of having no choice but to get really close. It's the feel of the string in your fingers and a wood bow in your hand. It's the pure concentration it takes to make a perfect shot, and the overwhelming feeling you experience when it all comes together.

"I shoot a 55-pound takedown recurve bow that I bought a long time ago at a local hunting shop. I used to use wood arrows to keep it traditional, but then I started to buy carbon arrows that look like wood because they shot a lot better. I have a leather three-finger glove I shoot with to keep my fingers from blistering, and I carry three arrows in a quiver mounted to the bow itself.

"I am not sure how much practice it takes to become an expert with a recurve. I shoot mine as much as I can, and I don't consider myself even close to expert status. Unlike a compound bow, where there is a decent amount of proficiency gained in a relatively short amount of time, a traditional bow is something that takes a lot of dedication to get good at. Even after a lifetime of shooting, you won't be as accurate at long ranges as a newbie archer with a tricked-out compound bow. For me, this is the appeal of traditional archery: simplicity combined with challenge.

"Although I had taken plenty of animals with a gun and compound bow, it took me a few years of hunting with a recurve before killing a deer with it. My first deer with a traditional bow was a huge 4-by-4 mule deer. After the shot I was shaking like it was my first hunt all over again. I was so overwhelmed by excitement and emotion I just had to sit there on the mountain and collect my thoughts. To be 100 percent honest, I thought I was going to shed a tear. I put a lot of work into hunting that deer, and when it all came together the moment was almost unbelievable."

HUNTING OPTICS

A hunting guide in Alaska once told a buddy of mine, "If I had a thousand dollars to spend on a gun, I'd put a hundred dollars into the rifle and the rest into the scope." That perspective is certainly extreme, but the old adage about getting what you pay for applies more fittingly to optics—rifle scopes, binoculars, spotting scopes, range finders—than perhaps any other category of hunting gear. The modern hunter spends a lot more time trying to locate game than he does trying to kill it, and you shouldn't skimp on these tools of the trade.

I'm ashamed to admit that I didn't realize the importance of good optics until I was well into my twenties. I just figured, like a lot of guys do, that glass is basically glass and that differences in quality could hardly justify the extra expense of premium brands. But my mind was thoroughly changed one August day when I was hunting caribou with my brothers and some buddies on the North Slope of Alaska's Brooks Range. We were butchering caribou meat in our camp when someone noticed a grizzly bear coming up the opposite bank of the river. My friend Chuck and I both scrambled to set up our spotting scopes so we could all take a closer look. Mine was a Chinese-made cheapo, but Chuck had a Leupold Gold Ring scope (plus a set of Nikon binoculars) that he'd acquired the previous fall while working for a moose guide in southwest Alaska. After a few minutes, everyone was waiting around for a chance to see the bear through Chuck's scope, while I had mine all to myself.

Curious to see the difference, I waited my turn and took a look through Chuck's scope. I wouldn't have been any more surprised if I had looked in there and seen a Martian. The bear in Chuck's scope seemed to be an entirely different animal from the one I'd been looking at, even though we were both using the same magnification and lens size. Through my scope I could see that the grizzly had a brown muzzle, but with Chuck's I could see that its nose was moist like a dog's and that it had a small scar above its upper lip. With my scope I'd been able to tell that the bear was basically a sort of blondish color, but with Chuck's I could see that it was actually tri-tone, as its coat faded from chocolate near the body to blond at the tips of its fur. But what struck me most was the way that the bear's hair parted in cowlick-like patterns that roved across the animal's body with each gust of breeze, a thing of great beauty that had been invisible to me through my scope.

Through the rest of that trip, I didn't miss an opportunity to do a sort of Pepsi Challenge between Chuck's optics and mine. Each time I did so, I noticed something different. While images through my spotting scope and binoculars were always a bit hazy around the edges, Chuck's offered crystal-clear images out to the edge of the field of view. While mine had a shallow depth of focus, Chuck's enabled me to look at objects at varying distances without having to constantly tinker with the focus adjustment. And while my optics were rendered basically useless by intense glare whenever I looked in the vicinity of a rising or setting sun, Chuck's stuff somehow managed to control that effect, allowing me to keep glassing during those early morning and late evening periods when animals tend to be most active.

These attributes didn't just mean greater enjoyment watching grizzlies, as fine as that is. They also meant that I'd be able to find more game and see it better, which is another way of saying that good optics make you a better hunter.

BINOCULARS

Good binoculars should provide you a crystal-clear image of whatever you're looking at, be it 10 yards away or 1,000. They should not fog easily. They should not cause your eyes to ache after a day's use. They should be glare free, even if you're using them in the evening when the sun is low above the horizon. They should provide an ample depth of focus, meaning you're not constantly fussing with the focus knob every time a deer takes a few steps closer to you or farther away.

Binoculars are usually described with two numbers separated by an ×. For instance, you might see binoculars described as 8×32, 10×40, or 12×50. The first number, the one that precedes the ×, refers to *magnification*. The second

A collection of high-quality optics and accessories.
A: Large spotting scope (Vortex Razor HD 85 mm). **B:** Lightweight spotting scope (Vortex Razor HD 50 mm). **C:** Tripod and head (Outdoorsmans compact medium tripod with Outdoorsmans pan head). **D:** Lens wipe with stuff pocket. **E:** Binoculars (Vortex Razor HD 10×50). **F:** Range finders (Vortex Ranger 1000 is an affordable option; Leica Rangemaster 1600 is a high-dollar choice). **G:** Binocular chest carrier (Bino Pouch by Alaska Guide Creations).

number, after the ×, refers to *objective diameter*. This is typically given in millimeters.

Magnification, of course, is the magnifying power of the binoculars (or rifle scope or spotting scope). A pair of 10× binoculars, for example, produces an image as if the viewer were ten times closer to the object, while 8× magnification produces an image as if the viewer were eight times closer. The amount of magnification you need depends on how you are using your binoculars. If you intend to freehand your binoculars (use them without a tripod), stick to 8× and 10× models. With any more magnification, the image is likely to appear shaky. Deciding between 8× and 10× is a matter of personal preference. As a general rule, though, 8× are great for eastern hunting applications, while the extra power of 10× binoculars comes in handy when surveying the wide-open expanses of the West.

As for the objective diameter, a pair of binoculars will produce increasingly brighter and sharper images as the objective diameter increases. A pair of 8×40 binoculars, then, will produce a brighter and sharper image than an 8×25, even though both enlarge the image an identical eight times. When shopping for binoculars, you'll see that many models are offered with three different objective diameters: 30, 40, and 50. (Or 32, 42, and 50.) For general, all-around use, an objective diameter of 40 is hard to beat. If you don't rely too heavily on binoculars and you value lightweight gear, go with the 30 or 32. If you feel naked without a pair of binoculars against your face and you don't mind the extra weight, go with 50.

Here are a few other things to keep in mind when shopping for binoculars:

Ocular Lens

Center Focus

Twist Eyecup

Strap Attachment

Locking Diopter

Rubber Armor

Objective Lens

Tripod Adapter Socket

1. Roof prism vs. Porro prism. Prism design refers to how an image is "righted" after passing through the objective lens of the binocular. You can easily tell them apart because roof prism binoculars typically have two straight barrels, while Porro prism binoculars have barrels that bulge out beyond the eyepiece. (Porro prism binoculars look more old-school; that's what your granddaddy had.) Porro prism binoculars will produce a brighter image than roof prism binoculars of the same magnification, objective size, and optical quality. However, roof prism binoculars are generally lighter, narrower, easier to hold, and better able to withstand abuse and water intrusion. Most manufacturers of quality hunting binoculars stick with roof prism designs, and you should, too.

2. Phase correction coatings are used in roof prism binoculars to enhance resolution and contrast. (Porro prism binos do not benefit from these coatings.) When buying roof prism 'nocs, make sure they have phase correction coatings.

3. A quality rubberized armor coating will provide a secure, nonslip grip and external protection. Make sure your 'nocs have it.

4. Quality optics are filled with argon or nitrogen to eliminate fogging inside the binoculars. Make sure your 'nocs have it.

5. Spend the money and buy binoculars with a lifetime warranty. Manufacturers that back their products with such force are usually building a product of value. Some of the companies will charge you for parts to repair a broken piece, while others, such as Vortex Optics, have an unconditional no-charge warranty: they will repair or replace damaged or defective products at no charge regardless of how it happened or whose fault it was.

6. Consider a chest carrier. Although many hunters still use a simple padded neck strap to carry their binoculars, there are much better alternatives. Chest carriers keep your binos handy and bounce-free, even when you're crawling on your hands and knees or squirming under a fence. The device also has a few small pockets for essentials such as a lens cloth, diaphragm calls, a lighter, and an extra couple of rounds of ammo.

7. Get a tripod for your 'nocs. No matter how stable you think you are while freehanding your binoculars, you're actually not. Wind, fatigued muscles, heavy breathing from exertion, and even your own pulse all make your binoculars jiggle around like a nervous chipmunk. If you don't believe me, mount your binoculars on a tripod and see the difference. With the stable platform, you'll start noticing small movements in the surrounding landscape that would have escaped your notice with a freehand hold: a chickadee flitting around in the bushes across a field, a porcupine uncurling from its slumber in the crotch of a distant tree, the slight twitch of a buck's ear in the shade of a juniper. Try this method and you are virtually guaranteed to spot more game. For an excellent tripod and adapter system that are compatible with most binoculars, visit the Outdoorsmans website (outdoorsmans.com).

SPOTTING SCOPES

Spotting scopes are not vital to hunting heavily timbered country, where visibility is limited to a couple of hundred yards, but when it comes to hunting open country they have several important functions. When I'm glassing big spaces with my 10× binoculars, I'll make a mental note of any areas that I couldn't quite pick apart to my satisfaction. These might include thick patches of cover, shaded areas beneath rocky overhangs or downed trees, or just interesting shapes that are hard to discern with my binoculars. Then, when I'm done with my initial scan, I'll bust out my spotter and give these areas a careful, up-close examination. The second great benefit of having a spotting scope is that you can analyze critters you've already located. This is especially important when you're dealing with legal size and sex restrictions. When I'm hunting for does, either at the request of a landowner who doesn't want to kill his young bucks or because I have an antlerless-only deer tag, I use my spotting scopes to make sure that I'm not mistaking a small spikehorn buck for a doe. And when it comes to hunting mountain sheep and moose, a spotter is great for determining whether an animal is of legal size. In much of the West, bighorn sheep need to reach three-quarter curl size in order to be legal; in Alaska, moose usually need to have either three or four brow tines (or a 50-inch overall spread) to be legal. In these situations, you want all the eyepower you can get. The difference between having a spotting scope and not having one can be the difference between having a dead animal and going home empty-handed.

When selecting a spotting scope, you should weigh your concerns about image quality against your concerns about portability. If you're strictly a long-range backpack hunter who humps into the Brooks Range, get a spotting scope that weighs around 2 or 3 pounds with an objective lens not greater than 60 mm and variable magnification of approximately 10×–30×. If you're a truck hunter who prowls the wide-open expanses of the Texas Panhandle, an 85 mm scope weighing 7 pounds with variable magnification of 20×–60× will suit you just fine. If you're looking for a single scope that can do it all, it's hard to beat a 65 mm spotting scope with variable magnification of about 15×–45×. (In truth, most spotting scopes, even the highest-quality ones, have a distorted image at their highest magnification settings. It's a dirty secret of the optics world.)

RANGE FINDERS

Carrying a range finder helps you eliminate uncertainty about distances when shooting rifles or bows. When you know the actual distance to the target, you'll have more confidence in taking the shot—or you'll know that it's too far away to risk it. The best models have a function that gives you the line-of-sight distance as well as the horizontal distance. When it comes to calculating the gravitational drop of a bullet or arrow during flight, the horizontal distance is all that matters; an angle-compensating range finder factors the line-of-sight distance as well as the look angle in order to give you this measurement. (Imagine yourself sitting on a 45-degree slope while looking downward at a deer that's 300 yards away. An angle-compensating range finder will give you the true horizontal distance—again, the only one that matters—of 250 yards.)

Another thing that differentiates a good range finder from a bad one is the device's ability to detect a small target. A range finder might boast a 1,000-yard capability, but then it only works when you're trying to range house-sized objects at that distance. Before buying a range finder, test it out. At the very minimum, you should be able to get a reading on a deer-sized target at whatever your maximum comfortable shooting distance is. While there are several good range finders on the market, the Leica Rangemaster 1600-B is one of the finest units ever produced for rifle hunters. If you're on a tighter budget or you're a bowhunter, check out the Vortex Ranger 1000.

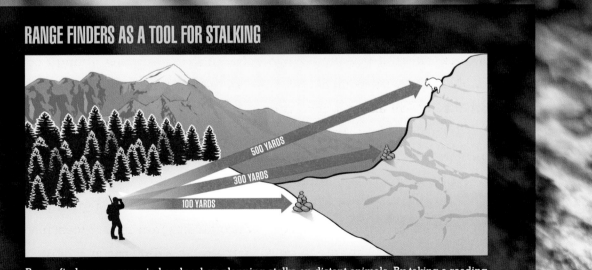

RANGE FINDERS AS A TOOL FOR STALKING

500 YARDS

300 YARDS

100 YARDS

Range finders can come in handy when planning stalks on distant animals. By taking a reading on the animal itself, as well as various topographical features between you and it, you can select prime shooting locations that lie within an optimal shooting distance of your prey.

BLADE TOOLS

I think of knives and blade tools as fun gear. They are cool to look at, exciting to buy, and a pleasure to toy around with. This creates a sort of problem for hunters, who tend to accumulate a lot of excess blades that they don't really need. If you've got endless funds for gear, this isn't a problem. But if your knife-buying habits mean you can't buy, say, a good pair of boots, they're impeding your ability to hunt as hard as you can. Which is to say, I've seen a lot of hunts ruined by foot problems, but I've never seen a hunt ruined by a knife problem. So what knives and blade tools do you really need? It depends on what you're doing.

Think ahead when selecting blade tools and ask yourself what you'll really need. Here, a bowfisherman uses his multi-tool's file to hone the edge of his machete on an overnight swamp hunt.

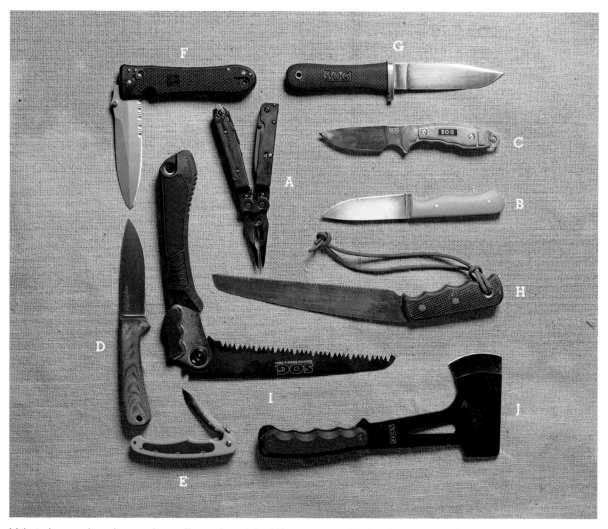

Multi-tool—never leave home without it. Your multi-tool should have a serrated blade, a bone saw, needle-nose pliers, and a bit receiver that can handle whatever bits are necessary to do quick repairs on your rifle, bow, or other equipment. Pictured here (A) is a SOG B66-N Power Assist. A great thing about SOG multi-tools is that you can customize them with whatever blades you want.

Skinning knife. While you can certainly hack your way through a skinning job with a multi-tool, a quality skinning knife is nice to have along. In fact, it should be regarded as essential. Excellent options include (B) custom knife by Brian Goode; (C) SOG Huntspoint skinning knife; (D) Phil Wilson Smoke Creek drop point; (E) Havalon Piranta (a replacement-blade razor knife that is lightweight, compact, and extremely sharp).

Utility knife. Lets you keep your skinning knife sharp and ready for its intended purpose; can be used for cutting everything from rope to wood to cheese. Pictured here: (F) SOG Pentagon Elite (folding, with serrated blade); (G) SOG NW Ranger (fixed, not serrated).

Bone saw. Useful when hunting big game, especially in the backcountry. Allows you to dismantle carcasses efficiently and cleanly, with no jagged bones, and to remove skullcaps when you want to keep the antlers or horns of an animal without having to pack out the entire head. Also handy around camp for fire making and various woodcraft tasks. Pictured here (H) is the Knives of Alaska bone saw.

Wood saw. Can easily double as a bone saw, but the more aggressive tooth pattern makes it better suited for wood. Great for building blinds, trimming shooting lanes, or cutting firewood and performing camp chores on extended backcountry trips. Pictured here (I) is a SOG folding camp saw.

Lightweight hatchet. A tad heavier and more cumbersome than a bone saw, but it's equally functional for butchering. Also works great as a camp tool for driving tent stakes, splitting kindling, and fashioning emergency tools and equipment from native wood supplies. Pictured here (J): SOG FO9-N hand axe.

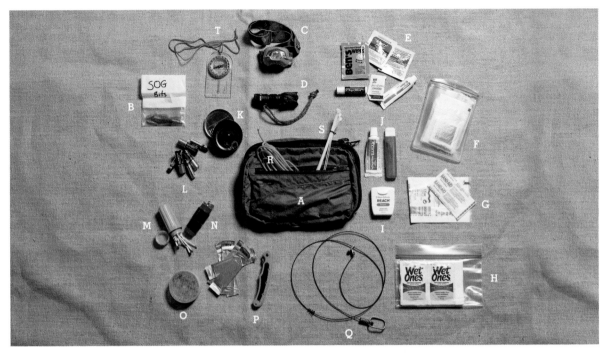

A basic hunting kit for overnight ventures. Weighs under two pounds when loaded for several nights afield. Fits easily inside a hip cargo pocket or pack lid.

A: OR Backcountry Organizer, size medium. **B:** Driver bits for basic firearm/bow/outboard engine repairs and adjustments; compatible with the ¼-inch driver on an SOG multi-tool. **C:** Black Diamond headlamp. **D:** SOG Dark Energy 240-lumen flashlight. **E:** Insect repellent wipes, Benadryl, Tylenol, ChapStick, lens cleaning towelette, antibiotic ointment. **F:** Resealable waterproof envelope for adhesive bandages, gauze, alcohol prep wipes, etc. **G:** Adhesive bandages and gauze pads. **H:** Wipes. **I:** Dental floss with heavy-duty needle tucked inside container. **J:** Toothpaste and collapsible toothbrush. **K:** Fishing kit. A chewing tobacco container containing a few flies, split shot, and 20 feet of 6-pound test. **L:** Spare batteries to fit flashlight, headlamp, GPS, and range finder. **M:** Waterproof matches in airtight container. **N:** Lighter wrapped with emergency supply of duct tape. **O:** Fire-starting paste. **P:** Havalon Piranta and extra blades. **Q:** Snare Shop survival snare. **R:** 25 feet of 4 mm utility cord. **S:** Zip ties. **T:** Suunto compass.

UTILITY/SURVIVAL KITS

Sensational TV programs chronicling the spastic antics of so-called survival experts have pumped a great amount of phony survival information into the American brain. These shows have promoted the idea that survival situations begin with the "victim" falling out of an airplane and landing on a deserted island with nothing but a large knife. The host then endures a number of misadventures, only to be saved by the well-timed discovery of a freshly killed zebra that's been left behind by a lion.

In real life, survival situations don't play out this dramatically. Instead, they begin when you wander away from your car or truck thinking that you're going for a quick hike on a day's hunt. Then you get injured or lost, and things go to hell. The key to surviving these situations isn't finding carrion or wringing water from a pile of animal dung; instead, it is proper planning and packing. Besides logging your starting point with a handheld GPS unit, a responsible hunter maintains a basic kit of essentials that he always keeps handy, either in a pack or in a hip pocket, whenever straying away from a vehicle or other point of departure.

A good kit does not consist exclusively of emergency survival material, as it should also contain a wide variety of small tools and materials that come in handy on a daily basis. Nor should a kit be static. I customize my kit before every trip, so it's always fine-tuned for the particular conditions that I'm likely to encounter. On a wintertime trip in the far North, for instance, there's no need to let insect repellent take up space in my kit when an extra canister of fire-starting paste is way more appropriate.

MAPS AND NAVIGATION TOOLS

Maps are imperative when hunting unfamiliar country, and even for gaining a better understanding of familiar turf. These days, maps come in a variety of forms, and they contain a wide array of information that is helpful to the hunter. Here they are broken into three categories, with explanations of what you need and how to use it.

1. Satellite imagery. Pictures taken from high above the landscape offer a detailed view of the vegetation that cannot be deciphered from topographical maps alone. This is important to hunters, as finding game often comes down to locating open feeding areas, thick bedding areas, and natural funnels and travel corridors. Knowing the exact location of a dry and brushy island in the middle of an enormous cattail marsh can be an invaluable piece of knowledge. Use tools such as Google Earth to pre-scout areas and get a feel for the land. Mark the coordinates of good-looking spots in your GPS, and then check them out on scouting trips. Also, bring along a laminated printout of satellite imagery. During the hunt, you can take a moment to peer at a satellite image and identify valuable details that perhaps didn't jump out at you before you had firsthand experience of the area.

2. Topographical maps. The problem with satellite imagery is that it's very hard to discern

the vertical character—the ups and downs, if you will—of a landscape. These are covered in detail on topographical maps. For hunting purposes, USGS quad maps in 1:24,000 scale are the best. Use these in conjunction with satellite imagery and you'll develop an intimate understanding of your hunting area before you even set foot on it. You can also get overlay maps, which combine satellite imagery with topographical lines and even land ownership details. The downside of these overlay maps is that details sometimes get lost when a map becomes overcrowded with information. (There are multiple sources for such maps; do an Internet search for "custom hunting maps.") Of course, you can get all of the above information from a GPS unit, but it's hard to beat the "big screen" of a paper map. And paper maps don't need batteries.

3. GPS. While all of us should know how to find our position on a map, it is faster and way more convenient and accurate to do it with a GPS. Today's GPS units can be loaded with detailed topographical maps and land ownership information as well. Armed with this info, the hunter never has to wonder if he is trespassing or if a big buck on the other side of the fence is fair game. By always remembering to mark your vehicle or camp, you will have the confidence to chase after distant game knowing you'll be able to find your way back after dark.

LAND OWNERSHIP MAPS

Land ownership maps (often called plat maps) used to be hard to track down, but not anymore. The Montana-based company onXmaps (HuntingGPSMaps.com) makes statewide digital topo/plat maps that are compatible with most Garmin GPS units. So far they offer products for nineteen states, and they continue to add more. You can get an entire state for about $100.

APPAREL

APPAREL INTRODUCTION

I grew up hunting in used apparel, from my dad's old wool army surplus clothes to home-made camos stitched together by my mother and then handed down to me once my brothers outgrew them. Even after I moved away from home, I still sourced my hunting apparel

from places such as Goodwill. When I was in an area with a lot of wealthy outdoor enthusiasts, such as Jackson, Wyoming, I'd scrounge the local thrift shops in search of apparel that had been cast off by those who were more fortunate than I was. I killed my first two elk while wearing a faded and torn camouflage shirt that I'd bought used and then refurbished with a needle and thread and recolored with a packet of RIT clothing dye. The blaze orange hunting vest that I'm using now, at forty years of age, came to me seventeen years ago as a preowned garment. This isn't to say that used clothes are somehow better than new clothes. Rather, I'm suggesting that resourcefulness is more important than money when it comes to hunting apparel—something that I certainly wouldn't say about optics. Once you understand what materials to wear and how to layer them, you'll find that you can get properly attired on just about any budget.

BASIC LAYERING

Layering allows you to be prepared for a multitude of conditions—in terms of both what nature serves up and how your body warms and cools during physical activity. By adding and subtracting the right layers, you can stay comfortable in all temperatures without carrying too much weight.

These hunters were well prepared for the wet conditions on this mountain goat hunt; still, they frequently had to start fires in an effort to stay dry and warm.

This hunter planned for the worst when packing for his archery elk hunt and was able to stay in the mountains despite snow and frigid temperatures.

Base layers are where it all starts. This layer, be it polyester or wool, is worn on every excursion. It should be modified only if you're headed into extreme temperature ranges. I'll wear my basic merino wool long-sleeve shirt and bottoms (A, B) from freezing temps up into the seventies. In hotter climates, I'll trade it out for a short-sleeved merino T-shirt without any overlayers or bottoms. In extreme cold conditions, I'll switch this out for an expedition-weight merino wool base layer.

Insulating layers lie between your base layers and outerwear. Common insulating layers would be a merino wool vest (C); Primaloft, down, or similar layers (D); or wool or fleece sweaters.

Your insulating layers are where most of the modifications to your layering system should occur. These layers should be avoided or minimized during heavy exercise such as hill climbing because you'll build up too much heat and start sweating.

The outer shell layer is your protection from snow, rain, and wind. In dry conditions, wool or nylon-blend pants (E) can be your outer layer. In wet conditions, pull a waterproof but breathable layer (F) over your pants. For upper layers, consider an insulated outer layer with a hood (G) when hunting in temperatures that are consistently cold—especially when stationary. In warmer temps, use a thin, breathable piece of rainwear (H) with a hood and armpit zips that can be opened for increased ventilation. Since nylon hardshells tend to be noisy, the use of a softshell outer layer has become very popular with hunters who rely on stealth. A typical softshell (I) will have a quieter, brushed-type surface. These shells are water-resistant but not waterproof, so a hardshell must come along in your pack. (Most softshells can double as an insulating layer, albeit a very light one.)

Light wool gloves (J) are good for concealment or cool mornings. Choose heavier gloves (K) for cold, wet conditions, and waterproof lined mittens (L) for extreme conditions.

A merino wool face mask (M) provides concealment and warmth. Pick a heavier stocking cap (N) (and coat hoods) for colder temperatures.

Insist on merino-synthetic blend socks (O). The merino gives warmth and comfort; the synthetic elements (usually nylon and spandex) give strength and stretch.

SYNTHETICS VS. MERINO WOOL

SYNTHETICS

- *Pros:* Dries the fastest of any technical fabric. Durable. Less expensive.
- *Cons:* Stinks, especially on physically active trips; is hard to deodorize; made from plastic (usually a polyester and nylon mix).

MERINO WOOL

- *Pros:* Dries fairly quickly; minimizes moisture from sweat; high warmth-to-weight ratio; naturally odor resistant; comfortable.
- *Cons:* Not nearly as durable as synthetics; more expensive than synthetics.

CAMO CLOTHING AND SCENT CONTROL CLOTHING: DO THEY WORK?

If only there were a simple answer to this question. While camouflage and odor-reducing clothes do have their merits, they are not nearly as important as marketers would have you believe. Scent control clothes work, at least theoretically, in two different ways: either the material is impregnated with activated charcoal, which absorbs odor molecules, or the garments are meant to seal off most of your body to prevent the escape of odor molecules. Some garments are said to do a combination of both. But simply put, there is no product available today—no clothing, no sprays, no camouflage patterns—that can negate the importance of understanding how animals perceive and respond to threats. The best way to learn these things is by spending as much time in the woods as possible in careful observation of your prey. Sneaking up on animals, or sitting tight and letting them walk up on you, not only teaches you what you can't get away with, such as fast movements and silhouetting yourself against the sky, but also lets you learn what you *can* get away with: things like moving only when a deer lowers its head to feed, or raising your bow on an elk when its peripheral vision is obscured by a tree, or relying on the downstream thermals above a cold mountain creek to carry your scent away from a black bear that you're stalking. Only when these skills are mastered do camouflage and odor-reducing technologies find their proper place in a hunter's tool kit, because only then will the hunter cease to rely on these things as a pair of crutches—crutches that will inevitably break down under pressure.

TIPS FOR STAYING COMFORTABLE IN EXTREME COLD

1. Stay dry at all costs.

2. Wear big, bulky insulating layers that trap lots of air. Down is excellent.

3. Use toe warmers and hand warmers.

4. Wear large, loose-fitting down mittens over your gloves. Wear down or synthetic insulated overboots on top of your regular cold-weather footwear.

5. Limit skin exposure to the cold air. Commonly missed spots are the neck and wrists. Use mittens or gloves with generous gauntlets and wear a neck gaiter.

BOOTS

I've seen more hunts ruined by foot problems than by any other cause. Luckily, most of these issues—problems such as blisters, sore ligaments, open lesions from chronic dampness, even debilitating athlete's foot—are completely preventable with proper boot selection and diligent foot care. I hunt across the country and throughout the year in just four pairs of footwear. You might think of this as the four-boot rule.

A: Medium-duty 6-inch all-leather, uninsulated hiking boots. A mainstay, good for everything from Florida spring turkeys to New Mexico antelope to travel days between your home and hunting grounds. They should be made of thick leather, preferably around 2.5 mm, which protects your feet from thorns, sharp rocks, and cold mornings. **B:** Backpack hunting boots are best for long hikes in rough country while carrying a heavy pack. At first glance, these should feel like overkill. Companies that produce footwear for serious mountain hunters, including Schnee's and Meindl, produce boots weighing almost 5 pounds (equivalent to about three pairs of standard tennis shoes). Manufacturers would certainly make these boots lighter if possible, but it takes a heavy package to incorporate all of the features necessary for serious backcountry hunts: thick leather uppers, heavily padded collars, heavy-duty midsoles; a breathable membrane such as Gore-Tex or eVent, rubber sole guards, Vibram or Vibram-style outsoles, and triple or double stitching. Typically, boots of such quality are completely waterproof. It's possible to wade or even stand in ankle-deep water for minutes at a time without getting your socks wet. What's more, they give you the necessary stability to handle side hills and steep downhill grades without injuring yourself while carrying heavy loads. **C:** Pac boots are for cold temps plus snow or ice. A dirty secret about the rigid rubber outersoles used on most hiking boots is that they become almost hard, like a nylon cutting board, when temperatures get into the teens and single digits. This isn't really a problem on dry rock, as they can still get a grip, but as soon as you throw snow and ice into the mix you might as well be trying to climb a hill on ice skates. When you know for a fact that you'll be dealing with low temperatures as well as snow and ice, switch to a pac boot with leather uppers and rubber bottoms, plus a more flexible style of outsole that's armed with Air Bob traction (or a similar design). The best designs fit almost as snugly and comfortably as boots designed for backpack hunters, but they'll keep you far warmer. Make sure to get the kinds that use removable wool felt liners, and buy two sets of liners if possible. On extended hunts, you can rotate your liners on a daily basis: one pair left to dry over the wood stove or in your sleeping bag, one pair on your feet. **D:** Knee-high rubber boots are for when you need to control odor and/or water. They are perfect for walking into tree stands and other ambush setups, because you can scrub them with muddy water to rid them of unnatural odors such as gasoline or your own stench—odors that might otherwise give you away. They are also perfect for hunting in flat, wet country, such as for chasing wild hogs on the Florida peninsula or stalking shoreline black bears in southeast Alaska. But definitely think twice about wearing rubber boots in steep terrain. The lack of ankle support can put you in a really bad spot, and your feet can get horribly blistered. Some of the best rubber boots, such as those made by Xtratuf, have smooth fabric liners that allow them to come on and off easily when wet without letting them slip and slide against your feet. Avoid any kind of liner that's fleecy or absorbent; you'll never get them dry.

CHEST WADERS: NOT JUST FOR DUCK HUNTERS ANYMORE

Chest waders fall outside the four-boot rule, but then you know what they say: rules are meant to be broken. When you need to stay warm for an extra-long period of time, consider donning a pair of the extreme-cold-weather chest waders used by late-season waterfowl hunters. These are made to keep you warm while standing waist deep in icy water as you get blasted by 40-mph winds, and they'll work equal wonders when you're lying out on a frozen field during a late winter goose hunt. They're especially handy when your hunt requires you to lie down in the snow or frozen mud for hours on end, because you'll stay dry even when your body heat starts to melt the surface you're lying on. Many ice fishermen have discovered this trick as well and have abandoned insulated bibs and boots altogether in exchange for cold-weather waders. For them, there's an additional benefit: if you fall through the ice in shallow water, you can just climb back up as dry as a bone and go about your business.

WET SOCKS GRIP ROCKS

A great benefit of wool-blend socks is that they stick like glue to wet, algae-coated river cobbles. When you need to cross a creek or river, keep your boots dry by lashing them to your pack and then cross in your socks. The rocks can be a little painful on your feet, but at least you'll have a greatly reduced chance of falling into the water and soaking yourself. Once you're safely across, wring out your socks before putting your boots back on. Or if you have an extra set of dry socks (you always should), then put them on and hang the wet socks on the outside of your pack to dry.

How do you properly waterproof leather hunting boots? Most important is to start with clean, wet boots. You can remove dirt and grime with a stiff toothbrush, and you can wet the leather either naturally (by being out in wet conditions) or by covering them in wet towels for an hour or so. Either way, you want the leather of the boots to be fully saturated. Next, use an old sock or rag to liberally apply your waterproofing agent to the leather. (Nikwax Waterproofing Wax and Sno-Seal are both good products.) Pay close attention to seams, stitching, and the areas around the eyelets. When you're done, let the boots dry for an hour (*do not* place them near a direct heat source) before you buff out the remaining paste. Then let the boots sit overnight to dry fully before you wear them outside. When water no longer beads up on your boots, it's time to repeat.

GEAR FOR THE BACKCOUNTRY HUNTER

Of all the forms of hunting discussed in these pages, backcountry hunting is far and away the most physically and mentally demanding—and also the most demanding on gear. Not only does the backcountry hunter have to *hunt*, he has to do it while balancing an extraordinary number of ancillary concerns ranging from where he'll sleep and navigation to how he'll avoid trouble with predators and how he'll deal with the downed carcass of a large animal that's potentially inaccessible to vehicles. With all this on the hunter's mind, there's little time or energy left for worrying about equipment performance. You need to make sure your gear is well constructed and well maintained or else things will go to hell in a hurry.

PACKS

THE DAYPACK

A daypack is useful for any kind of hunting that doesn't involve an overnight stay. It needs to have enough room for your essentials—food, water, safety kit, ammo, tools, and extra layers. It should be light, durable, and weather resistant. It should also wear well on long days of hiking and sitting. If your daypack is thoughtfully packed and organized, you'll insulate yourself from *oh shit!* moments when you realize you've left something important behind. When hunting big game out of a base camp or a vehicle, I prefer to carry a lightweight

The Outdoorsmans Muley Fanny Pack can be worn by itself or integrated into a frame pack system.

daypack that has the capacity to expand and carry out a load of meat. When transporting meat is not an issue, a simple fanny pack will suffice. No need to go big and fancy here; just get something comfortable that'll hold your gear and keep out rain.

BACKPACKS

Your backpack is the linchpin of your backcountry gear—it holds everything together. Whether you're on a week-long mountain bowhunt for elk or making day-long excursions into swamp country from a truck-based whitetail camp, you need a pack that's big enough to handle your gear, comfortable enough to wear all day, and configured in such a way that you can stay organized. There's a never-ending flood of hunting backpacks on the market these days that are advertised as being capable of the task. Some certainly are, but many more are junk. Here's a rundown of three very different backpacks that have what it takes to handle the rigors of backcountry hunting— each in its own way.

Easily one of the most versatile and durable backpack systems on the market, it's built around a lightweight but extremely sturdy pack frame that can be adjusted to fit pretty much anyone between Arnold Schwarzenegger and Justin Bieber. This frame can be used alone as a hauler pack for carrying heavy bone-in quarters of moose or elk weighing in excess of 100 pounds. If you need a small amount of gear and some water, you can add on a fanny-pack-sized bag as well as a water bladder and still pile on quarters of meat. (The fanny pack can be detached from the main body and worn on its own.) For all-day or overnight hunts, the main 6,000-cubic-inch bag can be added to the frame in seconds; this bag includes two large side sleeves that make packing—and accessing—your tripod and spotting scope a breeze. It also collapses easily to reduce bulk when unloaded, and has a liner that can be pulled out and washed once you get it bloody from hauling a fresh kill. Add the 1,000-cubic-inch external load pod, which can handle a one-man tent, a sleeping bag, and a compact sleeping pad, and you've got a total of 7,000 cubic inches of storage. It also has an integrated rifle/bow carrier that lets you keep your hands free while traveling long distances or use trekking poles when loaded with weight in rough terrain. So with one pack system, you're covered for everything ranging from a day hike to a week-long pack trip, and you've always got the potential to add a significant load of meat without having to return to your camp or the trailhead for a larger pack.

ARC'TERYX NAOS

If you do a lot of hunting in extremely wet places—coastal Alaska, Washington, and Oregon come to mind—then you can't beat this bruiser of a waterproof pack. It's essentially an indestructible roll-top dry bag mounted on an extremely comfortable and strong internal frame that can handle in excess of a hundred pounds without buckling. It carries extremely

well and keeps all of your gear dry as a bone—even when tossed into the water and used as a flotation device. While the pack itself is high-capacity, the main body lacks external pockets. It's annoying, but again, this pack is built to keep things dry, and it does its job extremely well.

MYSTERY RANCH NICE PACK SYSTEM

Now and then you get into a situation where the only thing you want out of a pack is the ability to haul heavy loads comfortably. Maybe it's a 20-mile pack-in on a Dall sheep hunt where you'll be coming out with 110 pounds of meat, horn, and gear, or maybe it's an extended mountain trip that requires you to tote along an inflatable kayak plus two weeks' worth of food. In these situations, you need something that can handle layer upon layer of gear, plus all manner of odds and ends—kayak paddles, a rifle, bearproof food canisters—bungeed and clipped to the outside. A number of companies make such rigs, and one of the best is Mystery Ranch. Their NICE pack frames are compatible with several different pack styles, including some smaller daypacks, but the system is especially suitable for their giant 7,500-cubic-inch bag. It's a heavy and stiff pack, for sure, and all the buckles and straps can be a little confusing, but it'll hold more gear than your shoulders will want to carry. It has plenty of pockets, including an ingenious pair of tubular vertical pockets that are perfect for fuel canisters, food, or any other odds and ends that you want to keep handy or well away from your clothes and sleeping gear.

A well-fitted pack should evenly disperse the weight of the load through the torso, with most of the weight falling on the centers of your shoulders and your hips. Carrying a burly load is never an exercise in comfort, but a well-fitted pack can really make a difference and reduce the level of hell that you'll certainly go through. When choosing your backpack, it's important to test the pack with weight in it. Start with around 40 pounds. (The best choice for this weight would be actual hunting and camping gear—an otherwise empty pack with a 40-pound dumbbell won't sit the same as a full pack, giving you a false fit.)

1. First, loosen all the adjustable load-bearing straps.

2. Find your iliac crests, otherwise known as your hip crests—these are the little ridges at the top of your hip bones. Center the hip belt over the crests, then buckle and tighten firmly.

3. Tighten your shoulder straps until they are snug and obviously bearing some weight. If there is space between your shoulders and the straps, then your pack is too long for your torso. Either shorten it if it is adjustable or try the next size down.

4. Finally, find the load lifter straps, which should be hanging between your shoulders and the top of the pack. Crank down on these until you find a natural balance point and the load feels evenly dispersed.

While it might seem that loading a pack is perfectly simple—just throw in your stuff and go, right?—there are a few tricks that will help you suffer less on the trail. For starters, keep the densest, heaviest gear centered in the lower third of your pack, where it's close to your lumbar spine. Think of things such as your tent, water jugs, sacks of food, or game bags full of meat following a successful hunt. Once these things are loaded in the lower center of the pack, they can be wedged into place with clothes, smaller gear items, or a sleeping bag. Keeping things centered is crucial; if your balance is off to one side, you'll have a fair chance of pulling a back muscle, injuring a hip joint, or damaging your knees. The rest of the pack should be organized according to your needs. Definitely consider where to put the things you may need at a moment's notice. Your rain jacket should be accessible, as should a quart of water, sunglasses, multi-tool, GPS, et cetera. Game bags, extra socks, and other nonessentials can be tucked into corners where they won't get in your way. Every backpack hunter has his own evolving sets of needs; experimentation will help you find a packing strategy that works best for your own style of camping and hunting.

A FEW EXTRA TIPS FOR EXTRA-BIG LOADS

1. There are two good ways to get a heavy pack up on your back. You can sit down, strap the pack on, and use your hands and knees to push up to standing. Or you can hold the two straps and lift the pack until the bottom rests on your bent knee, then quickly slide one arm through and swing the load onto your back.

2. Be very smart about how you move with this much weight on your back. Knees and ankles are incredibly vulnerable, especially when you're moving downhill. Your body will automatically move a little slower and more deliberately. Don't fight that. Carrying a big load out is something to take your time with.

3. Smile at your task. Try to enjoy the discomfort. Rather than thinking about the end of the hike, try pretending that there is no end. This is your life now, walking and suffering. Find a way to get cozy with that new reality.

4. Use hiking poles. They reduce stress on your joints by 30 percent and give you extra stability to prevent blown-out knees and ankles.

SLEEPING AND SHELTER: TENTS, BAGS, AND PADS

No matter how grueling a hunt gets, I can usually hack it as long as I'm able to get a decent amount of sleep at night. Sounds simple enough, but in the backcountry it can be a never-ending challenge. Wet clothes, soggy ground, cold temperatures, high winds, and uneven sleeping surfaces can work singly or together to make you miserable, pathetic, and whiny at a time when you should be content, focused, and silent. In fact, I'd say that getting quality sleep is one of the greatest challenges that face a backcountry hunter. Meeting this challenge is not a matter of accumulating lots of excess layers and gear. Organizing all this stuff and trying to keep it dry can actually lead to more problems and more lost sleep. Instead, sleeping success comes down to getting the right gear, mastering the right tricks, and knowing what things matter and what things don't. Remember: better sleep = better hunter.

There are many specialized tents that might have their place in a well-outfitted hunter's gear closet, but the vast majority of your hunting needs will be served by a freestanding three-season tent. Great options are available from Nemo, Mountain Hardware, REI, Kelty, Sierra Designs, and Black Diamond. When chosen properly, these are light enough to carry on a seven-day backpack hunt and durable enough to withstand several years' worth of intense use. They can shelter you from rain, wind, and sun, and will withstand all but the worst of winter blizzards if they're carefully staked out and supported with guy lines. Here are some other tent tips.

1. Insect repellents and sunblock can be extremely corrosive to tent fabric. Keep that stuff out.

2. A footprint or plastic ground cloth is a must-

When the weather turns wicked, you'll be glad you didn't skimp on your tent purchase.

have to protect against rain and/or ground moisture. In a downpour, take care that it is not sticking out and catching water that will pool and get you soaked.

3. Choosing a proper tent site is important. You'll sleep better if it's flat. A great way to test for this and also check for rocks and sticks that will jab you while you sleep is to lie down on your chosen tent location before you pitch your tent. Clear out any limbs, sharp rocks, roots, or other debris that can poke you. You're doing this for comfort and also to keep your tent from getting pierced.

4. Keep in mind large-scale risks such as dead trees or overhanging limbs, especially during windy conditions ahead of snowfall. You don't want to be sleeping there when that big cottonwood finally decides to tip over.

5. Take your boots off and leave them in the vestibule or outside the tent. This keeps dirt out of your living space, which is good for your tent's fabric and also good for your comfort. If you keep your boots outside, make sure to keep them covered—and also make sure you check them for scorpions or other critters before putting them back on.

OTHER TENT OPTIONS

TIPI SHELTERS

For large parties and long backcountry trips (and if your party is free of heavy-duty snorers), ultralight tipi tents are a great option. For the space they offer, they weigh next to nothing, and they can be paired with a titanium pack stove to create a portable heated structure.

Tipi tents are also great as communal cooking and eating shelters, especially during cold or wet weather. Check out the tipi-style tents made by Kifaru and Seek Outside.

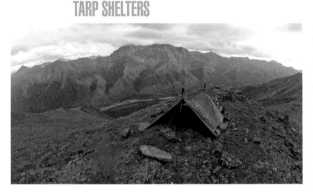

If you are going ultralight or ultra-hard-core, another great option is to learn how to make a simple shelter out of a tarp and parachute cord. A well-made tarp shelter can protect you from rain and snow, but keep in mind that they offer little in the way of insulation and nothing in the way of insect protection.

BIVY SHELTERS: WHY YOU SHOULDN'T BUY ONE

Bivy sacks always seem like a great idea when you're packing for a trip. What could be better than a miniature tent weighing a pound or so that stuffs down to the size of a water bottle? They're especially pleasurable to have along on those dry and sunny trips when you never actually have to get them out. You sleep under the stars, thankful that you're packing such a light and breezy load. The problem with bivy sacks comes when you actually need them. Then, with the rain coming down and the wind howling, you immediately realize that you're in a pickle. You can zip the thing up tight and soak your clothes and sleeping bag with the condensation of your own breath, or you can open it up and soak your clothes and sleeping bag with water from the heavenly skies. The best way out of this situation is to abandon the fallacy that bivy sacks are a reliable alternative to tents. For a great compromise, get a quality single-man tent that allows you to sit up straight and drag your backpack inside with you. When you emerge after the storm, dry and ready to go, you won't be lamenting those extra pounds that you have to tote around.

SLEEPING BAGS

The two most important factors to consider when selecting a sleeping bag are temperature rating and fill type. Temperature rating is just what it sounds like—the minimum projected temperature that you can comfortably endure in the sleeping bag while wearing base layers. (These ratings are famously inaccurate; you should always use a bag that's rated for at least 10° colder than what you'll actually encounter.) Fill type refers to whether the bag is insulated with down or synthetic materials. Down bags are lightweight and compress well, but they are useless once they get wet. Synthetic bags are heavier and bulkier, though they still function well enough when wet that you can enjoy a comfortable night's sleep.

Generally speaking, synthetic bags are the way to go unless you fetishize ultralight gear or hunt exclusively in arid environments.

As for temperature ratings, a 15° bag is a great all-around, all-purpose choice that'll keep you comfortable in the vast majority of hunting scenarios you're likely to encounter. You can unzip the thing in warmer temperatures, and you can add a fleece liner in colder temperatures. If you've got the money for a second or even third bag, round out your collection as needed with a 30° or 40° summer bag and a –15° cold-weather bag. If you encounter extreme cold, you can double up your bags or use a fleece liner to squeeze another 10° of comfort out of a single bag.

SLEEPING PADS

Always remember that you lose the majority of your heat through the ground, especially frozen ground, so do not underestimate the importance of an insulated sleeping pad in cold conditions. There are three main types of sleeping pads on the market: closed-cell foam, noninsulated inflatable, and insulated inflatable.

For the guy or gal who can sleep comfortably at home while lying on a tile floor, the closed-cell foam pad will suffice. The benefits of this style are ease of use and durability. Since there is no air inside, punctures are not a concern and you don't need to place a ground tarp between the pad and the earth. Because of its durability, the foam pad can also be folded and used as a seat while you're relaxing by the campfire—something you should never do with an inflatable pad. Look to Therm-a-Rest Ridge-Rest pads for high-quality closed-cell products.

For those requiring a little more comfort, inflatable pads deliver. While typical closed-cell foam pads give you ¾ inch of padding, inflatable pads offer from 1 to 3½ inches of padding. They easily cushion you against small rocks, roots, and other lumps you might be lying on. Noninsulated inflatables are by far the lightest option, some weighing just over 8 ounces. For cold weather, the insulated inflatables add another layer of protection between you and frozen ground. Manufacturers use both down and synthetics as insulating materials, and some use heat-reflecting materials to keep the warmth in. Insulation does add a little weight, if only a few ounces. For an all-around sleeping pad that can be used anywhere and anytime, the Nemo Astro Insulated sleeping pad is one of the best—maybe the best—on the market. The thing to remember about inflatable pads, though, is that they require great care. They are easily punctured by sticks, rocks, and thorns—even by rubbing against other gear inside your pack. Always place a tarp between the pad and bare ground, and carry a patch kit.

ADDITIONAL TIPS FOR STAYING WARM AT NIGHT

1. Before bed, boil some water, fill your water bottle, and tighten down the lid. Put the bottle of hot water inside a sock and place that on your abdomen or on the inside of your legs. If you've got a second bottle, put it down by your feet. If you're boiling creek water in order to sterilize it, you've now got two bottles of clean water waiting for you when you wake up.

2. Put clothes on, or take clothes off. Staying warm requires you to have plenty of room inside your bag for trapped air. Too few clothes can leave you feeling cold because there's not enough material to trap air; too many clothes can also leave you feeling cold if you're scrunched in so tight that there are inadequate pockets to accommodate warm air. In other words, a giant puffy coat might do more good on top of your sleeping bag than inside it. Or put that coat under your sleeping bag, where it can augment the effects of your sleeping pad.

3. Wear a hat and face mask. You lose a high percentage of your body heat through your head. A beanie or balaclava can keep your core temp where it needs to be.

4. Snuggle. Yes, snuggle. In a pinch, sleeping close to your hunting partner can greatly increase your collective warmth.

5. Maintain your bag. Clean it, dry it well, and store it by hanging it unpacked. Down bags can clump and be of no value if not properly handled, and synthetic bags will degrade over time if not taken care of. Don't just treat your bag as something that keeps you comfortable; treat it as something that keeps you alive.

COOKING: STOVES, COOKWARE, AND GRUB

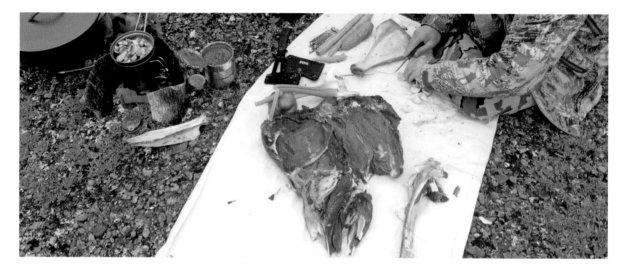

My dad always liked that old Napoleon quote about how an army marches on its stomach. During hunting season, he kept a plastic milk crate full of assorted goodies—jarred venison, corned meat, dried fruit, jerky, coffee Nips, crackers, toffee, peanuts—in the back of his Jeep Cherokee so that he could keep my and my brothers' spirits up when we might otherwise have turned tired and whiny. For sure, he and Napoleon understood something elemental about humans: we are better able to endure hardship when we're well fed. This is especially true on rugged backcountry hunts, where it can be nearly impossible to eat enough food to make up for what you're losing through climbing, walking, and staying warm. Packing the appropriate cooking equipment and food for a backcountry hunt doesn't need to be hard or expensive. Just follow these guidelines for a happy, well-fed hunt.

STOVES

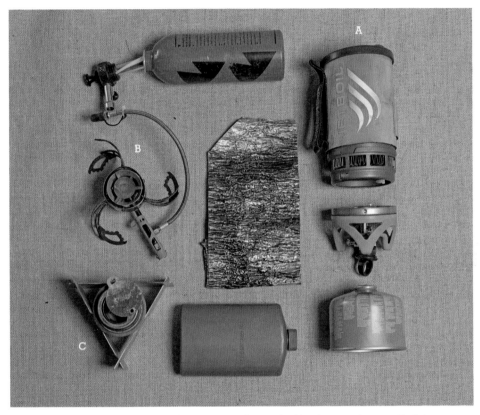

There are several lightweight stoves that can serve the needs of backcountry hunters. Each has its pros and cons.

A: Jetboil. A great option for hunts when you're using freeze-dried or dehydrated food. Pros: Highly efficient; simple design; easy to use and maintain. Cons: Poorly suited for anything besides boiling water; functions poorly in extreme cold; you can't fly with the canisters, so they need to be purchased on location; you're stuck with empty steel canisters that need to be packed out and then thrown away. **B:** Optimus Nova and aluminum windscreen (center). This is your all-around best option for camp cooking, as it is suitable for everything from making coffee to sautéing wild mushrooms to rendering black bear fat. White gas is the most appropriate fuel, but you can use regular gasoline or even diesel in a pinch. Pros: Variable flame; reliable in extreme cold and at high elevations; easy to find fuel. Cons: Loud, tricky to maintain and operate. **C:** Liberty Mountain Westwind alcohol stove. Alcohol stoves, which burn denatured alcohol, are the bargain hunter's best friend. These stoves are great for car camping and overnight backpacking trips, but they are inefficient; carrying enough fuel for an extended backcountry trip is a hassle. Pros: Extremely lightweight; virtually indestructible; maintenance free. Cons: Takes a long time to boil water; inefficient.

COOKWARE

The best cooking sets are made of stainless steel, anodized aluminum, or titanium. All are good, but titanium is best. Avoid plastic handles or lids, as you can't use these over a fire. Also avoid nonstick surfaces, because they don't last. A standard basic mess kit should include the following, in order of importance:

A: Small mug/pot with **(B)** frying pan lid. This alone will cover your cooking/eating needs. Performs as a cooking pot, a bowl, a mug, and a fry pan. Works on a stove or over a fire. Pictured here: 30-oz. Snow Peak Trek 900 titanium. **C:** Larger cooking pot. Handy for small groups, when you want to boil enough water for three or four folks to use at once. Also nice for more elaborate cooking projects, such as stews made from freshly killed meat. Pictured here: 2-qt. MSR Seagull, stainless steel. **D:** Spork. No explanation needed, though if you eat a lot of freeze-dried food from bags, consider the longer-handled options. Pictured here: Sea to Summit Alpha Lite spork. **E:** Oil and seasoning. Use these for cooking camp meat, wild mushrooms (carefully selected by a knowledgeable person, of course), and whatever unexpected foodstuffs you happen to run into. **F:** Portable backpacking grill. A luxury, but certainly convenient when you're doing a lot of cooking over a campfire. Pictured here: Purcell Trench Voyageurs grill.

BACKCOUNTRY MENU

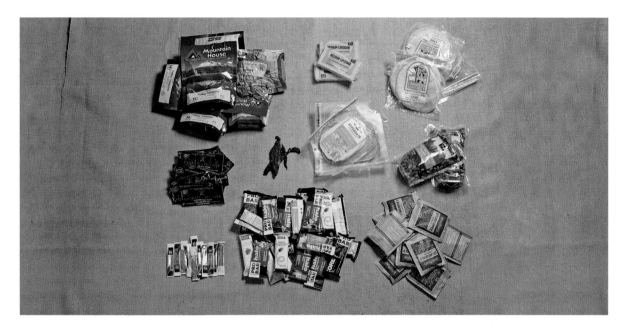

This is a very simple menu for backcountry trips that can be shifted or supplemented in a multitude of ways.

BREAKFAST
Instant coffee packets (2 per person per day)
Instant oatmeal packets (2 per person per day)

LUNCH
Flatbread (tortillas, pitas, bagels—something that resists crumbling and will last for up to a week in a pack)
Hard cheese (4 ounces per person per day)
Lunch meat (wild game salami or other cured wild game, or highly preserved packets of lunch meat; 4 ounces per person per day)
Mustard—it's worth it (a small bottle for a trip)

DINNER
Mountain House freeze-dried meals (buy the 2-serving bags, as each 2-serving bag is dinner for one person, and pack several extra bags per person for emergencies—the shelf life is thirty years, so don't worry about waste if you don't use them)
Small bottle of hot sauce

SNACKS, DESSERTS, EXTRAS
Drink mix pouches (2 per person per day)
Protein or energy bars (5 per person per day)
Assorted high-energy snacks—jerky, nuts, candy bars, hard candy, granola, etc. (pack according to expectations, but keep in mind that you will eat more of this stuff than you think)

FIRE AND WATER

Your water treatment and consumption gear deserves as much serious consideration as your bow or rifle. Here's a rundown of some basic water tools.

A: 1-quart bottles. Some people like stainless steel or aluminum bottles, which are just fine, but it's hard to beat the simple and ubiquitous Nalgene bottle. **B:** Bladders that ride inside your pack with a hose running to your shoulder strap are great for staying hydrated, because you drink more water if it's convenient to do so. The downside is that they can't be fully trusted. They sometimes burst open or leak, soaking your pack contents. And during subfreezing weather, the hoses will freeze and lock up. **C:** Collapsible canteens are great for long trips with scarce water supplies. Pictured here is a standard military-issue 2-quart collapsible canteen. A better though more expensive option are the Dromedary canteens made by MSR. They come in a variety of sizes, are durable, and weigh next to nothing. **D:** Water filter. Waterborne parasites are a bitch. They will ruin your trip, or even your life. Make it a general practice to purify all drinking water pulled from ponds, creeks, lakes, rivers, etc. Pictured here is the excellent MSR MiniWorks EX ceramic filter; the Katadyn Hiker Pro is another good filter. **E:** The Steripen, which uses ultraviolet light to purify drinking water, is a lightweight tool that is ideal for purifying small quantities of water; perfect for solo trips lasting just a day or two. **F:** Tablets or drops made from iodine, chlorine derivative, or other chemicals are simple and effective ways to treat water. Take care to follow the directions on the packaging and test them out before you head to the backcountry to make sure you can handle the off flavors. Follow directions carefully, giving the chemicals plenty of time to do their work. Pictured here are iodine Aquamira water purification tablets.

In a pinch, 3 to 5 drops of chlorine bleach will treat 1 liter of water. It tastes like a swimming pool but keeps you healthy. Water can also be treated effectively by boiling it for several minutes. **G:** Drink mixes such as Hydrate and Recover, an excellent product from Wilderness Athlete, help to mask the tastes of low-quality drinking water and also aid in combating dehydration and depletion from strenuous physical activities such as hunting in the mountains.

WATER BASICS

Staying hydrated in the backcountry is critical. Severe dehydration can lead to heat stroke and hypothermia; mild dehydration can lead to energy loss, a bad attitude, and poor decision making. Drink more water than you think you need, and don't be afraid to add powdered supplements or flavors if it helps you get more water down. In typical conditions, you should be pounding down 3 liters a day to stay in top condition. In hot or otherwise grueling conditions, go for 5 liters.

FIRE BASICS

It's hardly necessary to explain the appeal of fire; as a species, we have such an acute appreciation for controlled flames that we instinctively turn toward a campfire even when we're already warm and well fed. When times get hard in the woods or mountains—when you're cold, hungry, lost, or scared—your desire for fire can become almost unbearable. Learn the basic principles of fire making and you'll enjoy your time in the backcountry all the better. Even when you don't need a fire, it's comforting just knowing that you could make one if you wanted it.

It's wise to pack along fire-starting materials when hunting in wet country, and to pick up suitable fire-starting materials as you encounter them rather than waiting until you desperately need them.

A: A few strips of newsprint tucked inside a Ziploc bag can be a lifesaver. **B:** Commercial fire-starting pastes, such as Mautz Fire Ribbon, are cheap, simple products that take much of the stress out of fire building. A proper, well-organized pile of tinder and kindling on top of a quarter-sized dab of paste will rarely refuse to burn. Or if necessary, you can skip the tinder altogether and jump right to pencil-sized sticks. **C:** Coughlan Fire Sticks are waterproof and nontoxic, and they let off a strong and long-burning flame. **D:** Keep two lighters in your gear, and keep at least one of them in a sealable plastic bag. (It doesn't hurt to be overprepared, so carry a few wooden matches inside a waterproof match holder as well.) **E:** Dried bird's nests are excellent emergency fire starters. In rainy conditions, check tree cavities for bird's nests; often these are perfectly dry when everything else is dripping wet. **F:** The bark from paper birch burns amazingly well. It is full of resinous oils that repel water and ignite into a hot blaze when touched with a match or lighter. It is easy to collect; sheets will literally fall away from living trees. **G:** Fatwood, or heart pine, is a highly combustible kindling taken from the resin-impregnated heartwood of pines such as jack pine and longleaf pine.

A camp axe or hatchet is very helpful for limbing deadfall, gathering kindling, and splitting small to medium logs. Always remember that wet wood may be dry on the inside. A hatchet will get you into it. Using a knife, you can whittle away toothpick-sized pieces of kindling from the dry core and start a fire in even the wettest circumstances.

BACKCOUNTRY RISKS

The risks of a backcountry hunt include all of the normal risks associated with a typical hunt, plus many more. These risks are compounded by the physical distance that separates you from emergency assistance. For the unprepared hunter, a simple puncture wound can turn into a serious infection. A burn from an overturned pot of boiling water can lead to intense pain and a trip that's cut short. A sprained or broken ankle can result in an expensive helicopter evacuation. It's impossible to make a plan for every single sort of emergency you might encounter, as even the most imaginative person would never think of them all. Rather, you need to assume a general attitude of caution and preparation, and maintain a flexible safety plan that can evolve with the situation. Here are some suggestions:

- Keep a carefully inventoried trauma bag on you at all times.
- On extended outings, carry an expedition-sized med kit that is tailored to the size of your party and the duration of your

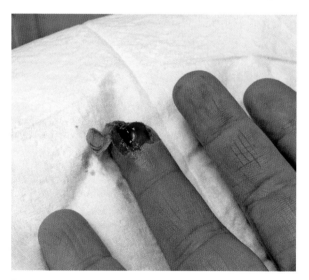

Backcountry risks abound. This javelina hunter's finger got caught between a rock and a hard place.

trip. Adventure Medical Kits makes great products.

- Invest in wilderness first aid courses.
- Always have a form of emergency communication. Be aware of cell service, or carry a satellite phone or satellite communicator.
- Take care to monitor weather leading up to your trip and adequately prepare for any severe conditions.
- Have a plan that every member of the party is briefed on. Be aware of evacuation routes and procedures in case of emergency. Know whom to call, and know the location of the nearest medical facility.
- Share your itinerary and plans in detail with someone who is *not* on your trip, and make plans to check in with that person before and after your hunt.
- Connect everyone's spouse or immediate family before a trip, so that they can reach one another in case of an emergency. That way, you can get in touch with everyone's family with just one phone call.
- Carry a GPS, physical maps, and a compass. Know how to use them.
- Stay calm. Think clearly. Be observant. The guy who pays attention to details is the guy who survives. The guy who panics is not.

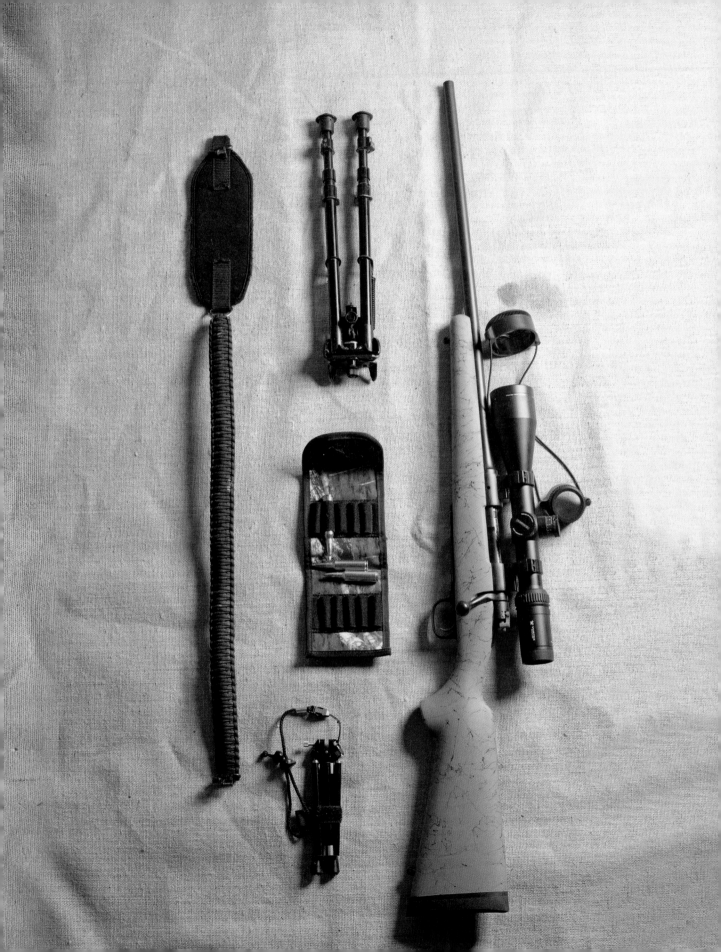

TACTICS AND STRATEGIES

WHERE TO HUNT

Before Europeans arrived on this continent, access to North America's richest hunting grounds was won and lost through warfare. The Nez Perce infringed on the hunting grounds of their enemies, the Blackfeet; the Blackfeet infringed on the hunting grounds of their enemies, the Sioux; the Sioux infringed on the hunting grounds of the Crow; the Crow attempted to steal the ancestral hunting grounds of the Shoshone. For Native American tribes, hunting land was something worth fighting and dying for.

Today, the battle for hunting lands in America is no longer bloody and violent, but it's still intense. The best hunters spend more time thinking about where they'll hunt than any other aspect of the hunting process. For them, identifying and gaining access to good hunting spots is more than a simple hobby—they treat it like a job. Year-round, they are studying maps, scouting locations, swapping information with their fellow hunters, and making phone calls to landowners and government agencies responsible for the management of public lands. All this effort goes into solving the primary question that should be on every hunter's mind: *Come hunting season, where will I be?*

For discussion's sake, let's divide all hunting lands into two categories: private land and public land. Private lands are privately owned parcels of land for which you need to secure permission from a landowner or land manager in order to hunt the property. Public lands are government-owned properties that are generally open to the public for hunting purposes. Bear in mind, though, that these are somewhat simplified definitions. There are many parcels of private land made open to public-access hunting through various state-sponsored programs; likewise, some public lands are managed by various branches of government as restricted-access hunting grounds, which are meant to provide high-quality hunting experiences to a limited number of hunters who are randomly selected through raffles and drawings.

Private and public lands each have their pros and cons. One of the best things about hunting public land is that you're exercising your rights as a citizen to access those areas and harvest publicly owned renewable resources of wild game. This right is distinctly American, as no other nation on earth has a public land and wildlife management system nearly as good as ours. There is no greater feeling than standing on a mountain knowing that you can hunt all day in any direction without having to worry about fences or No Trespassing signs, and that all of it belongs to We the People. But remember that public access means just that: you're going to be sharing the land with other people, and those other people are going to make your hunt more complicated—often in very frustrating ways.

In a nutshell, that's the great advantage to private land: limited access. You're sharing the ground and the animals with fewer people, which makes hunting a lot easier and often much more productive. This is particularly true in the eastern half of the United States, where public lands are less abundant and tend to be very crowded during peak seasons for highly desirable species such as deer, bear, and turkey. What's more, many private landowners practice superb wildlife conservation on their lands, and it's beautiful to witness the results firsthand. Yet private lands have their own drawbacks, especially for independent-minded hunters who want to operate with autonomy. Private landowners often exercise a lot of control over hunters on their land. They can tell hunters where and when to hunt. I have a good friend in Wisconsin who goes so far as to assign specific tree stands to each of the guys who hunts on his land. Also, many private landowners enforce restrictions that go far beyond the restrictions of the law. A hunter might *legally* be allowed to harvest any deer, buck or doe, but the landowner might stipulate that he kill only does. A final consideration is that private-land hunting permissions are tentative. At any time, and for any reason, a landowner might revoke your privileges or sell his or her land to someone who doesn't allow hunting. I still remember the hurt feelings that resulted when my family lost hunting permission on the farm where my two brothers and I all killed our first deer. The old farmer died, and his kids simply gave us the boot when they took over. They wanted those deer to themselves. I've met many hunters who actually quit hunting after suffering a similar loss of hunting access. These hunters had grown complacent in their search for hunting grounds, and they gave up after losing their "one good spot." Do not let this happen to you. Every hunter should maintain an active collection of viable hunting locations, either public or private. Here's how to begin.

PUBLIC LAND

All states have at least some public lands that are available to hunting, though exact amounts vary wildly. Percentages are in the low single digits in Rhode Island and Kansas, while the vast majority of Nevada and Alaska is publicly owned.

STATE-BY-STATE COMPARISON OF PUBLIC LAND OWNERSHIP

U.S. STATES LAND OWNERSHIP

RANK	STATE	% PUBLIC LAND	RANK	STATE	% PUBLIC LAND
1	AK	95.8%	27	TN	14.1%
2	NV	87.8%	28	KY	11.8%
3	UT	75.2%	29	SC	11.8%
4	ID	70.4%	30	MO	11.2%
5	OR	60.4%	31	MS	10.9%
6	AZ	56.8%	32	LA	10.7%
7	WY	55.9%	33	GA	9.7%
8	CA	52.1%	34	ND	9.1%
9	NM	47.4%	35	SD	8.9%
10	CO	43.3%	36	MD	7.6%
11	WA	41.9%	37	DE	7.4%
12	MT	37.5%	38	AL	7.1%
13	NY	37.1%	39	MA	6.3%
14	FL	29.2%	40	CT	6.2%
15	MI	28.1%	41	ME	5.7%
16	MN	23.5%	42	OK	4.6%
17	HI	19.0%	43	IN	4.5%
18	NJ	18.3%	44	OH	4.2%
19	NH	18.0%	45	TX	4.2%
20	WI	17.8%	46	IL	4.1%
21	AR	17.3%	47	IA	2.8%
22	VA	17.1%	48	NE	2.8%
23	WV	16.5%	49	KS	1.9%
24	PA	16.1%	50	RI	1.5%
25	VT	15.8%			
26	NC	14.6%		**USA**	**39.8%**

Note: Land ownership is fluid and these percentages are subject to frequent changes. This chart should not be regarded as completely accurate but is meant only to give the reader a general understanding of the availability of public land.

Public lands come in many forms, depending on the region and state. Some of the more common land designations are state parks, state game areas, state forests, state wildlife refuges, national parks, national forests, national wildlife preserves, national wildlife refuges, and Bureau of Land Management (BLM) lands. Typically, but not always, the terms *park*, *preserve*, and *sanctuary* denote land designations that are not open to hunting. (Don't confuse this with being unfriendly to hunting. Park and preserve lands serve a valuable role for fish and game by providing sanctuaries that help prevent overharvest; often, these areas serve as source locations that continually produce game that is harvested on neighboring lands.) The terms *forest*, *game management area*, *refuge*, and *BLM* typically denote lands that are open to hunting—but again, there are many notable exceptions.

Due to the nuanced nature of land designations, questions about hunting on public lands—both state and federal—should always be put to representatives of your state's fish and game agency. *It is the hunter's responsibility to determine the legality of hunting on any parcel of land before he attempts to harvest game on that property!* These agencies are responsible for the management of game within their state's boundaries, and they have a vested interest in helping you decipher the landscape of where you want to hunt. Since they rely largely on hunting license sales as a funding source, they want you to get out there and have a good time as much as possible, and since they are also tasked with the enforcement of game laws, it's in their own best interest to arm you with reliable information now rather than having to punish you later. In fact, many states actively promote awareness about public land hunting opportunities with websites devoted specifically to the subject.

STATE	WEBSITE
Alabama	www.outdooralabama.com
Alaska	www.adfg.alaska.gov
Arizona	www.azgfd.gov
Arkansas	www.agfc.com
California	www.dfg.ca.gov
Colorado	www.wildlife.state.co.us
Connecticut	www.ct.gov
Delaware	www.dnrec.delaware.gov
Florida	www.myfwc.com
Georgia	www.georgiawildlife.org
Hawaii	www.dlnr.hawaii.gov
Idaho	www.fishandgame.idaho.gov
Illinois	www.dnr.illinois.gov
Indiana	www.in.gov/dnr/fishwild
Iowa	www.iowadnr.gov
Kansas	www.kdwpt.state.ks.us
Kentucky	www.fw.ky.gov
Louisiana	www.wlf.louisiana.gov
Maine	www.maine.gov/ifw
Maryland	www.dnr.state.md.us
Massachusetts	www.mass.gov/eea/agencies/dfg
Michigan	www.michigan.gov/dnr
Minnesota	www.dnr.state.mn.us/fishwildlife
Mississippi	www.mdwfp.com
Missouri	www.mdc.mo.gov
Montana	www.fwp.mt.gov
Nebraska	www.outdoornebraska.ne.gov
Nevada	www.ndow.org
New Hampshire	www.wildlife.state.nh.us
New Jersey	www.nj.gov/dep/fgw
New Mexico	www.wildlife.state.nm.us
New York	www.dec.ny.gov
North Carolina	www.ncwildlife.org
North Dakota	www.gf.nd.gov
Ohio	www.dnr.state.oh.us
Oklahoma	www.wildlifedepartment.com
Oregon	www.dfw.state.or.us
Pennsylvania	www.pgc.state.pa.us
Rhode Island	www.dem.ri.gov
South Carolina	www.dnr.sc.gov
South Dakota	www.gfp.sd.gov
Tennessee	www.state.tn.us/twra
Texas	www.tpwd.state.tx.us
Utah	www.wildlife.utah.gov
Vermont	www.vtfishandwildlife.com
Virginia	www.dgif.virginia.gov
Washington	www.wdfw.wa.gov
West Virginia	www.wvdnr.gov
Wisconsin	dnr.wi.gov
Wyoming	wgfd.wyo.gov

But don't let your search end with published lists of public land hunting areas. Some of my best public hunting spots are under-the-radar locations that are not listed on any compilation. Growing up, we hunted squirrels, grouse, waterfowl, and even deer on a lot of property that was owned by the township, a type of governmental body in the Northeast and Midwest that holds varying powers. We identified township properties by looking at plat maps, which show legal property boundaries of land parcels as well as ownership. In this case, the plat maps showed the parcels as individual quarter-acre lots that were owned by the township, but together these small lots formed large contiguous tracts of undeveloped land that included some very productive marshes and hardwood forests.

Such under-the-radar public land locations might require an extra degree of research in order to ascertain legality. Answers about the permissibility of hunting might not be spelled out clearly, or even at all, so don't take the word of the first person you ask. For instance, a township clerk might say you can't hunt township land for the simple reason that he doesn't want to get himself in trouble by giving you permission. If you feel that you're not getting the full story from a government representative, ask for a thorough, legally based explanation of what activities are allowed, and not allowed, on the property in question. My paranoia about being misled by public officials comes from a firsthand experience that I had shortly after moving to Montana. I was interested in hunting BLM lands in the north-central part of the state, and I stopped in at the Lewistown field office of the federal Bureau of Land Management to inquire about maps. There I was told by an employee at the counter that I needed to ask permission from the rancher who held grazing rights on any parcel of BLM land before I could hunt there. This statement was misleading and categorically false.

Once you identify lands where you *can* hunt, you need to narrow those down to lands where you *want* to hunt. This is the hard part, and doing it well mandates that you spend hour upon hour in the woods, on the phone, and in front of the computer. The first and most obvious question that needs to be addressed is what lands hold the species that you're interested in hunting. Sure, you might have identified thousands of acres of prime grasslands and pine forest that are full of turkey, but that won't necessarily do you much good if you're dreaming about hunting wild hogs. The most obvious way to figure out what critters are living on a chunk of land is to put your boots on the ground and scout it out. I've done this many times in many places—drive or fly out to some potential hunting ground and start walking. Sometimes it's a three-day hike with a fully loaded backpack; other times it's a ten-minute stroll along a lakeshore within sight of my car. As much as possible, I try to time my scouting trips for optimal benefit in terms of

Map reading is an essential skill for anyone who's serious about finding prime hunting locations.

both season and time of day. If you're looking for a late-season whitetail location in the Upper Midwest, you can hardly rule out a location because you didn't see any fresh deer sign on an August visit.

While scouting a new location, it's wise to bring along a notebook as well as a GPS unit, topographic maps, and satellite imagery or aerial photographs. On your GPS unit and maps, record the description and location of relevant land features such as trails, parking areas, water sources, campsites, and so on. Mark and describe any animals or animal sign that you encounter, including tracks, trails, droppings, wallows, scrapes, rubs, and evidence of feeding. Record evidence left by other hunters, such as tree stands, ground blinds, or perennial campsites. (Buck poles and stacks of cut firewood often differentiate the campsites of hunters from those of more casual summer campers.) Don't just limit your observations to the specific species you happen to be looking for. If you find a beaver pond while scouting for deer, make a note. If you see brook trout rise from the depths of that beaver pond to take a mayfly, make a note of that, too. Be sure that your notes are clearly written, and stored in such a way that you'll be able to find them in the future. I can't tell you how many times I've had to call my friends or brothers to ask something like, "Hey, where were we that one time when there was a ton of snow and we saw a bunch of deer hunkered down in a little hemlock patch?" And when it comes to GPS, name your waypoints in a manner that will still make sense in a couple of months or even years. It's frustrating to look at your GPS and see numerically assigned waypoints that you never bothered to label. Is #46 a place where you found drinking water in a notoriously dry canyon several years ago, or is it just a place where you stashed your backpack and then took a waypoint to make sure you'd find it again?

TRAIL CAMERAS

Up until the advent of the trail camera, a hunter had to do most of his scouting on foot. Guesses on the whereabouts of certain animals had to be made by studying sign. Then along came this new technology, and suddenly a hunter can be in two places at once.

The use of trail cameras is easy. If you're curious about whether animals are using a certain area, or if you want details about animals that you know to be using a certain area, just hang

up the camera and see what images it captures. The only trick is posting the camera in places where animals will pass within close range of the trigger and lens, such as water sources, heavily used game trails, and natural funnels formed by topographic features. You can even home in on specific animals by positioning the camera near an old boar's wallow, a whitetail scrape, or a carcass killed by a predator.

Not only does the camera yield valuable insights about the size, quantity, location, and timing of animals that are using your hunting area, it can provide some big surprises as well. Besides having photos of your intended quarry, you'll end up with an inventory of many incidental species of wildlife that are roaming your neck of the woods. (This does not exclude the two-legged version. With infrared technology available, trail cameras will monitor a property for trespassers and poachers.)

Many hunters use trail cameras during the off-season, which is great, but don't make the mistake of thinking that the animals you captured will necessarily still be around in a few months. You can draw some insights, for sure, but you have to continuously monitor the area in order to have an accurate idea of what's going on as hunting season approaches. During the actual season, a single camera can be packed along with you while hunting. You can set it near fresh sign to see what's happening there, or post it near a prospective ambush location to see if anything passes through. (Check your state's hunting regulations before using a trail camera during hunting season. Montana has banned their use during the season, and more states may follow suit.)

Once you've set up a trail camera, test it before leaving. Walk in front of the camera at different distances to make sure the camera will trigger, and then review the photos to make sure everything is functioning properly. If there are trees with low-hanging branches within the camera's trigger zone, shake them to

Bushnell   09-28-2011 16:39:39

make sure they don't cause the camera to snap an image—you don't want to come back in a few days to find a thousand photos of the same branch blowing in the breeze. It's also smart to point the camera due north to reduce sun glare. If there are any cattle in the area, make sure to secure the camera out of their reach. Cattle love to rub trees, and they make no exceptions for those holding plastic-encased cameras.

Trail cameras set on private land are usually safe from theft, but thievery and vandalism of trail cameras are all too common on public land. Most trail camera companies sell locking kits to keep your camera where you left it, but this won't stop some loser from smashing your camera out of jealousy or spite. The best deterrent on public land is to camouflage your camera and use it only in out-of-the-way places where it's unlikely to be discovered by passersby.

There are dozens of trail cameras on the market today. A quick online search will result in a plethora of reviews and recommendations for units at prices ranging from affordable to astronomic. (Bushnell offers a number of great trail cams at fair prices.)

Scouting isn't the only way to get up-to-date information about your public land hunting areas. State fish and game agencies can be a great resource for this kind of material. Through various channels such as written surveys, online questionnaires, and interviews with hunters at check stations, they compile statistical information about hunting areas that can be quite detailed and localized to the particular areas you want to hunt. For instance, you can go on to the Alaska Department of Fish and Game's website and get hunter-success rates for particular river drainages and mountain ranges. You might find that moose success rates in one section of the Alaska Range have hovered as low as 5 percent for several years,

Hunting competition is a fact of life. Rather than cursing other hunters, learn how to make their presence work to your advantage.

Getting away from the crowds on public land involves creativity and energy.

while just across the range divide you'll see that success rates average as high as 30 percent.

Information that comes directly from regional wildlife biologists or enforcement agents can be even more valuable than the published results of hunter surveys. Serious hunters who value their time in the woods are always placing calls to state wildlife biologists to assess the situation in certain areas. Let's say you're interested in doing an elk hunt in Colorado's White River National Forest. You'd call the Colorado Division of Wildlife and Parks and ask for the phone number of the elk or big game biologist who's most closely associated with that area. Come right out and ask: "I want to hunt elk in the White River National Forest, and I'm hoping you can give me some insights." Often these individuals will limit what they will say. They can't give a specific set of GPS coordinates to every hunter who calls, because that would certainly diminish the quality of the area. But if you are persistent

and polite, they might throw you some tips. These tips take the form of "Well, I can tell you this much: the herd is looking really strong, and we're expecting a higher-than-average harvest this year"; or "If I were going to hunt that area myself, I'd be interested in checking out the South Fork of the White River. And I'd be especially curious about the area around Dry Buck Creek." When you get a tip like this from a biologist or warden, it's damn sure worth looking into.

While competition is certainly a downside to public land hunting, a smart hunter puts

A group of hunters "lines" canoes into otherwise inaccessible moose country.

that competition to use by collecting firsthand information from other hunters who've been there. Call sporting goods stores and archery shops in the area you're thinking about hunting and throw yourself at their mercy. Say you've never hunted such-and-such area but you're looking for some insights. Sure, you might get some bum information from guys who are trying to protect their locations from outsider intrusion. But by placing five or six phone calls to different places, and by checking these tips against information from your state fish and game agency, you'll be able to tell which insights are good and which are bogus. Another great trick is to track down hunters (friends, plus friends of friends) who used to hit a certain spot but then moved away. A guy who lived in western Montana for ten years but then moved to Alaska is going to be a gold mine of information about western Montana. He's no longer worried about protecting his spots, and often he'll divulge locations just because he's curious to hear about what you turn up. Bars in rural areas are another great spot. Buy a couple of drinks for an old barfly in Ennis, Montana, and you might be pleasantly surprised to hear him pass along information about his buddy's hunting locations and practices that his buddy would never in a million years want divulged. Online forums are a great resource, too. Let's say you're in-

Two hunters use horses to access prime elk ground.

terested in hunting wild pigs in Tuskegee National Forest. It's smart to sit down and do an online search with the key words "hunting wild pigs Tuskegee National Forest." Once you start scrolling through the hits, you're guaranteed to find folks talking very specifically about locations and methods and strategies.

A final thing that warrants mention here is that the public land hunter needs to plan around his competition. Of course, this isn't always necessary. Oftentimes, even in the East, the public land hunter can enjoy perfect solitude. But he needs to be aware that his solitude can be broken at any moment, and he needs to be ready to adapt to changing circumstances. And he needs to be realistic in his expectations. If you've been watching a half dozen whitetails feeding every morning in a meadow next to the parking lot of a state game management area, you can bet your ass that you're not the only person who's planning on working those deer. Before daybreak on open-

A sheep hunter employs an inflatable pack raft to transport his kill out of a remote hunting location.

Three llamas put this hunter into uncrowded elk country with a plush camp to boot.

ing day, they'll be spooked into the next county by a massive influx of hunters.

The best public land hunters have a knack for anticipating what the other guys are going to do, which in turn enables them to anticipate what their quarry will do. In Montana, my brother Matt and I used to hunt an elk herd in the Madison Range that behaved in a very predictable way on opening day. No matter where they happened to be feeding the night before, the first rifle shots of the morning would send them piling through a saddle on their way toward the protection of a heavily timbered valley. We would pack in to this saddle the day before opening day, even if the nearest elk was several drainages away. At daybreak, we'd be waiting for the elk. We filled a few freezers doing that. I have a friend who uses an advanced version of this strategy. He hunts a mountainside that often holds elk during the latter part of the season, but it's next to impossible to approach the animals without spooking them. So he'll actually wait until other hunters spot the elk and start climbing toward

them. Then he'll hustle up to the elk's escape route through a high saddle and wait for the animals to come through. He's been killing elk like that for twenty years.

Of course, there's more to public land hunting than heading off spooked critters. Many public hunters appreciate solitude and a quarry that is behaving in a natural, relaxed manner. To find these conditions, they seek out those areas of public land that are less likely to get visited by others. Generally, this means areas that are less accessible. A friend in South Carolina does all of his public land deer and hog hunting from a boat because he can reach areas that guys with cars cannot. Another friend of mine hunts deer and pheasant on the small islands of a river that has public land on both banks. For whatever reason, he's the only guy who thinks to do this and he has the islands to himself. It's so good, in fact, that he crosses the river using stealth tactics so that no one will steal his idea. I used to hunt whitetails on public land in Michigan using a similar strategy. By placing my tree stand in an area that was separated from the two-track by nothing more than a waist-deep channel of water, I had a huge expanse of marsh all to myself.

Stealth and sly thinking are not the only ways to get away from competition. My brother Matt and I use physical endurance to achieve similar results. We enjoy superb bowhunting for elk, often seeing hundreds per day, in a public land area that is absolutely devoid of hunters. It's a chunk of national forest that is very difficult to reach because there's a buffer of private property that separates the national forest lands from the highway. We get in there by making a circuitous 18-mile round-trip hike that dodges property boundaries. In a period of eight years, I killed three elk in there and my brother killed five or six. Packing multiple hundred-pound loads of meat that far is hell on your knees, but those steaks and burgers are awfully nice on your grill.

A hunter can access a lot of ground using nothing but his boots; he can access even more ground by using other forms of low-impact and nonmotorized conveyance. The following modes of travel are usually allowed in even the most sensitive and legally protected backcountry areas.

Pack stock. Horses and mules are great because they can carry you 20-plus miles in a day and lug more gear than you'd ever need. Horse camps often include everything from cast-iron skillets to electrified fences that help reduce the grizzly threat. But traveling in the backcountry with horses or mules is no simple matter. These are powerful animals capable of crushing human bones, yet they are also fragile in their own way. Good wranglers have typically grown up around horses, and they've crafted a lifestyle based on their love of the animals. If you take a horse or mule into the backcountry without the proper skill set, you

A hunter uses good old-fashioned boot leather to beat the crowds.

and the animal can end up in very bad shape—or worse.

Llamas. You can't ride a llama, but then they can't kill you, either. A full-grown animal will weigh between 300 and 400 pounds and can carry 40–60 pounds. They are user-friendly animals, far easier to care for than horses. Not only can they go almost anywhere that you can go, they'll eat just about anything and have very low water demands.

Watercraft. Rafts, packrafts, and canoes can all be used to get you into otherwise inaccessible areas. Packrafts are great because you can deflate them and carry them on your back; a common hunting method is to hike into the head of a drainage and then float yourself (or your kill) out. Canoes are good for more placid watercourses, and they're great for crossing lakes and reservoirs where you might be able to leave the competition behind simply by putting some water between you and your vehicle. Rafts are perfect for large-scale expeditions. With the right raft, a couple of hunters can float out all their gear plus a pair of moose.

Bikes. Considering how long mountain bikes have been around, it's surprising that they're only now getting widespread attention from backpack hunters. They are especially suitable for traveling logging roads that have been gated or otherwise closed to vehicular access—something that's becoming more and more common as the U.S. Forest Service shuts down roads due to a lack of funding for maintenance.

A bike can also make pack-outs easier if you drop an animal close to a trail or gated road. You can rig a heavy-duty cart by lashing two mountain bikes together using paracord and rigid poles cut from native materials. Or get a wheeled trailer for your bike; they can be built up from setups used for hauling little kids behind your bike.

PRIVATE LAND

If you're sitting around waiting for someone to offer you access to her game-rich chunk of private property, you're going to die of old age in your armchair while you wait for the phone to ring. Like almost everything of value, private land hunting opportunities usually go to the people who work for them. Since no two hunting permissions are secured in the same way, there's no exact formula for how to gain access to private land. The best you can do is study the tactics and perspectives of people who do

it well, and then try to incorporate these things into your own quest for hunting land.

Earlier I mentioned a farm where my two brothers and I all killed our first deer. The farm was owned by a man who went to our church. Over years of socializing at church-related functions, my father won that farmer's trust and earned a hunting permission that kept our family supplied with venison for a period of about twelve years. That type of permission—one that comes through a preexisting personal contact—is easily the most common form of hunting permission. These types of contacts come in many forms: immediate family, in-laws, neighbors, coworkers, friends of friends, plus fellow members of clubs, churches, fraternal organizations, or sporting teams. In fact, of the dozen or so active hunting permissions that I maintained as a kid around my home in

Twin Lake, Michigan, 90 percent were on lands owned by acquaintances of my parents or friends of those acquaintances.

Even if you have close contacts who own good hunting land, don't ever take for granted that they'll give you hunting permission. This sort of transaction needs to be carefully cultivated, regardless of how well you know the person. Remember, you're asking someone to allow an armed person onto that property, a property that might also contain buildings, pets, livestock, and a variety of other users. On top of that, you're likely to be coming and going while it's dark outside. What you're asking goes beyond a simple favor; it's a serious issue that needs to be handled respectfully.

To get a sense of how delicately I handle the issue of hunting someone else's land, consider the following story. My wife used to work with a woman who was married to a guy who was raised on a dairy farm in upstate New York. This couple was (and is) very close to us. The man in charge of this family's farm, which abounds in deer and turkey, was the father-in-law of my wife's friend—let's call him David. On multiple weekend visits to the farm I made sure to mention to David that I was an avid hunter. But despite my hints, he never

Leaving gates as you found them will keep you on good terms with landowners who are gracious enough to share access with you.

even came close to extending an invitation for me to hunt his land. I knew that he had several elderly friends who hunted there on occasion, and I figured he thought that was enough.

Not wanting to be pushy, I waited until I'd known him for a few years and then I asked if I could come out for a onetime squirrel hunt on a mid-January day. I picked that time of year because I knew that other hunters wouldn't be in the woods, so I wouldn't be putting David in an uncomfortable situation with his friends. At the end of that squirrel hunt, I stopped by the farmhouse to give David a few tokens of my appreciation, including some wine and a sampling of wild game sausages that I'd made at my home. I did not inquire about hunting there again. The next day, I followed up with a thank-you email. I attached to this email some photos of the meal that I'd made from the squirrels on his farm, because farmers are practical people and they like to see their resources put to wise use. Ultimately, my patience paid off. The next time that I spoke to the farmer, he mentioned that one of the other guys who'd been hunting there was no longer welcome. I could come out and hunt deer and turkey anytime I wanted. By that point, I'd known the man for a total of six years.

Not every place is that tough. Right now I'm sitting on another great hunting permission in the same region that came about through a good friend who lives in Anchorage, Alaska. This friend was visiting his relatives in Minnesota when he got to talking to a distant family member from New York who complained about a gross overabundance of deer on her property. My buddy shared some kind words about me, then promptly sent me an email urging me to reach out to her. I contacted her the next day and offered to provide letters of personal recommendation from other landowners whose property I've hunted in the past. She said not to bother, though the gesture clearly resonated with her. Without ever actually speaking to me, she granted me the first hunting permission that I had ever received over email.

These two examples are extremes on each end of the spectrum, but they demonstrate the adaptability and care that you need to use when approaching the subject of hunting on the land of a personal acquaintance.

THINGS TO CLEAR UP WITH A LANDOWNER BEFORE HUNTING THAT LAND, WHETHER IT'S YOUR BEST FRIEND OR A TOTAL STRANGER

1. Assure the landowner that you hunt with strict adherence to all rules and regulations, and then stay true to your word. Even if it's a seemingly silly law, like those stating that rifles and shotguns be cased at all times when inside a vehicle, adhere to it.

2. Be specific about what you want to hunt. Don't say you're going to hunt deer and then come walking out of the woods with a dead turkey—unless of course you were granted permission to hunt turkeys as well. Each landowner has idiosyncrasies about wildlife on his or her land, and it's your responsibility to find out what these are and then adhere to them. I hunt a lovely farm where the owner forbids the hunting of ducks and geese because she likes to watch them fly by. I used to hunt another farm where all legal animals were fair game except rabbits, because the owner's nephew liked to chase them with hounds.

3. Tell the landowner when you want to hunt. If you tell a landowner that you'll be hunting on Monday, don't show up on Tuesday without checking in first. Maybe the landowner has given someone else hunting permission for that day, or maybe there will be a fence repair crew coming in and a hunter won't be welcome on the land that day. Eventually, most landowners will tell you to come and go as you please. But until then, don't make assumptions.

4. Tell them who will be hunting, and then keep your word. This is the most common mistake that hunters make, and it infuriates landowners. If you ask permission for yourself, then don't bring a buddy without checking to see if it's okay. One time my brother Matt secured a great turkey hunting permission from a wheat farmer whose crop was getting devastated by the birds. At the last minute, though, Matt decided to take along me and our brother, Danny. Our intention was to clear this with the landowner before we started hunting, but we never got a chance. When we pulled up with three guys in the truck, the landowner angrily kicked us off his property before we could open our mouths to explain.

Securing hunting permissions from complete strangers is ten times harder and twenty times more awkward than securing them from acquaintances, but that doesn't mean it's impossible. In fact, I've done this many times, and I have enjoyed some great hunting because of it. My friends and I refer to this method of gaining permission as "banging doors." Here there's no room for patience or carefully orchestrated interactions. To make it work, you need to know when to ask, how to ask, and what to ask—and you need to do it quickly.

The "when" portion of the equation refers to timing, in terms of both time of day and time of year. Obviously, you don't want to scare some farmer's wife by banging on the door at 11:00 p.m. Rather than earning you a permission, that's likely to earn you an ass chewing. Instead, you should limit your landowner visits to business hours only. Some guys suggest that you try to plan your visits to avoid a farmer's dinnertime and peak periods of work activity, but it's nearly impossible to anticipate such things, and it can be like trying to hit a moving target. Instead, use common sense. Don't make a farmer shut down his combine in order to talk to you, but then don't make him uncomfortable by staring at him from the window of your truck for an hour while he eats dinner with his family.

As for the time of year, keep in mind that farmers and ranchers sometimes get so bombarded by hunters during hunting seasons that they begin to dread the sound of their own doorbell. A wise hunter pays visits to landowners during midsummer. This way, hunting season is close enough that the landowner doesn't feel as though you're talking about some abstract event in the distant future, but it's far enough away that he doesn't feel pressured to make an immediate decision. Under these circumstances a landowner might opt to defer his final answer until later, but that's fine. A month or two later, when you're a little closer to the season, you can remind the landowner about your previous visit and he's likely to treat you more charitably as a known person

Asking permission to hunt small game or waterfowl is a great way to get your foot in the door on private property. Many landowners who love to hunt deer don't really care about hunting small game, and they're happy to extend the privilege to polite, considerate hunters. In time, that permission might be expanded to include big game.

who had the courtesy to ask for hunting permission well in advance of the actual season.

When it comes to how you ask, think brevity and conciseness. The moment you walk up to a landowner's home and bang on the door, he's going to be wondering whether you're selling religion or fertilizer. Don't keep him guessing. Many articles on this subject suggest that you start out by complimenting the landowner on how beautiful the property is, but that only makes it worse. You just end up looking like a phony. Instead, say something simple like this: "Excuse me, ma'am. I'd like to ask about the possibility of doing some deer hunting on your property. I have references who can testify that I'm a trustworthy and respectful hunter. I'm sure you get permission requests like this all the time, but I want you to know that I'm more than willing to limit my harvest to does, or to do whatever is most beneficial to you. And I'd be happy to return the favor by helping out with any chores or errands that might come up between now and hunting season." By coming right out and stating your purpose, you do risk getting shut down immediately. But I'd venture to say that any landowner who says no right away would have still said no if you'd started out by saying how beautiful the grain silo looks in the light of the setting sun.

The "what" portion of the equation refers to what kind of birds or animals you'd like to hunt. Typically, the more romantic and coveted the species, the less likely you are to get permission from a stranger. If you drive up to a large cattle ranch outside Durango, Colorado, and ask the owner for permission to hunt the herd of bull elk that have been hanging around his irrigated pasture for the last two weeks, the answer's going to be no. For one thing, elk are big business in Durango, and there's a lot of demand from hunters and outfitters who are willing to pay top dollar for hunting rights. For another thing, if he was going to say yes to the first guy who drove up his driveway, that would have happened two weeks earlier when the elk first showed up.

Instead, get your foot in the door by asking about less coveted species that don't demand as much attention from other hunters. Squirrels and cottontail rabbits are obvious examples. Another great avenue of approach is to ask permission to hunt a deleterious species such as Canada geese. Often a farmer who's watching his alfalfa field get destroyed by geese will be in the mood to open his gates to a polite goose hunter who happens along. Antlerless deer and elk can provide great opportunities as well. Farmers and ranchers who are dealing with severe crop damage from grazing animals get sick and tired of hunters who pass up female deer and elk because they want to kill a trophy. Anyone with a snippet of knowledge about wildlife biology understands that ungulate populations are reduced through the harvest of females, not males. If you kill a male, you're removing just one animal. If you kill a female, you're removing her future offspring as well. Explain to a beleaguered farmer or rancher that you'd like to take a doe instead of a buck, and he might just give you the keys to the place. And once you get your foot in the door with squirrels or does, you can further earn the landowner's trust by showing yourself to be courteous, honest, and generous. If all goes well, you'll get the hunting equivalent of a promotion. Soon he might be calling you about those bull elk in his pasture.

A FEW MORE RULES TO KEEP IN MIND WHEN YOU'RE ASKING FOR HUNTING PERMISSION

1. Go alone when you ask permission, even if you're hoping to get permission for more than one person. No one wants to be outnumbered by strangers on their own property.

2. Ignore rule #1 if you plan on hunting with your kids. In that case, absolutely bring them along. Families make people feel comfortable (at least in small doses), and many landowners would be pleased to know that they are facilitating positive, out-of-doors interactions between children and their parents.

3. If you're a man and your wife will be hunting with you, have her ask permission. If nothing else, the landowner will appreciate the novelty.

4. Dress nicely. If you just got done working and you're covered in paint or you smell like a deep fryer, get cleaned up first.

5. But don't dress too nicely. Remember, you don't want to look like a salesmen or like you're gonna start passing out religious pamphlets.

6, 7, 8, 9, 10, 11, 12, and 13. Look the landowner in the eye. Stand tall. Don't mumble. Speak firmly and confidently. Be polite. Don't try to flatter the landowner; he'll see through it. If the answer is no, say thanks anyway. Finally, when the interaction is over and you've received permission, it's time to comment on how beautiful the property is. At this point he'll actually believe you.

THE PAY-TO-HUNT OPTION

If you are short on time but have plenty of money, you might consider a lease, trespass fee, or other pay-to-hunt option. These options are also good to ponder if you're older and "can't hike like I used to," or if you're trying to introduce young kids to hunting. The access to private land will almost certainly decrease the hunting pressure and increase the action, and that adds up to better hunting. For the older chap, it saves his knees; when taking kids hunting, it allows the focus to be on them and not on what your competition might be doing.

Leasing the hunting rights on private land can be either outrageously expensive or surprisingly cheap. A Tennessee hunter pays $2,000 annually to hunt whitetail deer and turkeys on a couple of thousand acres. He can shoot both does and large antlered bucks (which is what he's after) on the property. His buddy, who is only interested in having a secure spot to kill three to four does for the freezer, hunts the same property for $400 annually. He figures that each doe is well worth the $100 it costs him.

A group of Missouri hunters travels to Colorado to hunt elk every other year. They have a sweet deal worked out with a landowner. For $1,000 each, they get a cabin on 320 private acres; this private property adjoins thousands of acres of otherwise hard-to-access national forest. They kill most of their elk on the public land and seldom see other hunters back there. This group of hunters sees great value in their arrangement with the landowner. By shelling out a little cash, they have a far better hunt than they would otherwise experience. The reasons are many to pay for hunting grounds. It's up to each hunter to decide whether such gains are worth the expense.

TAGS AND LICENSES

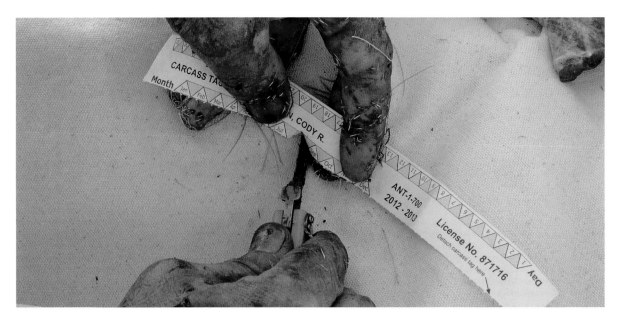

Hunting is a highly regulated activity in the United States. Wildlife is managed at the state level, with state game agencies, supported by license sales, deciding who gets to hunt what, where, and how. These rules and regulations can and do change annually and are published in a print booklet as well as online. Each state's regulations are different, and it's the hunter's responsibility to study the regs until you know the applicable laws inside and out.

Generally speaking, a hunting license enables a hunter to engage in the practice of hunting in a given state. For small game, a small game hunting license is typically all you need. But for big game, you often need to have a big game hunting license as well as permits or tags for the specific animals that you intend

to hunt. Think of it as an amusement park that charges you an entrance fee to get through the gate and then also a fee for each individual ride you choose to take. Oftentimes, tags or permits come in the form of carcass tags—literally a tag that is affixed to the carcass of an animal once it is killed. A tag might come with a host of legal requirements: it might be valid for only a male or female of the species; it might have specific dates for which it is valid; it might include weapons restrictions, such as archery-only or muzzle-loader-only; and a specific tag might become unavailable for purchase once the hunting season begins. (This prevents an unlicensed hunter from illegally killing an animal and then covering up his crime by rushing out to purchase a permit after the fact.) For these reasons and many more, it's imperative that you study your state's hunting regulations booklet before you head into the woods.

All states divide hunters into two classes when it comes to the sale of hunting licenses and tags: residents and nonresidents. Typically, states charge nonresident hunters much higher licensing fees than residents. In Colorado, for example, the cost of a resident license for bull elk is less than $50. A nonresident license for bull elk costs about six times as much. In Wisconsin, residents can get an over-the-counter deer license that allows them to kill multiple whitetail deer for just $24. A nonresident will pay about $160 for the same privileges. Typically, residents enjoy more hunting opportunities in their state than do nonresidents. In Arizona, for example, there is a 10 percent cap on how many limited-draw licenses can go to the nonresident pool of applicants. In the case of bighorn sheep, where only one tag is issued in some units, the application process is altogether closed to nonresidents. In Alaska, there are several species that are entirely closed to nonresident hunters unless the individual is hunting with a registered guide or a family member of second-degree kindred who is a legal resident of the state.

The most commonly purchased and widely available form of hunting tag is the over-the-counter tag, otherwise known as an OTC tag.

These tags are issued for species that are abundant enough in a given state to withstand widespread harvest—for example, whitetail deer hunting is over-the-counter across the vast majority of the eastern United States. Over-the-counter licenses can usually be purchased pretty much anywhere: sporting goods stores, online vendors, fish and wildlife offices, even some gas stations. If you meet the legal age and hunter's safety requirements, you can usually walk in and buy an over-the-counter tag and start hunting immediately.

A second classification of hunting tag is the limited-availability tag. This kind of tag is for hunts in which the state wants to cap the total number of people who can legally participate in a hunt. There are a variety of motivations for a state to limit the number of available tags for a given hunt, but it's typically for one of two reasons: (1) they want to produce high-quality hunts with low competition and a greater likelihood of animals living long enough to achieve trophy-class size, or (2) demand for a tag outstrips the availability of the resource.

To allocate limited-availability tags, state game agencies will use some type of lottery or drawing system. In greatly simplified terms, the names of all the interested hunters go into a hat and they pull out a few names and award those individuals a tag. Your odds of drawing some limited-availability tags might be well below 1 percent, while other limited-availability tags might carry 100 percent success rates in years when the hunt is undersubscribed—that is, when it turns out that there are fewer names in the hat than there are available tags. Because it's possible to apply for a tag for many years without receiving one, a lot of states use preference point or bonus point systems to reward repeat customers and enhance their likelihood of drawing a tag after one or more unsuccessful attempts.

Preference points and bonus points are a bit different, though the extent of the differences varies from state to state. In a typical preference point system, those hunters with the most points—called maximum point holders—will draw their tags first, while subsequent tags will be given to those with the next-highest amounts of points. Bonus points, which are also accrued annually, mean that your name goes into the hat that many more times each time you apply. For example, if Jay is applying for a tag for the first time, his name will only go into the hat once. But if Darr has been applying for that tag unsuccessfully for ten years, his name will be in the hat ten times. Keep in mind that this is a very rudimentary breakdown of the allocation process for limited-availability tags. Each state has its own nuances. For instance, Alaska, Idaho, and New Mexico do not currently offer bonus point or preference point systems; you're starting from scratch each time you apply, which is good news for new applicants and bad news for old applicants. Other states do a sort of hybrid between preference points and bonus points—some number of available tags are allocated directly to maximum point holders (similar to the preference point system), while the remainder are allocated to the general application pool (similar to the bonus point system). Again, this information should serve to drive home the point that you need to research your particular state's tag allocation system well before the hunting season begins.

If you really want to get aggressive about understanding the world of big game tags and licenses, you can learn pretty much everything there is to know by subscribing to *Eastman's Hunting Journal* or *The Huntin' Fool*. Both publications feature sections that are entirely devoted to deciphering the limited license draws and the applications that go along with them. If you're not in the mood to do the research yourself, you can hire a big game application service to help you select the proper hunts and do the paperwork for you. *The Huntin' Fool* (www.huntinfool.com/licenseapp) runs such a program, as does Cabela's (800-755-TAGS).

THE TOUGHEST TAGS

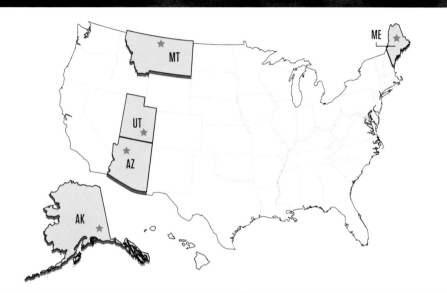

Here's a rundown of some of the hardest lottery tags to draw. These tags are coveted because either the experience cannot be replicated anywhere else or the available animals are of outstanding size.

A: Mule deer in Utah's Henry Mountains. Big, beautiful mule deer abound in this mountain range, but you can expect to apply for fifteen years before drawing the tag. **B:** Elk in Arizona's Unit 9. An archery hunter's dream: gigantic bulls, plenty of bugling, minimal hunting pressure. Plan to apply for about twenty years before you hit this tag. **C:** Bighorn sheep in Montana's Unit 680. This rugged and beautiful country is a sheep hunter's dream; it's where you go for world-record rams. Even if you apply for your entire life, it's unlikely that you'll ever draw the tag. **D:** Buffalo along Alaska's Copper River. It's an adventure just getting in and out of this area, not to mention doing it with a thousand pounds of meat and hide. Alaska does not do bonus points, so your odds of drawing this tag are in the single digits every year. If you do get lucky and draw it, you'd better make the best of the opportunity. It's literally a once-in-a-lifetime hunt, as tag holders are ineligible for future drawings. **E:** Eastern moose in Maine's north woods. Your best opportunity to hunt the eastern subspecies of moose in the lower forty-eight. The Maine moose population grew from 7,000 in 1950 to 20,000 in 1990 and now hovers between 60,000 and 70,000. While moose numbers rise, applicants are currently trending down, making it a great time to jump in the pool. For first-time nonresident applicants who buy only one chance, the success rate is 0.2 percent. But Maine does employ a bonus point system, bettering your odds yearly; it also allows nonresidents to purchase unlimited chances in bundles of ten at $55 each. (Since nonresidents and residents are not applying for the same tags, this does not affect the odds for Maine residents.) Buying these extra chances can greatly improve odds, though doing so is hardly essential to winning a permit.

Landowner tags are a third classification of big game tags, though they are generally relegated to hunters with hefty budgets. Basically, a landowner tag allows a landowner to sell a high-quality big game tag of the sort that would normally be given out only through a lottery. The thinking behind landowner tags is that they incentivize landowners to be good stewards of the land; in exchange for the landowner providing crucial habitat for wildlife—often at some expense to the landowner, through crop loss, property damage, or livestock depredation—the state awards the landowner a quantity of big game tags commensurate with the quantity and quality of property. The landowner can then sell the tags as he or she sees fit. Depending on the species and trophy quality of the animals in a given area, landowner tags might sell for anywhere from $500 to $15,000. This is a controversial type of tag; many hunters believe that landowner tags subvert the democratic nature of our nation's wildlife conservation model, under which wildlife is held in the public trust. Every tag that goes to a landowner, some folks say, is taken out of an already limited license pool in order to be bought by some high roller who's using his wealth to skirt the lottery process. What makes it even worse, they say, is that many landowner tags are valid for all public lands in a given hunting unit, which means that the landowner's tag isn't even being used on the landowner's property. Others hold that private landowners provide an invaluable service to North America's wildlife and that they should be rewarded financially in order to make it less likely that they'll have to sell off their land to developers who would inevitably bring along the scourge of suburban sprawl.

If you don't like the sound of landowner tags, you're going to hate the fourth classification of hunting tags: governor's tags. These tags usually carry extra privileges, such as expanded seasons or hunting zones, and they go to the highest bidder in an auction. How much money can such a tag go for? In 2012, a hunter paid $160,000 for a governor's tag enabling him to hunt mule deer on Utah's Antelope Island. In 2013, the same hunter paid $310,000 for the same tag. In 2014, he paid $305,000. Before you get too filled with righteous indignation, consider that 90 percent of this hunter's three-year, $865,000 mule deer hunting budget goes to wildlife conservation—in this case, habitat improvements on Antelope Island. But again, governor's tags do take hunting opportunities away from the common man and put them into the hands of the wealthy. Whether that's justified or not is open to discussion. (For more information on lottery draws, bonus points, and governor's tags, see page 177.)

THE METHODS: SPOT-AND-STALK HUNTING

Spot-and-stalk hunting is easily the most rigorous and demanding form of big game hunting. The method is well suited to open or semi-open spaces, where a hunter can locate his prey at a distance before stalking into effective killing distance without alarming the animal. The spot-and-stalk method is as applicable to a Dall sheep hunter who's looking at a ram on the top of a mountain that's 3 miles away as it is for a Florida hog hunter who needs to crawl across 100 yards of open pasture in order to get within bow range of a boar.

Beyond the unadulterated excitement that comes from stalking big game, the spot-and-stalk method gives you a number of tactical advantages over the less disciplined approach of just wandering around with a gun in hope of kicking something up. For starters, spot-and-stalk hunting lets you cover ground with your eyes instead of your feet—sometimes

(Left) This hunter, Matt Moisan, is pointing to the location of a black bear he's watching. By studying the bear from afar, he was able to determine that the bear was a reasonable-sized animal that did not have cubs. (Right) After a long and careful stalk, he killed the animal from about 30 yards away.

more ground in a glance than you'd be able to cover in a lifetime of tree stand hunting in thick timber. By perching yourself on prominent lookout points, you can cover all manner of habitat types and travel corridors without having to commit to a particular location until after you've found your quarry.

Another benefit of spot-and-stalk hunting is that it gives you a chance to accurately judge animals from a distance before you're absolutely obligated to make a decision about shooting. When most hunters hear the term *field judging*, they immediately think of trophy hunters trying to gauge the record-book quality of a particular animal before they kill it. But trophy status is hardly the only piece of information that comes from field judging. Many states have rules and restrictions that govern which animals of a species can be taken, and these are based on management strategies meant to ensure healthy and stable populations of game. In California, for instance, the harvest of spikehorn deer is illegal, even if you hold a tag that's valid for antlered deer. In much of Alaska, you cannot kill a moose unless the animal has at least four brow tines on one antler or a minimum antler spread of 50 inches. When hunting bears, it's strictly illegal to kill a sow with cubs. All of these distinctions can be difficult to make, especially when you're looking at a half-spooked animal through a veil of thick brush and you've only got a second or two to determine its legality before it bounds away. In short, making snap decisions when hunting can lead to serious ethical and legal trouble. Spot-and-stalk hunting helps alleviate the risk.

The act of looking for animals from a spot-and-stalk position is usually referred to as "glassing," since you're almost always using binoculars or spotting scopes. Success as a glasser begins with the ability to pick out the

This hunter has positioned himself below the skyline to avoid being silhouetted. He has unobstructed views in several directions and a comfortable seat for a prolonged glassing session.

right places to do your glassing from. The criteria for a good glassing position vary according to location, but generally you're looking for an area that gives you a relatively unobstructed view of the surrounding country. Often, but not always, such positions are located in areas that rise above the surrounding topography, providing a vantage point. But of course there's more to picking an observation point than just looking for a high spot.

Besides having good visibility, you should select a fairly comfortable position or you'll have a hard time staying put for any appreciable amount of time. Depending on the circum-

stances, you might need a spot that offers either a windbreak or a touch of breeze, or perhaps shade or direct sunlight—though you never want to set up where you're looking directly into a rising or setting sun. Experienced glassers will have spots that they prefer in the morning and others for the evening depending on where the animals have been seen before and where the sun is in relation to where they are looking. Glassing knobs with 360-degree views are great, of course, but so is that little shelf of rock that lets you peek down into a narrow wedge of a valley floor that includes a couple of prime game trails—especially if that little shelf of rock is close to a few other good vantage points. It sucks to put all your eggs in one basket by climbing to some lonely high point and then not having anywhere convenient to move to when it doesn't produce. In other words, it's a lot better to work a string of high spots that are connected by a continuous ridgeline than it is to scale an isolated peak.

Wind direction matters. It matters less and less as you get higher and farther from your target area, but it's of vital importance when you're sitting close to where you expect to see animals. If you're glassing a few meadows that are only 200 yards away and you have the wind at your back, you're running the risk of spooking all the game out of there. You also want to consider your visual presence. It's best to select areas where you can maintain a low profile. Having a backdrop of brush or rock is

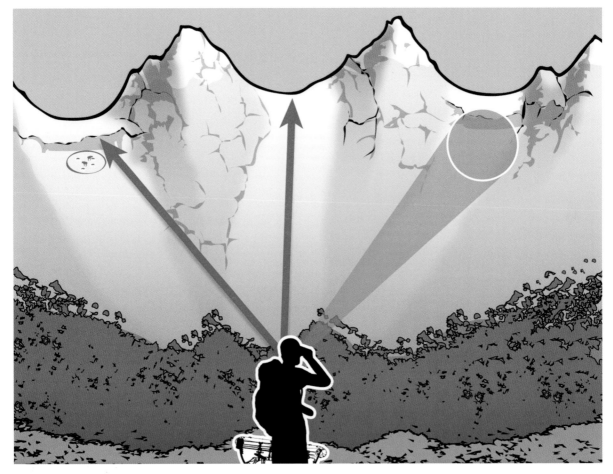

Many hunting areas, such as this alpine bowl, are best viewed from below rather than above.

helpful, because it keeps you from skylining yourself. Getting into the shadows is better than being in direct light, unless you're freezing cold and need the sun. And if you are in the sun, take care to hide or shade shiny objects such as watches, rifle barrels, and tripod legs. Nothing screams "I'm up here!" to an animal quite like a flashing beacon of reflected light that's bouncing off the lens of your spotting scope.

Not all good glassing spots are up high, either. There are certain types of country more suited to glassing from the bottom up. Such locations include cliffy areas, where climbing up high requires a serious investment of time and energy; open basins or hanging valleys; and semi-open hillsides that would be impossible to glass from above.

When you're selecting a glassing position, remember that your goal is to find an animal and then go after it. If you're up on a rock spire towering 2,000 feet above the valley floor, it's going to take you a long time to climb down when you do see something. Always consider the position of the sun and then be realistic about how much time you have to reach an

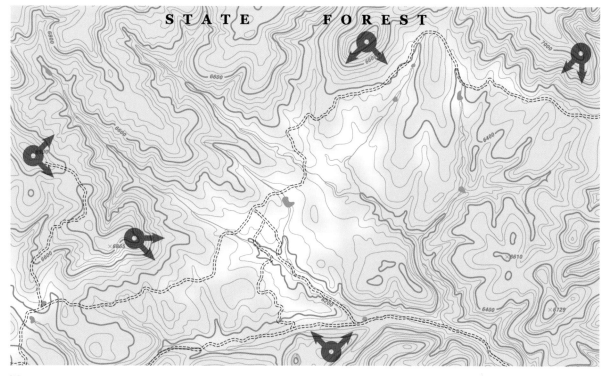

When hunting new areas, you can find some great glassing positions just by consulting topographic maps. Not only can you identify prime habitat features such as water and natural travel corridors, but you can pinpoint locations that will give you a commanding view of those areas. When actual scouting is out of the question, map reading is often the next best way to really familiarize yourself with an area prior to a spot-and-stalk hunt. (Or, for that matter, any kind of hunt.)

area that you're looking at. If you've got an hour of daylight left on the last day of the hunting season, it won't do you much good to be glassing a bunch of locations that are a mile away. Not only will you not be able to reach those areas today, tomorrow isn't even an option. If you're hunting in the morning, on the other hand, you have a much longer window of time in which to reach any animals that you happen to locate. And if you've got several days before the season ends, you can even change position on subsequent hunts in order to get closer to really far-out animals that you might have located. You might then need to find a new and closer glassing location in order

to locate those animals again once you get into effective stalking range, but that's all part of the fun.

Once you've selected a good glassing location and taken your position, it's time to actually start looking for animals. Now you're relying on your game eye, a term that refers to one's ability to spot animals in their natural habitats. It's nearly impossible to train someone to have a good game eye, as it can only be achieved through time and practice—and even then, some people will just never become good at spotting game. (It seems to have little to do with the natural quality of your eyesight. There are plenty of guys with 20/20 vision who can't spot squat, just as there are a lot of guys with bottle-bottom glasses who see animals that would escape the notice of 95 percent of other hunters.) That said, though, there are some tips and tricks that can help you do a better job of locating game.

Most experienced glassers use a divide-and-conquer strategy when confronted with a vast amount of turf that needs to be picked apart for animals. Basically, they break the landscape into manageable chunks and then scour those individual areas with the help of binoculars and/or a spotting scope. When doing this, start with the easy pickings. For instance, imagine a large hillside that's covered in vegetation types ranging from grassy openings to thick brush to scattered stands of mature timber. Cover those large openings with your binoculars first, simply because it's easy to quickly scan them and rule out the presence of any game that might be standing in plain sight. Next, check the smaller openings. If you still haven't found what you're looking for, it may be time to put your binoculars on a tripod or stabilize them against your knees and start doing some detail work. Go back to those openings and scour the edges, and give a careful look at any brushy patches out in the middle of the openings. Then start picking apart those large expanses of brush, looking for any holes or thinly canopied areas that you can see into. Use your binoculars to pry your way into every possible nook and cranny that

might be holding an animal: shadows cast by trees and brush, sheltered areas beneath overhanging rocks, the areas along or near game trails.

As you look into tougher and tougher locations, make sure to slow down more and more. No successful glasser would take just a quick glance at a promising hillside and then call it quits. Check everything multiple times, and make a mental list of any intriguing shapes or shadows that you can't see clearly. You can come back to examine these spots with a spotting scope once you've completed your initial few passes with a set of binoculars. All the while, remember that you're looking not just for animals but also for parts of animals: a bit of antler glistening in the sun, a twitching ear, a shadow cast by an animal's leg.

Another way to break down a large area is to glass it using a grid pattern. This works especially well in areas with a more homogenous appearance that aren't conducive to the

There's game out there, somewhere. Finding it requires a well-honed game eye.

When glassing big country, mentally divide the terrain into several pieces based on geographic features. Then work each piece individually with your binoculars. When covering larger pieces of ground, scan them using back-and-forth or up-and-down gridding patterns to ensure that you're not missing anything.

divide-and-conquer method. (It can also be used in conjunction with divide-and-conquer; see illustration above.) To grid, you divide the overall view into manageable pieces and cover those pieces with your binoculars in the same sort of back-and-forth pattern that a typewriter uses to cover a page. Simply pan your binos from one end of the area to the other, then tilt them up or down a slight bit and pan across the next strip of cover. For the sake of mixing it up, you can grid top to bottom if you like. Be sure to allow for plenty of overlap on each pass so that you don't miss anything. When looking at a small hillside, one or two passes

might be enough to rule out the presence of game. But in seriously vertical country, or when you're looking from a very high vantage point, it might take nine or ten passes to fully cover a patch of terrain.

Glassing strategies such as divide-and-conquer and gridding are hugely helpful, but when using these techniques it's only natural that you're going to focus the bulk of your energy on those areas where you most expect to see game. Identifying such areas is a learned skill that comes from a lifetime of hunting and observing animals. But there are some short-cuts to mastering this discipline. At all times, keep in mind the three basic things that critters need—shelter, food, and water—and look for the places that provide these necessities. For big game, shelter is typically synonymous with bedding areas, which are usually located in proximity to good avenues of escape. Some species, such as whitetail deer, prefer to bed in thick vegetation, where they are hidden from view. Others, such as mountain goats, bed out in the open, where they can see predators from a long way off and where they have steep cliffs to their back so that they can climb to safety when pursued. Food is most often found in open or semi-open areas where there's adequate sunlight to foster the growth of preferred low-lying big game grub such as grasses, forbs, and shrubs. Such openings might be found amid sparse stands of aspen, in creekside clearings or grazing pastures, at the edges of beaver ponds or the bottoms of avalanche slides, and in agricultural fields, orchards, or areas cleared by forest and brush fires. Water sources differ according to location as well. It could be a high-country seep in the Rockies, a man-made water catchment in the desert Southwest, a mud puddle along a dirt road in California, a bubbling brook in Maine, or a vast swamp in the Southeast. Learn how the animals in your chosen hunting area are using the habitat to get what they need, and you'll quickly become a better hunter.

Recognizing patterns is as important as, or perhaps even more important than, recogniz-ing habitat features. What this means is that when you see an animal you're able to figure out why it's hanging out where it is. You can then take that bit of knowledge and use it to your advantage by searching out other spots that offer the same sets of circumstances—and maybe animals as well. As an example, let's say that you're watching a big pasture. There could be many things about one corner that make it special: it's lower or higher than the rest of the pasture, wetter or drier, shadier or sunnier, breezier or calmer, closer to or farther away from a cattail marsh. Whatever the deciding factor might be, it's the smart hunter's responsibility to figure it out and then extend that piece of knowledge to the next patch of pasture that he happens to hunt.

Another thing you should strive to understand is how a particular animal looks in a particular setting. Hunters often find that it takes them a while to spot the first deer of the day, but as soon as they find one, they start spotting deer all over the place. Often, this happens because the hunter has suddenly figured out what a deer looks like in the context of a particular backdrop of vegetation and quality of light. In other words, finding a mule deer in dry grass (look for the white rump) is nothing like finding a mule deer in the snow (look for the brown body), which itself is nothing like the maddeningly frustrating task of finding a mule deer against a patchwork of snow and dry grass. But once you see an animal in a certain type of setting, something in your head clicks and you suddenly know what you're looking for. Achieving that moment of clarity is one of the many joys of spot-and-stalk hunting.

When you're sitting up on a glassing position for an hour or so without seeing anything, you'll inevitably start wondering how long you should wait before moving on. There is no simple answer to this question, as it really comes down to what animal you're hunting and what kind of terrain you're hunting in. If you're glassing an alpine basin for Dall sheep in Alaska, for instance, you'll pretty quickly determine whether or not there's a pure white animal standing against a backdrop of black shale and green grass. Conversely, if you're hunting the brushy mountains of Sonora, Mexico, for Coues deer (otherwise known as gray ghosts), you might spend two or three days in

This is a classic high-country basin where elk, mule deer, bighorn sheep, and mountain goats might be found. In this instance the glasser is looking for elk and deer. Red icons: These are big openings that are void of cover and should be glassed first. Animals here should be easy to find. Blue icons: Medium-sized openings with scattered cover should be glassed on the second pass. Finding game in these areas might take a little extra time. Green icons: Save smaller and more distant openings for later passes, after you've ruled out the presence of animals in more obvious locations. Look for bedded animals in these areas. A spotting scope might be helpful when studying the faraway areas. Black icons: These spots are not generally going to hold elk or deer, but you still might give them a careful examination in order to stave off boredom during a long glassing session. Who knows, you might find a sheep or goat to give you some much-needed entertainment.

one spot before you pick out the deer that you knew all along must be there. In that sort of terrain, you're not just glancing around for something white. Instead, your eyes are prying into every little nook and shadow in search of a leg, an ear, or an antler tine. In those situations, confidence plays a huge role. Sometimes you must force yourself to believe in your spot and know that something's out there—even if you don't actually *really* believe it.

Another reason to hold tight is that bedded animals will eventually get up and move around, and you need to be watching when they do. Many hunters are good enough to find bedded game on occasion, but only the best of the best can do it consistently. When an animal is on its feet, however, the movement will usually catch your eye long before the actual shape of the animal does. What's more, animals that are up on their feet aren't necessarily in view. Big game usually move slowly as they feed, often just taking one step every few minutes. You could easily be watching a hillside of oaks for wild pigs and not see a lone boar simply because he's spending an hour in a narrow out-of-view draw that hap-pened to collect a bunch of acorns that rolled down the slope after falling from their trees. Suddenly that boar steps out from the draw and there he is, seemingly emerging from thin air.

Another thing to consider is the shifting light. As the sun moves across the sky, shadows change and either lighten or darken an animal enough for you to see it. And the shifting rays of sun can reveal things as well. You could be staring at a huge patch of willows and not see a single thing, and then suddenly the sun bursts through the clouds and you see the palm of a moose antler as clearly as if it were a firefly lighting up in the pitch of night.

Speaking of light, many species of big game are crepuscular, or active primarily during the twilight periods of dawn and dusk. If you had two hours a day to glass for animals, you'd be wise to pick the first and last hours of the day. That's when you're going to spot 75 percent of the game you see. In general, it's very hard to rule out an area until you've had the chance to study it during those magical moments of rising and falling light.

BINOCULARS VS. SPOTTING SCOPES

There aren't many serious glassers who spend hour upon hour staring through a spotting scope. Not only can spotting scopes give you eye fatigue in short order, but the field of view on a spotting scope is typically much smaller than that of binoculars. Instead, do most of your glassing through a set of binos, preferably on a tripod. Use the spotting scope primarily as a specialty tool for investigating suspicious-looking (i.e., gamy) shapes and objects, and also for judging the size and/or legality of distant animals that you initially found through your binoculars. Now and then, of course, you'll use your scope to scan faraway country that's simply out of reach for a pair of binoculars, but give your eyes a break as you soon as you start to feel any discomfort. You'll want your eyes to feel fresh and ready when you finally get a chance to look through your rifle scope and make your shot.

Once you've found your quarry, it's time to start thinking about whether you should attempt to make a stalk. Sometimes the answer is perfectly clear. If you spot an antelope feeding casually out in a sage patch in an upwind direction and you've only got to make a 50-yard crawl to get to a good shooting position, you should probably start crawling immediately. But at other times, particularly when there's a lot of distance to cover, the answer might not be so clear. Considering the distance between the animal and you, will the animal still be there—or somewhere where you can find it—when you arrive at its location? This isn't the sort of question that can be answered with certainty, as animals are unpredictable in their movements and there are many unseen factors at play. For instance, you might be stalking a group of antelope that have been milling around in the same place all day, and then another hunter spooks them while you're closing the final part of your stalk on your hands and knees. There's just no way for you to control that sort of thing.

But you can make fairly accurate predictions about what an animal is going to do—and where it's going to be—if you take the time to observe both the animal and its surroundings. While there's no way to account for every scenario that a spot-and-stalk hunter will encounter in the field, there are a number of general guidelines that will prove helpful as you try to gauge whether to make an attempt on a distant animal.

During the breeding season, or rut, mating activity is one of the best things you can see. If you glass a male who's harassing or defending a group of females, chances are strong that he's going to stay in that area unless the females move. Conversely, it's generally a bad idea to take off in pursuit of spooked animals. If you hear a few rifle shots and then see a herd of elk disappear over a ridge, don't assume that they're going to be standing on the other side of that ridge when you get over there. Even if a nervous or spooked animal is standing in plain sight, it's still a good idea to hold off on your stalk until the animal calms down and goes back to feeding or resting. But not all fast-moving animals have necessarily been spooked. They might be cruising for mates during breeding season; moving between feeding, watering, and bedding areas; or traveling in search of new food sources. Regardless, try to determine where the animal is headed—and let it get there, preferably—before you take off in pursuit. This is especially true if the animal is moving away from you, as it's extremely difficult to overtake traveling animals without alerting them to your presence. That said, keep in mind that getting out in front of a traveling animal is an excellent strategy. If the animal's line of travel is predictable and you can head it off, go for it. Feeding is another good sign, as it means the animals are generally content and not at immediate risk of moving away too quickly. How-

Upon spotting these elk, the hunter is unable to get within rifle range before the animals disappear into thick timber. Assuming that the elk are going to bed down, he sets up an ambush where he expects the elk to reappear when they come back out to feed.

ever, they will move somewhat. If a group of animals is grazing, pay attention to which direction they are facing. (They will usually face into the wind.) Plan on them moving at least somewhat in that direction. Also consider the time of day when you're looking at feeding animals. In the evening, there's a strong likelihood that they'll stay in the same general area until dark. In the late morning, however, their feeding period might soon come to an end as they head to their bedding locations.

Speaking of bedding areas, there's a strategy utilized by highly disciplined hunters that's sometimes referred to as "putting them to bed." The strategy is useful when you've located an animal that might be difficult to approach, or when you're in a situation where you want to

absolutely minimize the chances of spooking an animal that you've selected as your target. It amounts to waiting for an animal, or a herd of animals, to settle into their bedding area before you proceed with a stalk. Sometimes, particularly with alpine game, you'll actually see the animal bed down. But it's much more common to have the animal disappear into some sort of thick vegetation or bedding cover. When a half hour or so goes by without the animal emerging, it makes sense to think that it might have bedded down. At this point, you can be moderately certain that the animal won't move for a while. If it's lying in a position where you can approach without detection, it's time to attempt a stalk. But don't make the mistake of thinking of a bedded animal as purely static.

Very few critters will bed down and then just lie for hours on end without moving. They get up and reposition for any number of reasons: to stretch, to find some shade or sun, to urinate, to have a few bites to eat, or to chase off a herdmate that's gotten too close. Every experienced spot-and-stalk hunter has had carefully planned stalks blown by supposedly bedded animals that were actually up on their feet and moving about.

Usually, your goal isn't to kill the animal while it's lying down. Not only is shot placement difficult on bedded animals, but getting into a position where you can actually see a bedded animal can often lead to mistakes and spooked game. It's generally preferable to stalk within range of where you expect the animal to emerge when it leaves its bedding area to begin feeding again, or to a place where you might be able to get a clear shot at the animal when it stands up. You then wait there, patiently, until your opportunity arises.

If you hunt often enough, you'll eventually locate an animal that seems virtually impossible to stalk. Maybe it's a wild hog that spends all of its time in an oak thicket where you'd never find it once you got close enough for a shot, or maybe it's a mule deer with a 360-degree view of the surrounding sage flat and there's no reasonable avenue of approach. In these situations, it's far better to observe the animal than it is to rush a stalk that will almost certainly fail. By observing an animal, you're doing something called patterning. That is, you're learning how and when the animal uses the overall context of its home range. Where and when does it eat? Where and when does it sleep? Where and when does it go for water? What routes does it travel when going from one of these areas to the next? By answering these questions, you can put together a schedule of the animal's habits and perhaps identify some places and times when it's vul-

Putting elk to bed is a common technique used by Colorado elk hunting guide Scott Graham. At daybreak, Scott spends time at high spots glassing for herds of elk. When he finds one, he watches the herd until it moves to its bedding location—usually a thick patch of timber. He then positions his hunters within rifle range of where he expects the elk to emerge for their evening feeding session. It's a proven, time-tested strategy. Above, top, Scott's client watches a herd of elk as they move toward their bedding area. Bottom, he poses with a nice Colorado bull.

Rocky Mountain elk or deer: Here the hunter has waited for the temperature to warm, causing an upslope thermal. Both stalks will require a wide loop and slow descent to the creek bottom to avoid detection. The creek bottom will then provide the cover for the hunter pursuing the elk in position B. The creek would also allow the hunter to peek periodically and keep tabs on the quarry. The hunter executing the route to position A would continue in a wide loop coming up the backside of the knob and then peeking over the top and down onto the target.

nerable to a carefully executed stalk. This might be a late morning moment when that hog you've been following crosses an opening in the oak brush on its way to a shaded bedding location. Or it might be a midday window of time when that mule deer you've been stalking disappears into a creek bed for water and stays down there just long enough for you to cross the sage flat without being seen.

Now for the actual stalk. Because losing track of the animal's location is perhaps the number-one mistake made by spot-and-stalk hunters, be sure to mark the precise position of your quarry before you begin approaching it. Do this whether the animal is 100 yards away or 2 miles away. Make a mental note of prominent or easily identified landmarks—trees, clusters of brush, rocks, et cetera—that can help you stay oriented during your stalk. Remi Warren, an avid and very successful big game hunter, often photographs his stalking route before he leaves his glassing perch, so

Sonora mountain Coues deer: Here the hunter can do a casual descent into the bottom and then use the band of rocks as cover until he or she is directly across from the animal.

that he can refer to the image if he gets confused about where he is. Another trick is to take a compass bearing on the animal's location, to ensure that you don't veer off course during your approach. Better yet, try to pinpoint the animal's location on a topographic map or GPS unit. In the case of GPS, you'll have the luxury of real-time information throughout your stalk about how much ground you've covered and how far you've still got to go. Make sure to mark the location of your glassing perch on your GPS unit as well, because it's helpful

to have that point as a reference while stalking. And if you're hunting in areas with high relief, make a note about whether the animal is higher or lower than your glassing perch, and then use relative elevation as yet another way to keep yourself oriented during a long stalk across a landscape that will almost inevitably confuse you.

Select the most direct route that you can without risking that you'll be in the animal's line of sight. You want to get there as quickly as possible without taking unnecessary risks

Alaska Range sheep: The route on the left side will allow the hunter to stay hidden behind a prominent shoulder of rock until he or she gets within shooting range and pops out above the sheep. Using the bottom route, the hunter will stay concealed thanks to the steepness of the slope. Once the hillside opens up, the hunter should be within shooting range of the target.

of exposure. In a perfect world, there would always be a ridge running parallel to your line of travel, and all you'd have to do is duck behind the ridge while closing the distance. But in the real world, stalking usually involves a route that takes advantage of many different features along the way. You approach the stalk like a dot-to-dot children's sketch, just moving from one position to the next with an end goal of arriving where you want to be. Use brush, rocks, and undulations in the ground. Wear camouflage or earth tones, and don't be afraid to get on your hands and knees or slither along on your belly like a snake. Sometimes you'll simply run out of cover, and then you have to move only when the animal is feeding or looking in another direction. (In unbroken landscapes, one might conduct an entire stalk by moving only when the animal is feeding.)

HAND SIGNALS FOR STALKING

When hunting with a partner, try having him or her stay at the glassing position while you move into range. With a few prearranged hand signals, your partner can help guide you toward the animal. And if the animal moves or spooks during the stalk, this information can be relayed to you in time for you to adjust your plan. The spotter is also a valuable asset in post-shot situations, because he or she will be more likely to see how the wounded animal behaves and which way it travels. In states where two-way communications between hunters is legal, it is possible to use radios in place of hand signals. But many hunters regard this as an ugly and unwelcome intrusion of technology, and reputable big game scoring organizations prohibit the admission of animals killed with the help of two-way communications.

At all times, remember to pay attention to the wind. Concealing your odor is even more important than concealing your body, and this can be done only by constantly monitoring the wind direction. Sometimes the wind is so faint that you can't even feel it on your skin, but it's still plenty strong enough to carry your odor to the animal and give you away. To monitor wind direction, you can use a commercially produced puffer, which puts out little clouds of easily blown talcum powder, or you can tie a bird's breast feather to the limb of your bow or the front sling stud of your rifle with a piece of dental floss. Milkweed seeds or cattail down kept in a chewing tobacco tin also work well; toss a pinch into the air and watch which way it blows. Whatever your method, check the wind often during a stalk. On flat ground, the wind is usually steady and predictable, but in the mountains or other rough ground the wind can be impossible to predict from one moment to the next. When the wind is favorable (blowing from the animal to you), proceed with your stalk. When the wind is unfavorable (blowing from you to the animal), back out and reassess the situation. Remember, an animal might question its own eyesight—sometimes it will see you and still not spook—but *never* questions its nose.

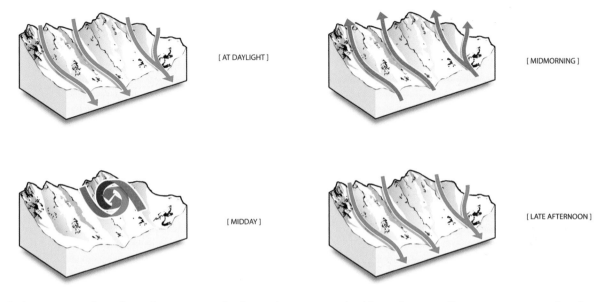

[AT DAYLIGHT]

[MIDMORNING]

[MIDDAY]

[LATE AFTERNOON]

In the mountains, thermals can bring a sense of order to otherwise unpredictable wind currents. Since warm air rises and cool air sinks, expect air currents to be moving downhill at daybreak, uphill when the day starts warming up, and downhill again when things are cooling off. Midafternoon, thermals tend to be replaced by gusty winds.

STALKING WITH A BOW

There's an old saying that goes, "Where a rifle hunt ends, the bowhunt begins." This refers to the fact that a bowhunter must creep in way closer to his quarry than a rifle hunter. At such close distances—anything less than a hundred yards, really—there are a million things that can go wrong. The rolling of a rock or the sound of brush against fabric is all it takes to send your animal bounding away. A bowhunter needs to be extra careful when choosing his route. As you draw near, make a plan for each and every placement of your foot. Look for grass clumps and soft dirt rather than dry leaves or loose rock. Movements must be slow, and never jerky or abrupt. Using a range finder can help immensely when selecting your final shooting position. If your maximum shooting range is 30 yards and your quarry is 60 yards away, use your range finder (see page 33) to select an object that splits the difference. This eliminates the need to use your range finder again when you're even closer to the animal, cutting out extra movements that might give you away. Finally, keep in mind that you'll need a final bit of protection when you rise to draw your bow, a substantial movement that generally will not go unnoticed. Use a tree, a patch of bush, a topographical feature, or a rock to hide the movement. Then, once you're drawn and ready, you can step away from the cover and rise to shoot.

A HANDFUL OF EXTRA TIPS FOR THE SPOT-AND-STALK HUNTER

1. Bring along a butt pad. It helps you stay comfortable while glassing, which helps you spot more game, which helps you harvest more meat. Good pads can be made by cutting off two sections from a Therm-a-Rest Z-Lite foam pad. It's a light and durable option, and if you split the cost of a pad with two or three of your buddies, it's also cheap.

2. When archery hunting, it can be difficult to carry your bow while trying to keep a low profile during a stalk. Attaching it to your back while belly-crawling will work, but the system requires fasteners and can put you in a tough position if you need to make a quick, unexpected shot. When the terrain allows it, a better method is to crab-crawl with your bow laid across your lap. You can do it with an arrow notched. And when the time comes, you can rise up to a kneeling position in one fluid motion and make your shot.

3. If you've finished your stalk but the animal is not where you thought it would be, stick with your plan and wait it out. Often the animal is just behind a tree or has bedded down. All it takes is a little patience on your part before the animal will move and give away its position.

4. In the final phase of a stalk, complete silence is a necessity. Many serious hunters carry a soft-soled form of footwear such as thick socks, running shoes, or manufactured "stalking shoes" such as Cat's Claws or Bear's Feet that can fit over one's hard-soled boots. These can all but eliminate the sounds of your footsteps.

AMBUSH HUNTING

An elevated blind provides both a better field of view and a comfortable shelter.

The ambush hunter lets his quarry come to him. This method of hunting accounts for the overwhelming majority of whitetail deer that are harvested around the country each season, and it is used as well by everyone from moose hunters in Maine to hog hunters in California. It could be argued that ambush hunting is the most universally applicable big game hunting strategy there is.

Ambush hunting relies on the fact that animals move in somewhat predictable patterns, and that it's possible for a hunter to anticipate these movements and then position himself in a specified location ahead of the animal's arrival. The location can be just about anything, depending on the species you're after: a winter-killed moose carcass for grizzlies, a livestock watering tank for antelope, a cultivated food plot for whitetails, a high mountain pass for Dall sheep. Once such features are identified, the ambush hunter selects a position that lies within comfortable shooting distance of where he believes the animals will pass through—a position that enables the hunter to see his quarry clearly without his quarry being able to see, hear, or smell him.

Speaking very generally, most game animals spend the bulk of their time either resting, feeding, or traveling to and from resting and feeding areas. Still speaking generally, an

The ambush hunter is generally wise to leave bedding areas undisturbed. Instead, try to ambush your prey along travel routes and near feeding areas.

ambush hunter is wise to avoid encroaching on his quarry's resting or bedding area. Upon arrival in its preferred bedding location, an animal is likely to lie down very quickly—often in a place where it's sheltered from view by thick vegetation that can make it hard or even impossible to see the animal, let alone place a lethal shot with a bow or rifle. More important, bedding areas are best left undisturbed because most game animals tend to be very intolerant of disturbances in their bedding areas. You might spook a critter in its feeding area and then see it again the next night. But if you spook a critter in its bedding area, you can kiss it goodbye.

The ambush hunter would be much smarter to focus his efforts on feeding areas. There are a few reasons for this. For starters, feeding areas are often more definable, more predictable, and more easily located than bedding areas. When hunting black bears in the spring and fall, for instance, feeding areas might ac-

count for just 2 or 3 percent of the total surrounding landmass, while bedding areas might comprise 70 percent of the surrounding landscape. For another thing, feeding areas tend to be located on more open turf than bedding areas. This allows the hunter a better chance to monitor a greater expanse of ground, and also to keep a safer distance from his quarry so that he reduces the chances of spooking it. Finally, feeding areas typically provide more and better shot opportunities. Animals are usually on their feet and moving around while they feed, affording the hunter a variety of shot angles and positions that can be exploited for a quick, clean kill.

When feeding areas are not clearly defined, or when there are so many feeding areas that it's impossible to guess which one your prey will be using at a given moment, it's wise to concentrate your ambush efforts along known travel routes that animals use as they move between their bedding and feeding areas or as they move from one feeding area to the next. When setting up an ambush along a travel route, it's best if you can identify funnels, or pinch points, that constrict the movements of animals and therefore bring even more predictability to their point of passage. Examples include isthmuses between large bodies of water for migrating caribou, fence-crossing locations for antelope, trails cutting through alder thickets along salmon streams for bears, shelter belts connecting bedding areas for whitetail deer, narrow canyon

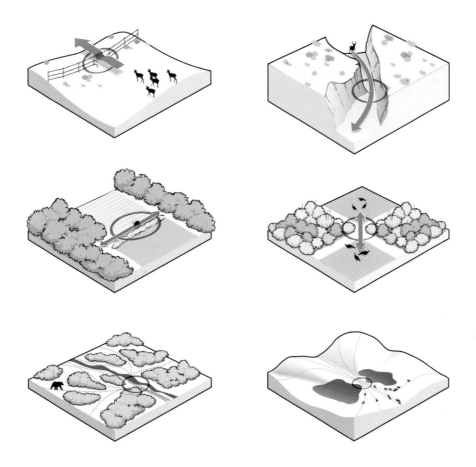

Ambush funnels, or pinch points, come in many forms. Observant hunters are able to read a landscape and anticipate those places animals are likely to pass through.

bottoms for mule deer, and tractor lanes connecting agricultural fields for turkeys.

The specific location where a hunter hides himself while ambushing prey can be described with any number of terms: *blind*, *stand*, *hide*, *pit blind*, *post*, *station*, and so on. While the terms are somewhat interchangeable, each does carry its own regional connotation. The word *blind* typically refers to an artificial structure or an assemblage of natural materials that form a visual barrier between a hunter and his quarry. Blinds can be fixed or stationary, ru-

dimentary or elaborate. Some hunters construct fixed blinds by interweaving pine or spruce limbs over a dome-shaped framework made from green tree limbs; others use commercially produced ultralight portable blinds made of carbon fiber posts and water-resistant fabric. Pit blinds are dug into the ground, or take advantage of natural depressions, in order to hide the hunter beneath the earth's surface. The word *stand* typically refers to an elevated position. These could be permanent or temporary platforms mounted in trees, known as tree stands, or they could be freestanding units supported by a framework of metal or wooden posts. Sometimes an ambush hunter's setup is so basic that it hardly deserves a name. He could be nestled against the base of a tree, sitting with his head poking above some tall grass, lying behind a hay bale, or tucked into a crevice in the rocks.

JEROD FINK, A WISCONSIN BOWHUNTER, WEIGHS IN ON HIS FAVORITE TREE STAND

"At no time in the relatively short history of commercially produced tree stands have there been so many choices for the hunter who prefers to hunt from an elevated position. Whether the goal is comfort or speed, there are endless choices in every sporting goods store or catalog that you encounter. There are double-wide and triple-wide tree stands that you'd need a pickup truck to haul into the woods, and there are ultralight microstands for hunters who like to slip in quietly with their gear on their back. Picking the right stand for the right situation can be downright confusing, but I've managed to beat the tree stand selection game with one simple setup that I've used for all sorts of hunting over the past five years.

"It's called a tree sling. It's lighter than even the lightest metal tree stand. And once you get past the seemingly confusing system of webbing and buckles, the possibilities with a tree sling are virtually endless. You can use them in pretty much any tree, anywhere. The feature I most enjoy, though, is the ability to shoot 360 degrees around the tree. There are no blind sides when using a sling. In fact, on more than one occasion I've shot multiple deer in the same night thanks to this feature.

"Tree slings are also highly transportable. Instead of having a metal tree stand banging around on your back, you simply stuff the sling into a backpack and you're off. There is no more metal banging on metal, or aluminum pipes slapping against saplings in the predawn blackness—something that always seems to happen when you're trying to be stealthy. And once you get used to the feel of your body in the sling (it takes three or four uses to achieve this), the comfort is second to none.

"Unfortunately, my preferred brand of tree sling is no longer being produced, but other companies are beginning to pick up the slack and produce comparable models. That is a good thing, because at this point I simply can't imagine going back to a regular tree stand. When I'm hunting, I just can't deal with that sort of weight, noise, and immobility."

The elaborateness of one's setup is dependent on how wary your quarry is and how close you need to get. Someone who's bowhunting for whitetail deer, an exceptionally shy species, needs to get within 10 to 40 yards of his target for maximum efficacy. That is best accomplished by hunting from an elevated stand, where the hunter is above the deer's natural line of sight and where his odor is less likely to be detected by the deer's outrageously acute sense of smell. On the flip side, take someone who's hunting with a rifle for moose. These animals are not nearly as wary as whitetail deer and the rifle hunter doesn't need to get nearly as close as the bowhunter. For him, it might be enough to just hunker down at the edge of a willow patch or lean against a spruce tree about 100 to 300 yards (depending on his shooting abilities) downwind from where he expects the moose to appear.

Whatever the quarry and the method of take, the ambush hunter must consider the three S's when selecting his position: smell, sight, and sound. Smell is the most difficult to control, and perhaps the most important. If an animal that's been hunted before smells you, it's going to vanish faster than you can shoot. While there are hundreds of kinds of sprays, lotions, and clothing that promise to diminish or neutralize human odors, the best way to avoid an animal's nose is the original method: stay downwind. Often this means having multiple blinds or stands for a single ambush site, which allows you to change position according

When ambush hunting, don't assume that game will appear only in anticipated places. On the day he killed this buck, Janis Putelis was attempting to ambush deer along a heavily worn game trail at the bottom of a draw (left). If he wasn't being careful, he might not have noticed this whitetail buck (right) that was bedded among some pines on the opposite hill.

to the dominant wind directions. A hunter on ambush should be prepared to switch positions or even postpone his hunt when he encounters an unfavorable wind.

As for dealing with your quarry's sense of vision, it's important to remember that movement is your worst enemy. Big game animals, as well as turkeys and waterfowl, have a remarkable ability to detect even the slightest shift of your arms, head, or weapon. A deer might look you straight in the face at 30 yards without registering your presence, but a simple blink of your eyes might catch its attention. When you're waiting on ambush, position yourself in such a way that your physical movements will be minimized or nonexistent when your quarry appears. Keep your weapon trained in the direction of where you anticipate shooting, and have a plan for how you're going to make the shot. If you're using a rest, such as a backpack or tree limb, test it when you first settle

in to make sure that it's going to work. Inevitably, though, you'll get into situations that are hard to anticipate. You might be watching a bait for black bears and then have a big boar come in directly behind you, where you least expected the animal to appear. In these cases, you need to pick your moments. If possible, move when the animal is facing another direction or when its head passes behind a tree. Or move when the animal is distracted by eating or by other animals. When you do move, move slowly and steadily. Avoid jerky motions.

After movements, your outline, or silhouette, is your second-worst enemy. Animals that receive a lot of hunting pressure come to recognize human shapes and outlines and are sensitive to their presence. Animals that do not receive a lot of hunting pressure still tend to be wary of the human form—perhaps because they are wary of any unusual or out-of-place shape. To avoid unwanted scrutiny,

The ambush hunter is wise to utilize a natural or man-made backdrop that will break up the human outline.

position yourself (or utilize your blind) in such a way that you have cover in front of and/or behind you. Of course, your front cover has to be sparse enough that you can still see and shoot through it. Backdrops, on the other hand, can be solid. The best backdrops have some complexity to them, with depth and texture and darkness. Think spruce trees, rock outcroppings, and the like. Such surfaces tend to swallow and conceal whatever lies in front of them. As an added precaution, the use of camouflage clothing can provide an extra level of protection against being seen.

There's also the issue of sound. This is the easiest to deal with, as much of the work can be done at home. To begin soundproofing your equipment ahead of an ambush hunt, put on everything that you'll be wearing and then do a few slow-paced jumping jacks. Potential trouble spots will be revealed as clicks and clacks and swishing sounds. These can be addressed individually until the only thing you hear is the sound of your boots hitting the floor. When you establish your stand, make sure to soundproof your surroundings as well. Clear any dead leaves or dry twigs from beneath you. Before settling in, you should also move around a little bit. Practice aiming your bow or rifle in all directions where you might possibly take a shot. (Do this slowly, of course, and remain alert for the passage of game.) Cut away any twigs or limbs that might catch your clothes. Pay special attention to things that might rub against your hat or the limbs of your bow, as these are somehow easy to miss upon first inspection.

Finally, as you settle in for an ambush, ask yourself how badly you want success. If the answer is "not much," then feel free to fidget about and doze off and then leave early. But if the answer is "real bad," then prepare to hold tight and stay long. The best ambush hunters have the discipline and dedication to remain on stand for an entire day, dawn to dusk, if that's what it takes. And then they'll get up and do it all over again the next day. Assume this level of dedication for yourself, and your ambush hunting is guaranteed to bring you a sense of satisfaction and also a lot of memories of critters that you saw but that did not see you.

A HANDFUL OF EXTRA TIPS FOR THE AMBUSH HUNTER

1. Listen carefully while attempting to ambush game. Often, a slight bit of noise will alert you to the arrival of an animal long before it shows up—giving you plenty of time to get ready before the animal is close enough to detect the movement of raising your weapon. Always remind yourself that sounds don't just happen on their own; if you heard something, there's a reason. Stay tuned to the direction of the sound until you can rule out the presence of game.

2. A comfy hunter is a deadly hunter. Don't be afraid to bring along a foam sitting pad, extra layers of clothes, and hand and toe warmers. This will keep you from fidgeting and shivering, which make noise and distract your attention from your surroundings.

3. If you bring along food, make sure you can get to it easily and eat it quietly. A big handful of venison jerky stuffed into your pocket is a great snack, because it doesn't make noise when you chew and there's no crinkly package to deal with. On the other hand, a sack of potato chips is a poor choice.

4. A lot of guys listen to music or play video games when waiting in their blind or stand. Don't do this. It is childish and it is disrespectful to the woods. It also will distract you.

5. If you absolutely have to take a nap while ambush hunting, don't get too comfortable. If you're in a less-than-perfect sleeping position, you'll wake easier and sooner.

STILL-HUNTING

Still-hunting combines the simple pleasure of walking in the woods with the excitement and discipline of being on a hunt—let's call it a perfected sneak. Because you could encounter your quarry at any moment, you need to maintain constant focus and move slowly and carefully enough that an animal might perceive you to be standing still. It's like being on the final leg of a careful stalk, except it lasts for hours and you're never sure of the animal's

Aspen groves are prime locations for still hunting.

location until it's time to raise your bow or rifle and shoot. It is this sense of the unknown that makes still-hunting so rewarding.

Along with stealth, route selection is one of the most important aspects of still-hunting. In a general sense, your route should obviously take you through regions of good habitat that you've already identified through research and scouting. But on a more specific level, your route should take you through areas where you can travel quietly and enjoy enough visibility to see animals before you're right on top of them. The opposite of a good still-hunting route would be one that takes

you through the bottom of a draw that's covered with 6 inches of dry leaves and choked with head-high alders. Here you're going to make a ton of noise and you won't be able to see a thing. Conversely, edge habitats often provide quiet travel and good visibility. There are as many types of edges as there are types of terrain: where dense forest meets open meadow, where alder thickets give way to alpine tundra, where swampland adjoins hardwood forests, where agricultural fields join heavy thickets, where riparian zones meet valley walls, where sage flats meet aspen stands. Such places are animal magnets be-

Slipping through an aspen grove with the wind in his face, this hunter hopes to intercept an elk as it moves from its bedding area in the thick evergreens to its feeding grounds in the open aspens and sagebrush.

cause they provide close proximity to both feeding areas and secure shelter areas. By working these areas, you're likely to encounter animals that are moving back and forth between different habitat types or lingering along the edges. This is especially true during the low light periods of morning and evening, when animals are most actively traveling between bedding and feeding areas.

Many ridgelines provide heavenly conditions for still-hunting. Wind keeps the ground relatively free of leaves, and you're looking at country on both sides of you from an elevated angle. ATV trails and access roads that cut through feeding and bedding areas are also fantastic, because you have quiet walking conditions and good visibility ahead of you. Active game trails can also be excellent, though things can happen almost too quickly if you happen to be moving against animal traffic in thick cover.

Managing human odor is a huge factor with still-hunting, and this is best done by playing the wind. This isn't such a big deal for small game or turkey hunters, but it's of paramount importance to big game hunters. If the wind is wrong (blowing in the same direction as you're traveling), you're at a tremendous disadvantage. Either wait for the wind to change or alter your line of travel. It's not that the wind needs to be directly in your face, but it should at least be at a 90-degree angle to your line of travel. In crosswind situations, focus more effort on glassing and looking to the upwind side of your route, as downwind animals might have smelled you and then traveled into the wind to escape.

There's an old saying, "May the wind always be at your back. May the sun shine warmly on your face." Just as the wind portion of this saying is wrong for still-hunters, the sun portion has it completely backward as well. For reasons of visibility—both for your own and the animal's—it is much better to have the sun at your back. This way, your body is not brightly illuminated, yet there's a better chance that your quarry will be well lit. What's more, staring into the sun can be taxing on your eyes and leads to diminished awareness on your part. However, if it comes down to having either the wind or the sun working on your behalf, go with the wind every time.

When still-hunting, you need to use your binoculars habitually. Too many hunters figure they can see everything just fine with the naked eye. Sadly for them, it's just not true. Even at close distances of under 100 yards, binoculars provide not only magnification of your vision but also a tightening of your focus that allows you to peer into small spaces where you might pick out the fine details of a leg, rump, or antler tine. But don't focus on these small spaces at the expense of the bigger picture. You need to alternate between detail work and broadscale scanning of the landscape ahead of you, alongside you, and even behind you. Since you never know where game will appear, you should expect it everywhere.

As hard as a still-hunter searches for his prey, his prey is searching ten times harder for predators. Every day of the animal's life depends on its ability to spot trouble before

When still-hunting, look for portions of animals, not just the whole critter.

On left: The crest of the hill is all that's needed to block the view of the elk and hide the hunters in the green positions. The hunter in the red position has skylined himself by standing right on the crest. On right: From the animal's point of view, left to right: The first two hunters (in green) have stopped well short of the crest of the hill; they are mostly hidden by the horizon. The middle hunters (in red) have approached too close to the crest of the hill and are now skylined. The two hunters on the right (in green) have advanced to the edge, but by keeping a backdrop (trees for one, a close mountain for the other) they've kept themselves from becoming skylined.

it's too late. You're competing with the animal in a game of who-spots-whom-first, and you need to do everything possible to swing the odds in your favor. First off, move slowly. (Still-hunting really ought to be called "slow hunting.") Take two or three steps and stop. Then take a few more steps and stop again. Give yourself plenty of time to listen. And whenever you start thinking that you're moving slowly enough, slow down even more. You'll find that walking slowly actually takes a little practice; it's a difficult thing to do, especially for energetic people who pride themselves on getting a lot done. It also takes a certain type of muscle control and concentration that aren't really cultivated by normal life. At first you'll find that you trip more often than you do when walking quickly, which is certainly strange. But stick with it and you'll get better and better at slow movement.

Try to maintain a backdrop as you move along. Zigzag in such a way that you put trees, rocks, or brush behind you as much as possible. These things absorb your form and help keep you hidden. In areas of varied topography, avoid skylining yourself at all costs. A skylined human (that's when you're silhouetted against the sky) is very easy for animals to detect. Be especially careful about this when hunting ridges and other high ground, but keep it in mind as well when hunting terrain with even minor ups and downs. Even a small rise in semi-timbered country can get you into trouble. Standing on it, you are not technically skylined, since there are trees behind you, but your movement and presence are certainly more noticeable.

When you approach any sort of rise or promontory, be it a major ridge or the crest of a small swale, slow your speed down to that of a three-legged turtle. Every step you take increases your field of view immensely, and all of this new terrain deserves close inspection. Give your brain time to process the new ground. Depending on your abilities, it might take a minute or more for the brain to register that it's looking at the back of a feeding deer and not just another gray rock.

By moving slowly as you travel around and over terrain features, you allow the terrain to camouflage your body. Even if an animal senses something and looks your way, it should only see you from the eyes up—and that might not be enough to alert it. But what will certainly alert the animal is the silhouette of a man from the waist up scrambling to get his rifle sling off his shoulder while muttering profanities because he should have moved slower and more carefully.

The still-hunter must also deal with the issue of noise. In particular, hunters must be aware of making unnatural noises. Popping a stick with your boot is not the end of the world, since sticks pop in the woods all the time. But the sounds created by a thorn against canvas pants, a Velcro closure being torn open, or a bow limb smacking against a belt buckle are all unnatural. They will not go unnoticed by game. The still-hunter's footsteps should be the only noise he makes, and that noise should be minimal. You can diminish the sound of your footsteps by choosing routes that take you over soft vegetation, bare ground, and large rocks rather than dried leaves and loose gravel. Also consider your footwear. Big, clunky mountaineering boots are not what you're looking for. Instead, seek out light hikers or even trail runners when the weather permits.

The soles of these shoes are much softer and quieter, and they'll allow you to feel the ground under your feet. This way, you can sense impending noisemakers such as dry sticks and loose rocks before they give you away.

If you're careful about movement and noise, you could get away with wearing a Santa Claus outfit in many still-hunting situations. That might sound funny, but it's meant to emphasize the point that camouflage is not nearly as important as other basic principles of stealth. However, you'll never regret the use of camouflage clothing, and it might very well save you from getting busted by a prized animal. Regardless of whether you use camo or not, you should think about wearing gloves and a head net or face mask in order to hide the glare of your bare skin—especially white skin that might be shiny from sweat and natural oils.

Weather conditions can have a serious impact on a still-hunter, and not always negative. Moisture from rain or melted snow is perfect for still-hunting, because it quiets the leaves and grass. But be careful during cold weather, because when that rainwater freezes into a crust it becomes some of the loudest stuff you'll ever traipse across. High winds can also be beneficial. Apart from loud metal-on-metal-type noises, most sounds will be canceled out by a fierce wind rattling every bush and leaf. And since the vegetation is moving with the wind, your physical movements will be partially concealed as well. Remember, animals don't get the day off because it's windy. They will, however, alter their bedding locations. They look for the lee side of topographic features and tend to bed in more open areas where they can see better. This is a plus for the still-hunter, as it makes game easier to spot from a distance.

Your mental attitude is one last thing you should consider before you enter the woods on a still hunt. To keep the heightened level of focus needed for still-hunting success, you need an optimistic and positive frame of mind. By always believing your quarry is just around the corner or just over the next rise, you'll keep your eyes working for the duration of the hunt. The moment that pessimistic thoughts such as *I picked the wrong spot* or *I should've gone somewhere else instead* enter your head, you'll sling your rifle over your shoulder and take a few careless steps. Just then, the bedded buck you worked so hard to sneak in range of will burst out from a thicket and leave you standing there to contemplate whatever it was that distracted you from the work of hunting.

With the morning thermal falling, the Jaunarajs brothers still-hunted along a creek bottom as they scanned the aspens above them. Soon after daylight they spotted this bull feeding 170 yards up the hill.

A HANDFUL OF EXTRA TIPS FOR THE STILL-HUNTER

1. Because bumping into animals is an inherent part of still-hunting, the hunter must be always ready to make a quick shot. Carrying your weapon in the cross-body field position instead of slung on your shoulder will shave a precious second or two off your response time. But don't discard your sling altogether. It'll come in handy when scrambling up a steep face, crawling through a thicket, or any other time when you need both hands.

2. Even the best still-hunter will inadvertently spook game. To capitalize on this reality, the friends and family of a Wisconsin deer hunter named Doug Duren have perfected a variation of still-hunting that they call mooching. On a mooch, two or more hunters coordinate their still-hunts in the hope of bumping deer toward one another. (For a complete breakdown on mooching, see page 293.)

3. Another still-hunting variation is to add calling to your hunt. A South Carolina deer hunter named Robert Abernathy will stop every couple of hundred yards on a still hunt in order to do a rattling sequence. "Even if an animal doesn't come immediately charging in, the hunter might still draw animals into the general vicinity and then encounter them during the course of his hunt." The same strategy can be applied to many species besides deer.

4. It's easy for big game to pick out the rhythm of human footsteps. When walking on noisy ground, walk in an arrhythmic pattern and never take more than three or four steps at a time between pauses.

5. Turn your scope to its lowest magnification setting when on a still hunt. This will help you find your target faster, especially at close range.

6. Use your nose to sense what's ahead of you. Many critters, especially elk, wild pigs, and javelina, have pungent odors that you can sometimes smell long before your eyes find the animal.

DECOYS AND CALLING

Calling and decoying big game is so much fun because it's just about the only time in life when you can justify deception, double-crossing, hoaxing, fraud, dupery, and dishonesty. Here, the goal of the hunter is to mimic, through visual and audio trickery, the same critters that he's trying to harvest. It's an exciting, challenging, and interactive discipline that forces you to learn detailed information about your quarry—information that will inevitably lead to more successful hunts and a deeper appreciation for the animals that we are blessed to share the woods with.

For our purposes here, a decoy is defined as an artificial animal used to entice a real animal into range of a bow. (For the sake of safety, big game decoys should be reserved exclusively for bowhunting. These are lifelike decoys that can fool animals and hunters alike; obviously, you do not want another hunter shooting in your direction.) The tactic of using decoys for big game is still in its infancy. In recent years, there's been a steady proliferation of decoy types, and now you can find some sort of decoy for many species of big game, ranging from antelope to elk. The most versatile and effective decoys are 3-D picture decoys that use high-quality images of animals printed on an elastic fabric that can be stretched over a thin wire frame. These are lightweight and

packable. For some species, you use a female decoy to draw in males during the breeding season. For others, such as antelope, it can be more effective to use a decoy of a small male—this elicits an aggressive territorial response from dominant males. (Decoy use for each animal is covered in the dedicated species sections.)

In fact, the territorial response of the males of some species is so strong that they'll be attracted to anything that suggests the presence of another male. A simple white flag on a stick or a wearable hat made to look like a male antelope will sometimes draw in antelope bucks who want to bully the suspected youngster and drive him away. Hunters also use antlers of deer, elk, and moose to the same effect. Flash the antler from behind a tree or bush to give the impression of a rival male. This might just draw your quarry in close enough for a shot. When hunting predators such as bears, decoys made to look like wounded or distressed prey can be effective. Waving a patch of fur or an animal tail on a stick can get the attention of a black bear and perhaps bring him close enough for a shot.

Calling for big game is a much more established strategy, and it's much more difficult to master. You need to understand the proper sequences of calls and also the proper pitch, tonality, and cadence. Not only are you trying to learn the "words" used by animals, you're trying to build proper sentences as well. To understand this, imagine a high school party. Suddenly there's a loud banging on the door accompanied by either "This is the police" or "Pizza delivery." Although both statements are in the English language, they will have completely different effects on the partygoers.

The same goes for hunting. Using the wrong call, making a call at the wrong time, or calling with improper tone can have the opposite effect of what you want. Mastering these animal languages requires a ton of practice and care-ful study of the sounds made by actual animals. Thankfully, there are many DVDs, downloadable videos, and YouTube videos that explore this information. (Hint: Any instructional material by Will Primos is going to be excellent.) Great callers listen and practice year-round, even keeping a few calls on the dashboard of their car or truck so that windshield time equals practice time. Warning: Calling practice in the home needs to be done in moderation, as it can cause serious marital strain.

There are many types of big game calls available to hunters. Internal and external reed calls are the most widely available and easily learned. It's easy to imagine that the original version of a reed call was someone holding a piece of grass in his fingers and blowing on it. Today reeds are usually coupled with tubular structures made of wood and/or synthetic materials with either an open reed on one end or an enclosed reed inside the tube. The size of the reed and the tension at which it is held dictates what the call will sound like. Predator calls, elk calls, and whitetail buck calls are all made in this style.

Diaphragm calls, or mouth calls, are the next most popular type of big game call—particularly for predators and elk. These are placed inside your mouth, against the upper roof, and air is blown between your tongue and the call's latex reed. These are a little harder to master but have a great advantage over other calls in that

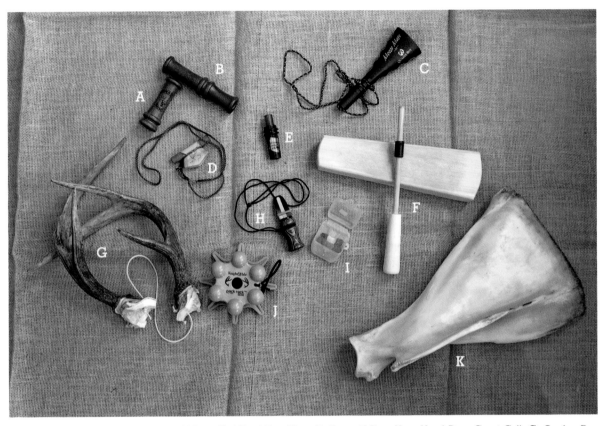

A mixture of big game calls. **A:** Down-N-Dirty SlickHead Doe Bleat. **B:** Down-N-Dirty HawgHead Deer Grunt Call. **C:** Quaker Boy Moose Mate cow call. **D:** Handmade blacktail deer fawn bleat. **E:** Arizona Game Calls J-13 javelina distress call. **F:** Quaker Boy Bulldozer moose call. **G:** Whitetail rattling antlers. **H:** Phelps E-Z-Estrus elk call. **I:** Assorted elk diaphragm calls. **J:** Knight & Hale Pack Rack whitetail rattling call. **K:** Moose scapula used to mimic the sounds of a bull raking brush with its antlers.

they are completely hands free and generally more versatile. To amplify the sound and give it a more genuine quality, diaphragm users can blow into a tube.

Rattling and scraping calls are different in that they don't imitate the sounds that animals make with their vocal cords; rather, they imitate the sounds they make with their antlers. Many whitetail hunters have rattled two deer antlers together to imitate the sound of two fighting bucks in order to lure in a competitor or curious onlooker. Artificial calls or devices have been made to replicate this sound as well. A rattling bag is simply a dozen or so dowels placed in a loose bag that resembles a tube sock. Held between two hands, the bag is rolled back and forth, creating a sound simulating antlers clashing. A dried moose scapula from a previous year's hunt can be used to emulate moose antlers scraping brush. This method of calling moose is particularly effective during the pre-rut, when bulls tend to fraternize for a period of time before turning into mortal enemies during the breeding season.

Electronic calls, which do the work for you, are very popular among predator hunters.

Uldis Jaunarajs and Janis Putelis bumped this bull during their morning still-hunt. With loud, aggressive cow calling they were able to make the bull stop for a look, which presented a shot opportunity.

These devices can store thousands of sounds, which can be played back with the push of a button. However, their use is almost categorically prohibited for big game. Before using any electronic call, check your state's regulations regarding their use. The opposite extreme from electronic calls is attempting to use your own unaided vocal cords. Moose calls are fairly easy to produce on your own, but turkey calls are a nightmare. Other animals fall between these two extremes. In general, it's difficult for adult males with naturally deep voices to consistently produce the high-pitched sounds of game animals. But if you can figure it out,

it can be deadly. Natural callers are some of the best in the business.

In general, big game animals make calls for three reasons: for mating purposes, to signal distress or alarm, or to enforce herd dynamics and conduct various social interactions. The bugling of bull elk and the grunting of deer and moose are closely associated with mating, though it's true that they will sometimes make these noises outside of the breeding season. Not unlike humans, the males of big game species are often overcome by poor judgment when pursuing the opposite sex or defending their love interests against rivals;

quite often, they lose their inhibitions and make poor decisions, which can work to the advantage of the hunter. Not all effective game calls are communicated between males and females. The sound of a male's antlers rattling together or thrashing brush can be very seductive to another male, who might approach out of curiosity or territoriality—basically, he wants to see what the guys are up to, and maybe get involved himself.

Distress calls are meant to mimic the sound of dying, wounded, or panicked animals. Such noises can bring in hungry predators looking to capitalize on another creature's misfortune, or they might bring a member of the same species that's coming to the rescue. The sound of a screeching javelina might sound like a dinner bell to a black bear, but to a pack of javelina it will sound like a call to arms.

Social calls exploit the gregarious nature of herd animals, who generally find comfort in the company of others. The sound of other herdmates not only implies safety and companionship but can signify an available food source as well. And since wild animals are so easily habituated to food sources, the sounds of sources themselves can be enticing to animals. There are many instances in which hunters have observed grizzly bears moving toward the direction of a rifle shot in order to scavenge a fresh gut pile. In places like Texas, where the practice of feeding deer with corn is well established, the deer are attracted to the noise created by whoever disperses the corn. In most cases, this is an automatic feeder. When the feeder turns on to sling corn, the sound of the whirring propeller and the corn hitting nearby foliage is enough to cause a minor stampede. In the North Woods of Maine, the sound of a chain saw is known to attract whitetail deer during the winter. For them, the chain saw means a freshly felled tree, which equates to fresh browse that's been knocked down to ground level. Such mechanical sounds are not used for hunting purposes in any widespread fashion—at least not yet.

No matter how good you are at decoying or calling big game, you're relying on a certain bit of gullibility on the animal's part. But once a critter has survived one or two encounters with fakery, it can become extremely suspicious of anything that isn't absolutely genuine. As a hunting season wears on, the standard decoys and calls used by many hunters become ineffectual and can even begin to work against the hunter. As the animals wise up, you need to employ new sounds and tricks in order to stay competitive, or else move on to other strategies altogether. Just forty years ago, for instance, no one knew how to make cow elk sounds because you didn't have to; hunters knew how to make the bugling sound of bulls by blowing turkey diaphragms through plastic tubing, and elk would come running to every bugle—real or fake—that echoed through the mountains. Once elk began to

A buck such as this one has been successfully evading hunters for a long time; unless your calling is perfect, the odds are good that he'll retreat instead of coming your way.

grow suspicious of bugles, about thirty years ago in some areas, hunters started learning how to produce rudimentary versions of the whistles and mews used by cow elk. Then that, too, became an overused and ineffective strategy. So game call manufacturers began marketing ever more realistic-sounding cow elk calls, and the old calls became obsolete. (Nowadays, if you blow an elk bugle in a competitive location, you're more than likely going to send elk running in the opposite direction.)

Around 2002, a push call came on the market that produces very realistic cow elk calls. With this call in your hand and a diaphragm in your mouth, you could sound like a small herd of elk. This strategy really brought bulls running in. The problem was that this call was very easy to use and well marketed, and soon every elk hunter had one. Within five years the novelty wore off, and the push call became a sure-fire way to repel high-pressure elk.

You can watch a similar phenomenon happen overnight if you're hunting javelina. The first time a herd hears a javelina distress call they will trip over themselves to come rushing in your direction. Go back to that same pack of javelina the next day and try it, and they'll disappear in a cloud of dust. Game animals are quick learners, which isn't at all a bad thing. After all, intelligent game makes for intelligent hunters.

A HANDFUL OF EXTRA TIPS FOR THE HUNTER USING DECOYS AND CALLS

1. Be careful not to overcall. It sounds phony and suspicious. It's not uncommon for an experienced caller to go fifteen or twenty minutes between making sounds. Listen to the animals themselves and mimic the frequency with which they talk.

2. To add realism and depth to your calling setup, use two callers. It creates a herd dynamic, and you'll sound a lot different from most hunters, who are using just one call.

3. Try moving around when calling, especially when you're working an animal that won't come in close. Often, a little movement gives your setup the necessary realism. Also try making some natural sounds to go with your calling, such as rustling leaves or the raking of an antler. Do it subtly at first, and make sure you get a positive response before repeating.

4. Mouth calls, or diaphragm calls, come in many configurations; the frames have different shapes and thicknesses, and they use different types of latex cut in different ways. Even mouth calls of the same brand and model might sound different because of inconsistencies in the latex. If you can't get the sounds you want, try another mouth call. Eventually you'll find one that works for you.

5. Practice, practice, practice! That is the only way that you'll ever get good at calling big game.

DRIVE HUNTING (OR CONTROLLED CHAOS)

The Folsom site at Wild Horse Arroyo. Near the end of the Ice Age, hunters using sophisticated stone spear points slaughtered a small herd of bison here. They were almost certainly using drive tactics.

The term *drive* has nothing to do with vehicles. Instead, it is used to describe the strategy of chasing game toward waiting hunters. It is an ancient method that requires careful coordination between multiple individuals. In fact, linguists and anthropologists have postulated that the challenges of drive hunting may have helped spur the development of human language; our early African ancestors needed a way to coordinate their hunting activities, and so they learned to talk.

Here in North America, the archaeological record abounds with the evidence of successful drive hunts. The Folsom site, in northeastern New Mexico, revealed the remains of more than twenty *Bison antiquus* (an early ancestor of the modern buffalo) killed by Ice Age hunters who drove the animals into an arroyo and then slaughtered them with spears.

Across the Great Plains, from southern Texas to southern Alberta, there are dozens upon dozens of locations where Native American hunters drove buffalo over cliffs—sometimes hundreds or even thousands at a time. Some folks might argue that these "buffalo jumps" don't really represent game drives as we understand them today. It was the cliff that did the killing, they'd say, not hunters. But a careful examination of these sites reveals the opposite. It is common to find great abundances of arrowheads—sometimes thousands—mixed among the slaughtered bones at the bases of the cliffs. It seems that the cliffs usually did little more than injure the animals. Hunters did the rest.

Today, drives are used effectively on several big game species, ranging in size from javelina to elk. It's the only hunting strategy in which you're actually trying to spook your quarry. It can be exciting, fast-paced, and sometimes quite hectic. In a perfect situation, two hunters are all it takes to orchestrate a drive; one guy goes into a thicket to spook up the quarry, the other guy kills it when it comes running out. But in reality, drives aren't usually so precise. Instead, they are built around a number of unknowns, and these are addressed by the use of additional hunters. It's often going to take more than one guy to find your quarry and get it moving in the right direction, and it's often going to take more than one guy to cover the possible escape routes. Realistically, most drives require between four and eight hunters to do things right.

Each hunter in a drive is assigned a role, either as a pusher or a stander. Pushers are responsible for getting the game up and moving, usually by walking through areas of thick bedding cover. Sometimes the pushers will get shots at game that they've kicked up, but it's usually the standers who get the shots in. These are the hunters who are responsible for covering the escape routes used by the quarry, which is where most of the action typically occurs.

Whitetail deer are particularly conducive to drive hunting. Here, a group of hunters in Wisconsin celebrate after conducting a successful deer drive that has produced dozens of whitetails over the years.

It's probably no surprise that most hunters prefer to be standers. But it's the pushers, at least the good ones, who deserve the respect. Instead of blindly walking through the woods, trusting that he'll scare out game and that it will go in the right direction, a pusher needs to engage in constant analysis. He has to let his movements be guided by the terrain and the available evidence of animals. If he's doing a deer drive and he sees some semi-fresh deer beds beneath hemlock trees, he'll veer out of his way to pass beneath every single hemlock in the woods. He'll also alert the other pushers of his find, so they can do the same. And if he cuts a fresh track, he'll dodge off course to follow it. If that track goes into a particularly dense thicket that might hold the deer, he'll enter the thicket in such a way that the deer is likely to bound away in the direction of the standers. And if the wind is blowing toward this thicket as he approaches it, he'll adjust his course so that his odor doesn't arrive ahead of him and potentially spook the deer out in the wrong direction. What's more, the pusher remains on high alert at all times for a critter that has detected the standers and attempts to double back and make its way through the line of pushers. In addition to these considerations of strategy, the pusher needs to be a disciplined worker who's willing to bust through the nastiest briar thickets and brush-choked hellholes that Mother Nature can throw his way.

Obviously, there is more to being a stander than just shooting at game. A good stander approaches his role in a drive with some of the same care and thoughtfulness that an ambush hunter uses when picking his location. When hunting a species with a sensitive nose, such as deer or elk, he positions himself with a mind toward the wind so that he's not letting his odor reveal his position to the game. He anticipates potential shot avenues and makes sure that he's got enough room to maneuver and get his weapon in position. He remains extremely alert, watches in all directions, and expects sudden surprises. Most important, he maintains a constant awareness that his hunting partners are out in front of him somewhere, and he *never* even thinks about taking a shot that might send a bullet or arrow in their direction.

At this point, it's helpful to take a look at a couple of hypothetical drives, one for whitetail deer and one for elk. While no two drive scenarios are the same, these two illustrated examples (see next page) will give you an idea of the thinking that goes into a drive. Consider these examples and then apply the methodology to the situations that you'll encounter on your own hunts—regardless of what you're after or where.

The first is a whitetail drive in a classic farm country setting of mixed croplands, woodlots, and wetlands.

The hunters know that late-season deer tend to seek shelter in the thick brush and cattails around a small pond, as well as along the brushy ditchrow that separates the lower fallow field from the south cornfield. The two pushers (red routes) will push out all the bedding areas while the two standers cover the most likely escape routes. Since this is late season and the deer have already been subjected to some hunting pressure, they will want to stick to cover as much as possible once they spook. The pushers have considered this and positioned themselves accordingly.

Here's another drive situation, this time for elk. Bear in mind, however, that elk drives are not nearly as easy to pull off as deer drives. The vastness of the country and the steep topography make it hard to anticipate the movement of an elk herd. But this situation will help shed some light on the general sort of thinking that goes into a drive as you factor in topography, cover, and the known habits of the quarry.

In this scenario, the elk are thought to be bedded in a smallish patch of evergreens near the top of a mountain slope. This particular patch is worth driving because it has a natural border (cliffs and scree fields) at its upper end that will keep the elk from going straight up and over the mountain. The hunters are aware of a heavily used elk trail through the saddle and another traversing the sage-covered opening heading to another patch of timber. Maybe the most important part of pulling off this drive is the ability of the standers to get to their locations without alerting the bedded elk. This

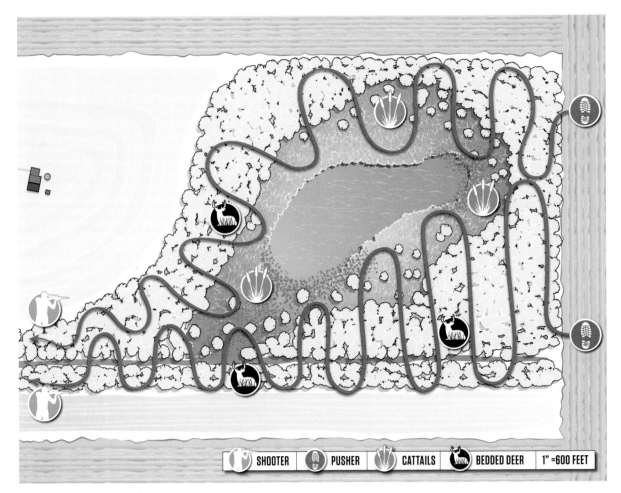

Drive scenario: Whitetail dear

| SHOOTER | PUSHER | CATTAILS | BEDDED DEER | 1" =600 FEET |

might mean a wide loop up the backside of the mountain, requiring a couple of hours of hiking. Once the standers are in position, the pushers start at the lower end of the timber. As the pushers zigzag through the timber, their scent is carried uphill by a rising thermal. It is important that the pushers traverse the hill completely to ensure that their smell wafts up through the entire section of timber. It is the scent of humans that will drive the elk out, not the noise or sight of a pusher. The elk will sneak out, following the known escape routes through the saddle and along the trail. If everything goes right, they will pass within easy range of the standers.

The more you experiment with drives, the more you'll see that each particular game drive is like a jigsaw puzzle: it may be hard to put together the first try, but it gets easier and easier each time you do it. The most effective drives are perfected over many seasons of hunting. Eventually, through success and failure, you learn what the animals in a given situation are going to do—even if you never

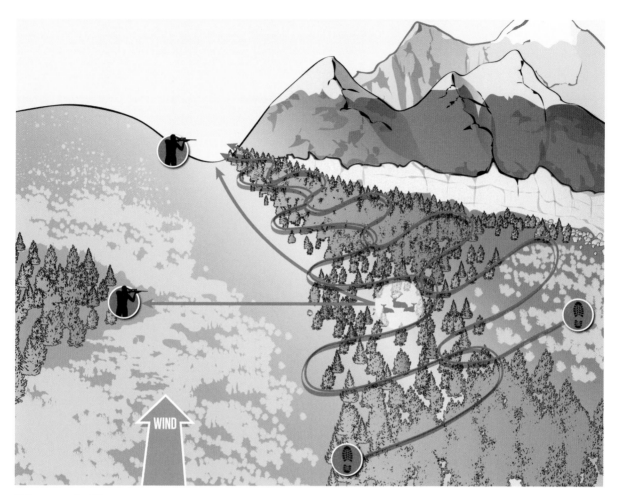

Drive scenario: Elk

really understand *why* they do it. Such lessons are learned from direct observation of the animals themselves, and also by checking for tracks in the snow or mud after an unsuccessful drive. Doing so, you might find that an animal went off in a completely unexpected direction and never came near your standers, or that it passed within easy shooting distance of your standers but avoided attention through the intentional—or just lucky—use of slight dips and rises in the landscape. Through these investigations, and through direct observation of the animals, you'll learn that animals in a particular area favor certain ridges and shun others, or opt to travel on one side of a creek and not the other, or tend to cross a field on the north end rather than the south end. You can then incorporate these lessons into next year's hunt—hopefully with deadly results.

A HANDFUL OF EXTRA TIPS FOR THE DRIVE HUNTER

1. Don't drive a particular area more than once or twice a year. If you do it too often, you'll force the animals that are using the area to abandon it.

2. When it comes to deer drives, save them for the last day or two of the season. By then, more deer will be hunkered down in the thickest, least accessible regions of your hunting area, which are the best areas to drive. Also, you won't have to worry about the drive impacting your ambush hunting prospects.

3. The standers on a drive should sneak quietly into their positions and maintain absolute silence when there. No talking, no coughing, no fidgeting around. If animals detect the presence of the standers, they will choose an alternate route of escape.

4. One pusher can do the job of four if he uses the wind to his advantage. Rather than walking through an area to scare out deer, let the wind carry in your scent and do the work for you.

5. Consider your weapon and ammunition before a drive hunt. Because your quarry is likely to be moving, set variable-power scopes at low magnification levels so you can find game in a hurry through the lens. For fast access, cradle your firearm rather than slinging it over your shoulder. And keep extra ammo ready, so you don't need to dig for it in a moment of panic.

THE BACKPACK HUNTER

When a hunter is carrying everything he needs to survive on his back, the thrill of taking an animal becomes almost secondary to the thrill of staying out on the land and fending for oneself for a period of days or even weeks. But that's not to say that the backpack hunter is

somehow less interested in having a successful hunt. Backpack hunters are committed to
searching out the richest and least exploited
hunting grounds, and they're willing to suffer
in order to reach them. Often the payoffs for
these efforts can be extraordinary. Many of the
finest public land hunting opportunities in the
United States belong solely to the backpack
hunter because he's the only one who's willing
and capable of reaching them.

A good backpack hunting location is any
area that's inaccessible to hunters who are
operating out of vehicles. Such areas might
be inaccessible for a variety of reasons, including a complete lack of roads or else a closure of existing roads due to legal restrictions
or weather conditions. Some areas, such as
Alaska's Brooks Range, Idaho's Frank Church
Wilderness, or Montana's Bob Marshall Wil-

derness, are almost wholly inaccessible to
vehicle hunters. These are the great famed
bastions of the backpack hunter, though backpack hunting opportunities are certainly not
restricted to pure wilderness locations.

In fact, some of the finest backpack hunting
opportunities are on the fringes of vehicle access
areas, in places that lie just beyond the reach
of road hunters but not so far into the backcountry that you're competing with outfitters who
pack in large groups of hunters on horses or
mules. In some cases, an hour-long uphill climb
is all that it takes to prevent vehicle-based hunters from visiting an area. Typically these guys
will stay within a mile or so of their vehicle, and
they'll almost never stray more than 3 miles
away. In the rare instance that a vehicle-based
hunter does walk more than 3 miles, he usually
won't reach the farthest point of his wandering

A backpack hunter must be physically and mentally prepared for the arduous task of hauling meat.

Of course, the range of a backpack hunter is limited to how far he can feasibly pack the meat of his kill. Deer-sized animals, once they're boned out, can usually be transported in a single (though sometimes grueling) load. Other animals, such as moose, might require a hunter to make six or seven trips while carrying 100-pound loads. Before heading out on a backpack hunt, a hunter needs to be realistic about how much he can endure. One time, my brother Matt and I backpacked into the mountains a distance of 9 miles and shot two cow elk. After killing them, we quartered the carcasses and hung them in a tree where they were safe from grizzlies. Then we boned out 200 pounds of meat, loaded 100 pounds into each of our backpacks, and headed for the truck. It was well past dark when we got there. We camped at the trailhead that night, then left before daylight the next morning to make another run. After 18 miles of walking, we were back at the truck after dark that night with

A typical backpack hunter's lair: not cozy, but enough to keep him or her in the field while others sip cocoa at the local diner.

until the midday period, when hunting conditions are at their worst. In order to avoid nighttime walking, he'll start heading back to his rig well before the prime-time dusk period. The game animals in such areas are sometimes completely chilled out, as they haven't experienced any hunting pressure. What's more, other animals from pressured areas tend to congregate in these places after getting bumped from their usual haunts. The backpack hunter is uniquely equipped to capitalize on such hunting grounds because he doesn't waste valuable time and energy traveling back and forth from a distant vehicle or camp.

Minimize your backcountry funk by washing when the opportunity arises.

another 200 pounds. We then did the same thing the next day, moving the final 200 pounds over the same trail that we'd now traveled a total of six times—all while enduring single-digit temperatures. It took us about a week to physically recover from that trip. Now I regard the distance of 9 miles as being the outer limit of how far I'll walk for an elk.

Many backpack hunters specialize in the spot-and-stalk hunting strategy, mainly because the locations that are most suitable for backpack hunting occur in the Rockies and Alaska—places where open expanses and varied topography are the norm. In these regions, it's often possible to spot game from a long way off and then execute a carefully planned approach. But the backpack hunter is hardly limited to a spot-and-stalk strategy. Archery elk hunters in Arizona will backpack into their favorite mountain ranges and then use calling strategies almost exclusively once they get there. Black bear hunters in California

will backpack into remote areas and then spend their entire trip setting up ambushes at the edges of likely feeding areas. A blacktail deer hunter in Oregon might backpack into an area that's primarily suitable for still-hunting; day after day, he'll carefully work mile upon mile of brushy and timbered terrain while sleeping wherever he happens to be at nightfall. More typically, though, a backpack hunter needs to be elastic in his approach. Because he's traveling long distances over unfamiliar terrain, he needs to be ready for anything. For instance, you might hike into an area for mule deer and then spend your first day glassing from a peak to see if you can identify some distant areas with a lot of deer activity. The next day, you might still-hunt a ridge where you saw some deer the day before—albeit from a couple of miles away. If that fails, you might spend an entire day ambush-hunting on a canyon-bottom trail that seems to be getting a lot of deer traffic. If nothing turns up there, you might climb to yet another peak that gives you a fresh perspective on a new patch of ground. All along, you shouldn't be worried about switching from one tactic to another. You're hunting in ways that the situations dictate, doing what makes most sense in the moment.

A disadvantage of backpack hunting is that you're creating extra disturbances in your hunting area by "living" in close proximity to your quarry. Without access to showers or laundry facilities, your stench can get pretty bad during warm weather hunts. Game can wander into your camp at night and get spooked out of the area without you ever knowing that it happened. The simple chores of camping, such as cooking, collecting water, and clearing a comfortable tent site, all add to the problem. These negatives can be limited by taking a careful approach to hygiene and campsite selection. When possible, pack along a fresh set of underwear and a fresh set of socks for each day you'll be out. Use moist towelettes to wash yourself at night, and apply an unscented body powder to your groin, armpits, and feet. When hiking long distances, go shirtless or wear just a merino T-shirt if the weather allows; this will keep your clothes from getting too sweaty. Wash yourself in small creeks, even if it's so cold your bones ache. When it comes to sleeping, try to make your camp a mile or more from where you plan on hunting. You're still within easy striking distance, but your disturbance is somewhat re-

This hunter slept above a few Coues deer does; he woke up to find some bucks had joined the group. He killed one from a shooting position that was just a short crawl from where he slept.

moved. Camping in thick timber or in the bottoms of narrow drainages can help keep you hidden from surrounding wildlife.

Sometimes, though, walking to and from your hunting or glassing spot makes more commotion than just sleeping where you are. In these cases, don't make fires and forgo the tent if at all possible. Try to find a low spot that's out of the wind and lay out your sleeping bag on a tarp or pad. Then get into your bag, lie low, and keep movement to an absolute minimum. One of my most memorable nights in the mountains was spent literally surrounded by Coues deer in the Arizona desert. I had hiked up to a good glassing area, only to realize that I had does in every direction. Rather than risking a hike back down to the canyon floor, I crawled into my sleeping bag at dark and forced myself to eat 2,000 calories' worth of energy bars rather than mess around with a Jetboil. Four bucks showed up below me at daybreak. I shot one just a short crawl away from camp.

On backpack hunts, it's often a good idea to stash the bulk of your gear where you anticipate spending the night. This allows you to do the morning and evening hunts with a lighter load. But be careful not to travel *too* light. You should stay prepared for long days (and emergencies) by bringing along a few extra layers of clothes, plus food, water, and a basic field kit. You can put all of this gear into a regular backpack, then cinch the pack

When hunting in grizzly country, safety procedures should take priority over your hunt plans.

down to reduce the profile. If you make a kill, you can expand the pack and haul a load of meat back to camp. What's more, this partially filled pack often comes in handy as a rifle rest for prone shots. If you're traveling a long ways from base camp, or if you're hunting in an exceptionally rugged area where nighttime travel is difficult or dangerous, pack along your sleeping bag as well. This way you can bivy out for the night if you stray too far from camp and can't get back before dark, or if you kill an animal and have to sleep next to it in order to protect it from bears and other scavengers. Keep in mind, too, that you should always pay careful attention to where you stash your gear. Use an easily identified landmark, and mark it with a waypoint on your GPS. If you come stumbling back in the dark, exhausted and overburdened with meat, you don't want to have a hassle trying to locate your food and gear.

As for bears, particularly grizzlies, the back-

Air-drying the quarters before you place them into game bags will allow a crust, or rind, to build on the outside of the meat; this helps protect the meat and limits moisture loss.

pack hunter needs to be prepared for them. Grizzlies inhabit most of Alaska plus much of the backcountry habitats in Montana, Idaho, and Wyoming. Currently they are expanding their range beyond these areas; in the near future, they may very well become a fact of life (and a welcome one, in my opinion) in Colorado, Washington, Oregon, and perhaps elsewhere. When hunting in grizzly country, you need to maintain maximum awareness at all times. This is especially true after you've made a kill. A grizzly will contest the ownership of the animal and he'll fight you for it. You'll want to get carcasses quartered quickly and then get those quarters hung high in a tree as soon as possible. Ideally, you should hang the meat 10 feet high and about 4 feet away from the tree's trunk. This will help keep grizzlies as well as black bears and coyotes away from it. If there's no tree that can support the meat, then move the edible portions of your kill as far as possible from the gut pile. This will help buy time, as bears will want to consume the soft organ tissues first. Drape the meat with dirty clothes and any extra odds and ends from your backpack in order to increase human odor and to make the carcass seem as unnatural as possible. When approaching your meat cache on return trips, make a lot of noise and come in, slowly, from an upwind direction. This will let any bears know that you're coming, and hopefully they'll scoot out. Keep in mind that it is illegal to kill a grizzly bear that has claimed your animal unless it poses an immediate threat to your life. If a grizzly takes your kill and you can't scare it away by using safe and reasonable measures, then walk away and report the incident to a game warden. In most cases, the warden will issue you a new tag.

Here's one trick for backpack hunters that I've never seen or heard anyone else mention: pay attention to backpackers. I mean this in two ways: one, let them do some scouting for you; and two, pay attention to their technologies. As far as scouting goes, backpackers are far more open about what they've seen on their journeys than hunters are. That's because backpackers aren't typically worried about keeping their spots secret. Time and again, I've asked backpackers about their most recent journeys into the mountains and received valuable up-to-date information. In one case, I met a pair of backpackers near a trailhead in the

Bitterroot Mountains. I started yakking them up, and they bragged of having just seen three black bears on a ridgetop that was covered in huckleberries. I went up there and found two of them, though I didn't kill either one. At other times, I've picked up information about elk, mountain goats, and mule deer from backpackers. Most of the time, I simply asked backpackers I bumped into at trailheads or along well-traveled backcountry routes if they'd been seeing a lot of wildlife.

While I'm not suggesting that you lie, I do think it's wise to conceal your identity as a hunter if possible when discussing critters with backpackers. It's an unfair generalization to say that backpackers are opposed to hunting (since many backpackers *are* hunters, myself included), but you'll find that they'll be freer with information if they don't think you're putting "their" animals at risk. Also, it's wise to spend time on the Internet to see what backpackers are saying about certain areas. Recently, I've been doing some online scouting for a mountain goat tag that I drew in southeast Alaska. So far, the most valuable information that I've found has come from a backpacking blogger who made his way to a particular backcountry lake last summer and saw a bunch of them. He even shared his route of travel.

As for technology, the backpacking industry has managed to stay way ahead of the hunting industry on lightweight and functional equip-ment. Up until a few years ago, when a hand-ful of hunting apparel companies began to make high-performance gear for mountain hunters, I dressed almost completely in clothes meant for mountaineers and backpackers. I found them to be better fitting (your average backpacker is way thinner than your average hunter), longer-lasting, and more comfortable than traditional hunting garb. As for other in-tegral categories of gear, including water pu-rification systems, sleeping systems, tents, and cooking equipment, you're still better off shopping at backpacking websites than hunt-ing websites.

But the backpack hunter who's preparing for his first backcountry trip shouldn't fixate on gear to the point that it detracts from more important issues. The primary piece of equip-ment that deserves 95 percent of the backpack hunter's attention is his own body. The major-ity of hunters, even many of those who consider themselves to be in good shape, are incapable of withstanding the rigors of a backcountry hunt. Just ask any Dall sheep guide and they'll tell you: the number-one thing that keeps their clients from success isn't shoddy backpacks—it's lack of stamina. Quite simply, people get into the mountains and start to fall apart: blisters, sore muscles, pulled tendons, chafed skin, and exhaustion. And this isn't because these people are lazy or weak. Rather, it's be-cause backpack hunting demands that a per-son be able to walk long distances over rough terrain while carrying a heavy load—not a combination of abilities that is honed by typical exercise regimens. In order to prepare yourself for a backpack hunt, you should plan on doing several months' worth of running or biking, weight training, and hiking long uphill distances while wearing the exact same boots and backpack that you plan on wearing during your hunt. With proper training and preparation, your backcountry hunting experience will almost certainly become a defining point in your life. You'll never feel as free and alive as when you embark into the wilderness with a pack and rifle, the land opening ahead of you.

A HANDFUL OF EXTRA TIPS FOR THE BACKPACK HUNTER

1. When hunting in the mountains, consider camping where several forks of a river drainage come together. You can hunt a different stem of the drainage each day while using the same base camp.

2. In areas with limited water, bring along several collapsible canteens. (Nalgene and MSR both make good products.) This way, if you have to hike a long way for water, you can return to your camp with several days' worth.

3. When hunting in areas with extremely limited water, make a few preseason trips into your hunting area in order to stash a supply of water. Figure on 3 to 5 liters per day, depending on temperature, humidity, and exertion. It'll keep you in the mountains longer, and it's a great way to help you get into shape before your hunt.

4. If you're comfortable with your hunting partner, you can save on space by sharing a low-profile two-man mountaineering tent. At the end of the day, you'll be so tired that you won't mind the extra company.

MAKING THE SHOT

The only way that you'll ever reach a high level of proficiency with your firearm is through trigger time. Not only do you need to know how to put your bullets where you want them, you also need to acquire an intimate understanding of your weapon's capabilities and limitations. The more time you spend with your gun, shooting and hunting, the more you'll understand it. There are no shortcuts.

While training to shoot, make sure to familiarize yourself with a variety of shooting positions—not just from a bench equipped with sandbags. Of course, benches are ideal for getting your rifle sighted in, but once that's taken care of, you need to explore postures and positions that are likely to be encountered in real-world hunting situations. By doing this, you'll have a better understanding of which shooting postures work best for you at various distances. No matter what stance you're using, ask yourself the following questions before you take a shot: Do you have a good rest? Is your breathing under control? Is your grip on your rifle secure, but not so strong that it's torquing the rifle? What is your point of impact? Have you picked the exact spot that you want to hit? (You can practice this checklist in your spare time at home by dry-firing your rifle. It's a great way to familiarize yourself with your hunting weapon.)

Each of the above positions would be improved by the use of a rest. A rest is anything that helps steady the rifle for the shot. When standing, you can rest the rifle against a tree to get more stability. When kneeling, a set of shooting sticks or a propped-up backpack can work. For prone shots, you can use about anything: wadded-up clothes, sleeping pads, fixed or detachable bipods, even a rock.

The prone position is inarguably the most stable position for use in real-world hunting situations.

OVER-THE-SHOULDER SHOOTING TECHNIQUE

This shooting method is used by so few people that it qualifies as a secret. When a natural rest cannot be found, and when ground cover rules out shooting from a prone position, you can use the back of your hunting partner to get a solid rest and radically increase your effective shooting range. When you're ready to fire, tell your buddy to hold his breath and plug his ear. Then run through your normal shooting routine. It's deadly. (For the target, that is.)

SHOT PLACEMENT FOR BIG GAME

If you have the time, it is always best to let the animal turn and offer a broadside shot. Broadside means the animal is perpendicular to you, facing left or right, not looking at you or away from you. In a broadside situation, a shot placed behind the crease of the shoulder will result in the bullet traveling through both lungs. The lungs and heart are your primary target when trying to kill an animal. A hit in the liver can also produce a kill, but it is not quick. Shooting just behind the shoulder hits only minor bones in the ribs, preserving most of the meat. When a major bone in the shoulder is struck by a bullet, bone fragments destroy much of the surrounding meat. Quartering shots are also valid, but the meat of one of the shoulders will be jeopardized.

In some instances it is necessary to drop the animal in its tracks, also known as "anchoring." In alpine situations, where steep rock faces and cliffs exist, this might keep the animal from tumbling thousands of feet. Other times, when hunting a small parcel of land, stopping the animal instantly keeps it from jumping onto the neighboring property, where retrieval might be difficult. Dangerous game also requires shot placement that anchors the animal. Bears, known for not bleeding well, are good to try to anchor, shortening the tracking job.

In a broadside situation, aim square in the center of the shoulder if you want to anchor the animal—imagine you're hitting it in the center of the scapula. On an elk, for example, your only change in aim is moving the crosshair left or right about a foot, depending on which way the

This antelope is facing the shooter. A shot that lands a few inches to the left or right of the bull's-eye will certainly kill the antelope, but there will be substantial meat loss in the shoulder.

The antelope is quartering to the hunter. Any shot placement here is likely to ruin one of the shoulders.

This bull is slightly quartering away, but not enough for major adjustment of shot placement. Placed right behind the shoulder, the bullet will travel through both lungs and possibly clip the heart.

At this moment the doe's left shoulder is blocking the vitals and a shot would ruin meat. By letting the doe take one more step, the bullet will have a clear path through ribs and both lungs, avoiding unnecessary damage to the shoulder. But if there's no time to spare and the shot needs to happen now, this placement will kill the doe almost instantly.

A black bear's heart and lungs are positioned a bit more forward than in members of the deer family. Even though this bear is broadside, the hunter would be wise to let the animal move its right leg forward before taking a shot. That way, the vitals would be more vulnerable and the meat loss in the shoulder would not be as catastrophic.

By placing the shot high on the shoulder of this mountain goat, the hunter will anchor the animal in place and help prevent it from going over a cliff and landing in a place where retrieval might be impossible.

Big animals such as moose require careful shot placement. The target area is big, but so are the bones and muscles in the shoulder. Animals such as this call for high-quality ammunition and hard-hitting rifles in addition to good marksmanship.

Broadside but slightly quartering, this mule deer requires shot placement that is tight to the shoulder. Being a few inches off could result in a shot that misses the lungs entirely.

This sheep is standing perfectly broadside; the shot placement will send the bullet through both lungs and the heart.

When an animal is quartering away, like this whitetail buck, aim for the front leg on the far side of the body. This will likely send the bullet through both lungs.

This buck has his left front leg positioned forward. This makes for an unobstructed path to the vitals and minimal meat loss.

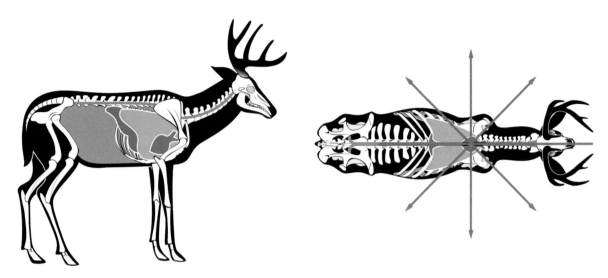

The lungs and heart are the primary target. The arrows represent quartering away, broadside, quartering to, and head-on shot angles from both sides of the animal. With proper penetration, the bullet will go through the lungs and often the heart in each scenario.

This mountain goat was shot up at the hunter's fingertip. Had the hunter anchored it properly, it would have stayed up here. But faulty shot placement allowed this goat to make it to the edge and take a 1,200-foot plunge. Much of the meat was destroyed and the horns were lost.

elk is facing. By shooting the shoulder, you accomplish three things that help in bringing down the animal quickly. One, the shoulder itself is broken, making the animal less mobile. Two, the shock moving through the area disrupts the spine and nervous system. Three, the bullet, along with bone fragments from the shoulder, travels into and sometimes through both lungs. All this combined usually results in a very fast kill. The one downside to this approach is that a good portion of the shoulder meat can be lost to damage.

AFTER THE SHOT

The trigger was pulled, the bullet or arrow sent toward the animal. So what do you do now? If the animal has dropped dead in its tracks, you can take a few moments to feel grateful for your fortune and to thank the animal for the gift of its meat. If you scored a hit but the animal ran off, you'll have to put your celebrations on hold. There's an incredible amount of information that needs to be gathered in the immediate moments following a shot.

First off, watch the animal for evidence of the actual shot placement. Look for a spot of blood on the animal's side indicating the location of the bullet's entrance. This is sometimes magnified when archery hunting, because the fletching portion of the arrow might be visible at the point of impact. The animal's reaction to the shot can reveal significant information as well. For instance, a leap straight into the air with a hunched back indicates a well-placed shot—likely to the heart. A slinking, hunkering reaction points to a shot that hit too far back, probably in the stomach or intestines. A flailing limb can mean very bad news, as it could indicate a shot that has missed the body but clipped a leg.

If the rear end drops but the front legs are still pulling, the spine has most likely been hit. Sometimes spine hits will cause the animal to fold all four legs and fall straight to the ground. (If this happens, don't expect the animal to be immediately killed. You might have to act quickly to avoid any suffering and put another round into the animal's neck or through its lungs.) Although you should refrain from aiming for these locations, head and neck shots will also result in a dropped animal that will usually die much faster than an animal hit through the lower portions of the spine.

Whether you're hunting open or dense habitat, you need to mentally mark the precise location where the animal was standing when it was hit, plus the location of the last place you saw the animal. If you are hunting in a forest, visual contact may cease within fractions of a second; in open country, you might watch the animal for several seconds before it disappears. A wounded animal typically makes a fair amount of noise as it crashes off, so pay attention to that as well and try to get a mark on the location of the last noise you heard. Stay quiet and attentive. Sometimes, after a period of silence, a final crash or guttural moan might give you some valuable information about the animal's condition and whereabouts. At this point, mark your shooting location with a piece of clothing or plastic surveyor's tape. Then pull out your compass and take note of the directional headings to the various locations you marked and estimate the distances. If it was a long shot, study the area where the animal was standing with binoculars. Notice rocks, trees, logs, vegetation, or any other identifying features that might help you pick out the exact area once you get over there. You can also use your range finder to mark the distances to various landmarks; once there, you can measure back to your shooting position to determine if you're in the right spot. When you do leave your shooting position, go immediately to your mentally marked locations and mark them with surveyor's tape or additional clothes such as your hat and gloves. If you're hunting with a partner, have him or her remain in the shooting position in order to help guide you to the necessary locations.

Generally, you should wait about forty-five minutes to an hour before tracking a wounded animal. That way, there's less of a chance that the animal will get up and run after it lies down to die. You can add or subtract time according to how confident you are in your hit; if it's a heart-shot animal, it's probably been dead since a minute or two after you shot. If it's hit through the stomach, you want to give it plenty of time before you start pushing it. So instead of plowing ahead, take a moment to replay everything that happened. Ask yourself: How confident are you about your shot placement? Did you rush the shot, or did you calmly squeeze the trigger? Was the animal standing still or walking? What side should the entrance

wound be on? Try to remember these details. They might come in very handy later in the tracking job, especially if things go poorly and you can't immediately find the animal.

Hopefully you'll find blood right away, within a few yards of where the animal was standing. Also check for any hair or bone fragments. If you can't find blood, look for the tracks of a fast-moving and startled animal. They frequently have a skidded appearance or are deeply bedded. These will often lead you to the beginning of the blood. When you find blood, don't disturb it. The color, amount, and contents of the blood will give you clues about the type of hit and the condition of the animal.

1. A lung or lung/heart hit will produce a bright, almost pinkish blood. Often you will see foam or bubbles in the blood, which is a very good sign.

The blood might be so profuse that it looks as though someone was running through the woods with two cans of red spray paint with the nozzles held open. If that's the case, the animal is probably already dead and will be lying close by. If it was a quartering shot, it's possible that only one lung was hit. This could mean less blood and an animal that might travel for several hundred yards or more—though it will certainly die and you should be able to recover it with minimal effort.

[MUSCLE]

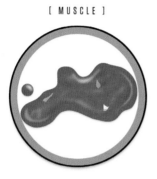

2. Muscle wounds tend to generate a crimson-colored blood that is darker than pink lung blood. Heart shots can result in a similar-colored blood, but it's so copious that there's little trouble in following it to the dead animal.

But when this bright crimson muscle blood comes in spatters and pin drops, you should be very worried. Small chunks of bone are often found with this type of blood, which could indicate a wound that may not be fatal. Common shot locations that produce this type of blood are lower legs, brisket, and neck shots that missed the spine. With luck on your side, a major artery might have been cut. This could cause the animal to bleed out and expire. In the case of a hit to the femoral artery, the animal could leave a strong blood trail and bleed out very quickly. But with a blood trail that starts strong and then peters out to pin drops that are spaced 10 to 20 feet apart, there's a

strong chance you've got an animal with a nonlethal muscle hit. It could certainly die from an infection in days or weeks, but there's a strong possibility that the wound may clot and heal. There are always exceptions to the rules, though, and every blood trail should be followed until you've exhausted all possibility of finding the next droplet.

[GUT]

3. Blood with grass or other food particles or digestive material mixed with it points to a shot in the stomach or intestines.

This isn't good, but it's not necessarily entirely bad. A lot of different things could happen here, but you need to wait before proceeding along the blood trail. Give the animal at least four hours. This gives it time to lie down and, hopefully, expire. Since shots to the guts don't tend to bleed much, an animal bumped from its bed and pushed becomes exponentially harder to find. If you start trailing the animal and find where it has repeatedly laid down and then gotten back up again, give it more time before you continue the chase. Patience may be the only thing that's on your side.

4. When the blood looks so dark crimson that it's almost black, a liver hit should be suspected. Again, extend the waiting period to four hours. Shot livers do kill animals, just not as quickly as the other vitals. With due diligence, you should be able to recover this animal.

5. If hair is present, try to match the hair color and texture to an area on the animal to help decipher the shot placement. A lot of hair at the shot site might indicate a grazing or raking shot. You may not even find blood, as the wound could be superficial or nonexistent. But you still owe it to the animal to spend several hours at the location doing a careful examination for any other evidence of a more serious wound.

READING AN ARROW

When blood-trailing a wounded animal, make sure to mark the last blood you found before advancing ahead to find more. You need to treat the area in the way an FBI forensics expert would treat the scene of a crime. Walk slowly and deliberately, and find every clue without destroying any evidence. Too much hurrying and tromping around disturbs the forest floor and could possibly hide that one drop of blood that might ultimately help you find the animal. Walk in a crouched position so that your eyes are closer to the ground. Crawl when necessary. Besides looking directly on the ground, look for blood on grass, on bushes, on branches. Check both the upper and undersides of vegetation. Note the height of the blood on standing vegetation; this will help you decipher the location of the hit.

Keep your nose in the game. Many bears and rutty bucks have been found when the tracker passed directly downwind of the fallen animal and smelled the creature's natural odor. Do not quit, even if it means crawling around on all fours for a day, and then waking up the next day in order to divide the area into a grid pattern and cover each and every square. This animal is your responsibility. You wounded it, and you need to find it. A blood trail is no place for quitters.

A recovered arrow can tell you a lot about your shot as long as you can read the clues within it. This arrow demonstrates good penetration, as it's coated in blood along its entire length. The fact that the arrow is broken 6 inches back from the tip points to an exit on the far side of the animal, where it was broken by movement between the shoulder and the ribs. The bubbles in the blood indicate it was a lung shot. The same types of blood found on the ground along a blood trail may also be found on a recovered arrow, and they can be interpreted in the same way. (See blood sign illustrations in "After the Shot," pages 163–164) Another clue to look for would be a bent shaft or broadhead indicating contact with a hard material such as bone. An arrow that's completely devoid of blood might indicate a clean miss. Any arrow recovered has a story to tell, even if it's not the story you want to hear.

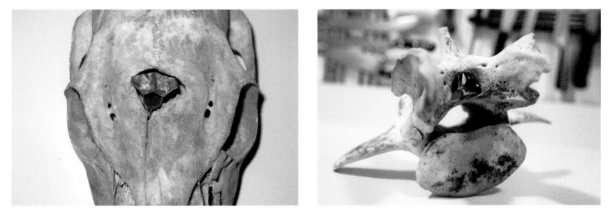

Good luck, bad luck. Each of these shots is the result of poor aim, but only one hunter lucked out. The whitetail deer on the left snapped its head toward the sound of the arrow's release and caught a steel broadhead in its skull. The bull elk on the right had a broadhead miss his spine by ¼". The bone healed around the broadhead.

BIG GAME: SPECIES AND METHODS

ANTELOPE
SCIENTIFIC NAME: *Antilocapra americana*
A.K.A.: American pronghorn, speed goat, prong buck.

More than any other creature, antelope are emblematic of the lonesome, wide-open spaces of America's Great Plains. It's a hostile and barren environment, in which the animals face temperature ranges from −40° to 110° Fahrenheit. Passing trains sometimes kill dozens at a time as the animals seek out the snow-free conditions of plowed railroad tracks, and in the summer they've been known to stand within the slender ribbons of shade provided by telephone poles in order to escape the crackling heat of an otherwise featureless environment.

BARROOM BANTER: The American antelope, or pronghorn, is the fastest land mammal on the continent, capable of reaching speeds in excess of 55 mph. The only faster mammal on earth is the African cheetah, though the antelope can sustain top speeds longer than the cheetah thanks to its relatively enormous lungs, heart, and airway. Paleontologists believe that the antelope coevolved on the Great Plains with the now-extinct American cheetah, which helps explain its swiftness.

PHYSICAL CHARACTERISTICS: Colored an orange-hued tannish brown, with prominent white markings on sides, rump, and throat. Males have a conspicuous black marking over their mandible. While some female antelope have either one or two small, underdeveloped horns, males carry prominent horns made of a hairlike substance that forms as a sheath over a bone core. This sheath sheds and regrows on an annual basis. Mature males weigh 90–140 pounds, females 75–110.

DIET: A wide variety of forbs, shrubs, grasses, and cacti, including many that are toxic to livestock.

LIFE AND DEATH: It's common for antelope to reach ten years of age. They've been known to live as long as fifteen. Predators include bobcats, mountain lions, coyotes, and golden eagles. Fawns are particularly susceptible to predators. Habitat loss and blocked migration corridors are the primary long-term threats to antelope.

BREEDING AND REPRODUCTION: Antelope typically breed in mid-September; the females drop calves in late May.

HABITAT: Grasslands, typically, but also desert and brushlands with predominantly knee-high vegetation that doesn't impair the animal's vision. Large concentrations are sometimes found on the Great Plains, notably the eastern portions of Montana, Wyoming, and Colorado. Smaller, more isolated herds can be found in intermountain valleys and atop large mesas and benchlands in mountainous regions.

TELLTALE SIGN: Sign isn't so important with antelope because they inhabit open country and are easily located. Besides tracks and scat, you can look for shed horn sheaths and tufts of hair clinging to the bottom strand of barbed wire at well-used fence crossings. (Antelope cannot jump fences; they have to go under.)

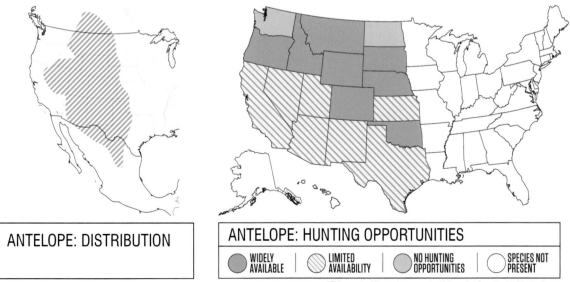

ANTELOPE: DISTRIBUTION

ANTELOPE: HUNTING OPPORTUNITIES

WIDELY AVAILABLE | LIMITED AVAILABILITY | NO HUNTING OPPORTUNITIES | SPECIES NOT PRESENT

*This map should be used as a general guideline only. Information is subject to change.

EDIBILITY: Antelope meat gets mixed reactions from the general public due to a strong, sometimes musky flavor, though wild game connoisseurs almost invariably express appreciation for the flesh. Good for any red meat application.

HUNTING OPPORTUNITIES: State residents generally find that antelope tags are easy to come by, though they are rarely issued as over-the-counter tags. You usually have to apply for a tag several months in advance, though units in many states, including Montana and Wyoming, are undersubscribed and tags are all but guaranteed. Tags in the Southwest are a bit harder to come by, though persistent applicants will be rewarded within a couple of years of starting the draw process. Nonresident tags are widely available, though not as abundant as resident tags. If you want a nearly guaranteed draw, look to Wyoming and Montana. Archery hunters have an even easier time getting antelope tags. A bowhunter can hunt antelope across the West every year if he or she wants to.

HUNTING METHODS: For the big game hunter, finding antelope is not the challenge. They live in open country, where it's possible for the hunter to see great distances, and they've got a prominent patch of bright white hair on their flanks—in direct sun, a herd of them looks almost as conspicuous as a clothesline full of bedsheets hung out to dry. Often, small dust clouds kicked up by their hooves reveal antelope that are out of sight beyond contours in the land. If you spend a day or two in your antelope hunting area without seeing any, you can be pretty sure you're in a bad spot.

But don't let the ease of locating antelope fool you. The challenge is getting into reasonable shooting distance of these exceptionally wary critters, and then connecting with a clean, long-range kill shot on a target that is considerably smaller than your typical whitetail buck. To do this consistently, a hunter needs to learn how to "read" the landscape in order to plan and execute superb stalks. And he or she needs to be able to shoot under circumstances that are far less favorable than the rifle or archery range. Plan on long belly crawls, long shots, and knees and elbows full of cactus thorns.

Rifle hunters take the vast majority of their antelope using spot-and-stalk methods. As mentioned above, locating antelope is not difficult. In good antelope country it's common to see a dozen or more (sometimes *way* more) of the animals per day, though they could be a couple of miles away. Thankfully, you can tell the males and females apart at distances of a mile or more if you're using good optics, so if you're hunting on a sex-specific tag you should be able to select your desired animal before you begin what might become a painful and arduous stalk. You don't want to walk a 2-mile half circle in 90-degree heat just to get within crawling distance of a lone antelope and then discover that you're stalking a buck when all you've got in your pocket is a doe tag.

A peculiarity of stalking antelope is that the animals sometimes bed down in places where they can't be stalked. It's frustrating. They'll lie on open expanses of table-flat ground where it's virtually impossible to approach within half a mile of them without getting busted. In these situations, it's smart to be patient. Wait for your quarry to get up and move—it eventually will—and then try to determine where it's headed. You'll find that antelope tend to pick a direction of travel and then stick to it. They don't zigzag wildly or change course unless something spooks them, and even when they do spook, they will assume a new course and then adhere to that. Unless the animal is headed directly away from you, at which point it'll be very difficult to catch, you want to pick an avenue of approach that'll help you get out ahead of it. Sometimes this is quite easy, such as when you can drop behind a ridge and run directly to your desired objective. At other times, this requires long, roundabout journeys in order to get to a place where you can put a hill or butte between you and the animal. (Antelope hunters sometimes find themselves walking directly away from an antelope in order to get close to it.)

The beauty of getting out ahead of a traveling antelope is that they aren't that good at picking out stationary objects. (At least not as good as they are at picking out moving objects, which is their specialty.) So make sure to select a potential shooting position that offers a wide field of view, a place where you can wait without having to move around too much. If the animal was following the bottom of a valley or dry wash, then make sure you can usually cover the entirety of the valley. If it seemed to be headed toward a gap between two mesas, make sure you can usually cover the entire gap. You don't want to be lying there for an hour and then start wondering if the animal passed you by without your knowing it. Keep your rifle ready at all times, be patient, and hold dead still. When the antelope comes into sight, there's a very good chance that you'll get a shot before it sees you. But if you're getting up on your knees to sneak glances at the approaching animal over the tops of the sagebrush plants, or shifting around too much from place to place because of cactus thorns in your legs, you might find that the antelope never shows up. You got busted, and it ran off without your seeing it.

When stalking stationary or bedded animals, the use of topography still applies. Use rocks, hills, buttes, arroyos, old homestead buildings, or anything else that will hide you as you creep into range. Not all antelope are easily spooked, but you should treat them like they are. Knee pads and elbow pads are a great asset. In country with a lot of sagebrush or other low-lying ground cover, it's possible to belly-crawl straight in if you keep below the vegetation. Either drop your backpack or push it ahead of you as you crawl. And don't carry your rifle on your back, as the barrel will wave around too much. Keep it in your hand as you crawl, or cradled in your arm. Another trick is to put it in a soft-sided case made of durable fabric and tow it behind you (unloaded, of course). If the antelope is standing or rises to its feet during your stalk, watch its body posture. An antelope that's feeding is almost certainly unaware of you. An antelope that's staring in your direction or walking away with the hair on its rump poofed out almost certainly is. If that happens, it's time to either make your shot or back out and try again later. If neither of those options is tenable, try waving a white handkerchief at the antelope. This is an old plainsman's trick. Maybe the antelope think it's another antelope, maybe it's just curious, but sometimes it'll bring the animal toward you or at least stop it from getting farther away.

A stalking situation should not become a shooting situation until you're so close that you're 100 percent positive of making a clean, one-shot kill. This might happen at 50 yards or 600 yards, depending on environmental conditions, the position of the animal relative to its surroundings, your marksmanship skills, and the type of weapon you're shooting. But when it is time to shoot, remember that the animal can potentially see you whenever you can see it. So move *very, very* slowly as you get your weapon into a well-supported shooting position. If everything's done properly, the antelope won't know what hit it.

Due to the extremely wary nature of antelope, it is often difficult for bowhunters to kill them using spot-and-stalk strategies. Not only is it tough to get within effective archery range of an antelope, it can be even tougher to get into an effective shooting position. Whereas a rifle hunter can make his shot from a concealed prone position, an archer needs to rise to a kneeling position before he can shoot. At close quarters, this extra bit of movement is all that it takes to send an antelope tearing across the prairie.

By setting up an ambush position inside a pop-up ground blind, bowhunters can get extremely close to antelope while still having the necessary protection to draw their bow and make a shot. The most common ambush locations are watering holes, particularly during the dry conditions of late summer. Your best bet is to spend a day or two trying to pattern the antelope in your hunting area. Find out what water sources they are using, and when they are using them. Two days of scouting might save five days of uneventful waiting in your blind. If you have the time, place your blind and let the antelope acclimate for a couple of days before you hunt it. That'll reduce their wariness. And while it's smart to set the

Rutting antelope bucks become so focused on potential rivals that they miss some of the finer details—in this case, a waiting hunter.

blind in a downwind position from the water source, don't get too carried away. Commercially produced pop-up blinds help prevent the dissipation of your odor, enabling you to place your blind in the best position for the best possible shot opportunities. Ideally, you want to be less than 50 yards away from the furthest portion of the water hole. Finally, you have to be patient. Plan on sitting in your blind the whole day, sunrise to sundown. This is not a strategy for fidgety hunters.

Decoying is probably the most exhilarating way to hunt for antelope. It's a method for the archery rut season, when bucks are feeling amorous toward does and hateful toward other bucks. A decoy hunt begins as a spot-and-stalk hunt. You need to locate a mature buck that appears to be fired up, chasing around other bucks and generally acting belligerent. Then plan a stalk that'll get you close, ideally within a couple of hundred yards. At that point, you "show" the decoy to the buck, usually by having your hunting partner stand up while concealing himself behind the decoy. You, the archer, stay hidden behind the partner and the decoy. The most effective decoys are of younger, immature bucks, which will sometimes get an aggressive response from the older buck. (That's why this technique can only be used during the archery season; you don't want a far-off rifle hunter taking aim at the paper "buck" you're hiding behind.) Experienced antelope hunters say that perhaps one in ten bucks will come charging in. Slightly more will come cautiously, posturing and posturing as they approach. As the buck draws in, your hunting partner uses a laser range finder to take distance readings. Don't plan on getting a close shot. Instead, when the buck reaches your maximum effective range, it's time to rise to your knees and draw back. When you say go, your partner lowers the decoy enough to give you a clear shot. Hopefully the buck will give you a few seconds to aim as he tries to figure out why there's a person kneeling in exactly the same place where a rival buck was standing just moments ago.

When hunting in open country on sunny days, be wary of sunlight flashes against the lenses of your optics. When pointing rifle scopes, binoculars, or spotting scopes toward the sun, shade the objective lenses with a cap or piece or clothing. If you don't, the bright flash might send your quarry heading in the opposite direction.

BIGHORN SHEEP
SCIENTIFIC NAME: *Ovis canadensis*

Bighorn sheep, along with their northern relatives the Dall sheep, inspire a level of devotion among hunters that is unparalleled by any other game animal. After getting a taste of what it's like to chase these massive horned creatures in their rugged and dangerous habitats, some hunters experience a fading interest in all other outdoor activities as they devote themselves increasingly to the discipline of being a "sheep fanatic." The irony, and part of the appeal, is that bighorn sheep hunting opportunities are extremely limited. The demand for bighorn sheep tags far outweighs the supply of bighorn sheep, and the animals are managed very conservatively. Less than a thousand bighorn tags are issued annually in the United States. Many guides and outfitters who specialize in bighorn sheep hunts have never killed a ram and likely never will.

There are disparate views on the subject of bighorn sheep subspecies, including whether what's called subspecies have enough genetic differentiation to deserve that term. But from the perspective of a contemporary big game hunter, there are four: Rocky Mountain, desert, California, and Baja. All of these occur in huntable numbers and account for the totality of bighorn sheep hunting opportunities.

BARROOM BANTER: A bighorn ram can withstand a blow to the head sixty times greater than what it would take to fracture your own skull. When two of the rams collide in battle, they often do so at a combined speed of 50–70 mph. Multiplying that figure by the combined weight of the two animals suggests an output of 2,400 foot-pounds of energy. For perspective, that's a hundred times more force than your shoulder feels when shooting a .300 Ultra Mag, a cartridge that many hunters avoid because of the kick. The rams can absorb this pressure thanks in part to special sutures in their skulls, which zigzag more widely than those found in many other horned mammals and enable the plates to flex and compress upon impact. Sometimes a pair of rams will fight for twenty hours.

PHYSICAL CHARACTERISTICS: Coloration varies throughout range, from dark brown in the north to a pale tan in the deserts. The belly, rump, and back of the legs are white. Rams and ewes both appear stocky and heavily muscled. Ewes have short, backward-curving horns similar to a barnyard goat. Mature rams have exceptionally massive horns, curling to near 360-degree circles and measuring up to 3 feet long with base circumferences of 15 inches. Ewes have body weights up to around 200 pounds. Rams can weigh well over 300 pounds.

DIET: Grasses in summer, switching to woody browse such as willow, sagebrush, and rabbit brush in winter.

LIFE AND DEATH: Ewes often live to fifteen years, but a ten-year-old ram is regarded as fairly old. Bobcats, lynx, wolves, golden eagles, and coyotes can all kill bighorn sheep. Moun-

tain lions are especially adept bighorn predators, as they can ambush the sheep in the precipitous, cliffy country where bighorns spend much of their time. The primary long-term threats to bighorn sheep are diseases transmitted from domestic livestock.

BREEDING AND REPRODUCTION: Bighorns breed from late fall to early winter, depending on latitude and elevation. Females will drop a single lamb between mid-April and late June, after a gestation of six months.

HABITAT: Inhabits open, precipitous terrain with a mixture of sharp ridges, deep canyons, rocky outcrops, and sheer cliffs, ranging from cool climes in the high mountains to extreme heat in the low deserts.

TELLTALE SIGN: Look for frequently used beds pawed into ridgetops and below rocky outcrops that sit above precipitous terrain. These are usually about 4 feet across and 6 to 12 inches deep and ringed with droppings. Well-used bighorn trails can often be seen from far away, especially where they cross steep slopes of loose rock. Multiple trails will appear to be stacked up the hillside like off-kilter ladder rungs.

EDIBILITY: Widely renowned as excellent table fare. In the 1800s, commercial meat hunters extirpated bighorns from much of their range in order to satisfy demand from burgeoning frontier towns. Suitable for all red meat applications.

HUNTING OPPORTUNITIES: Extremely limited. (See below.)

| BIGHORN SHEEP: DISTRIBUTION | BIGHORN SHEEP: HUNTING OPPORTUNITIES |

WIDELY AVAILABLE | LIMITED AVAILABILITY | NO HUNTING OPPORTUNITIES | SPECIES NOT PRESENT

*This map should be used as a general guideline only. Information is subject to change.

HUNTING METHODS: Rather than discussing specific hunting tactics for bighorn sheep, it's a far better use of time to discuss the ways in which a hunter might get a bighorn tag. These can be broken into two basic categories: paying and winning. The paying option requires a minimum of around $30,000 and a maximum of around $400,000, which is obviously far beyond the reach of the vast majority of hunters. For that reason, we'll start with winning.

The following states hold lottery drawings and/or raffles for bighorn ram tags that are open to residents and nonresidents alike: Arizona, California, Colorado, Idaho, Montana, Nevada, New Mexico, North Dakota, Oregon, Utah, Texas, Washington, and Wyoming. In any given year, the odds of a first-time resident applicant drawing a sheep tag in any one of these states are less than 1 percent. Because many western states cap the number of bighorn tags that can be given to nonresidents (there's a 10 percent limit in Montana, for instance), those hunters face chances that are way, way less than 1 percent. While many devoted would-be sheep hunters apply in every state every year, they still face depressingly low odds of drawing a sheep tag.

Many states have incentive systems to reward the loyalty of returning applicants, and also to bring a degree of fairness to the drawings. (When an applicant has been applying unsuccessfully for twenty years, it's grating to see someone pull a tag on his first attempt.) These are called "bonus point" or "preference point" systems. Typically, they serve to give unsuccessful applicants from previous drawings a statistical advantage over applicants who have made fewer previous attempts. In some states, your name goes in the hat once for each time you've applied in the past. Other states, such as Nevada and Montana, will square your bonus points and put your name in the hat that many times; currently, there are Nevada bighorn applicants who have accrued 26 bonus points. In the next drawing, their name will be in the hat 676 times as opposed to once for a first-time applicant.

That it's possible to apply for a Nevada bighorn tag twenty-six times in a row without success demonstrates that bonus points hardly guarantee a tag. To further alleviate this apparent lack of fairness, some states mandate that certain percentages of available tags go to "max holders," or hunters who hold the highest number of points. Wyoming gives 75 percent of their sheep tags to those who are currently sitting on 19 points. Thus, a first-time applicant in Wyoming is vying for only 25 percent of the total available tags, and he's competing for these against hundreds of other applicants whose names are in the draw multiple times each but who have yet to reach max holder status. To further complicate matters, nonresidents are limited to only 25 percent of all available sheep tags in Wyoming. So, in reality, a first-time nonresident applicant in Wyoming is eligible for only about 6 percent of the total available tags. And these drawings aren't cheap. Many states require you to pay for the tag up front, and then they refund your money after the draw. This eliminates the hassle of having applicants who can't afford to pay for a tag once they've won it. If a hunter applies for a bighorn sheep tag in every state that allows nonresident applicants, he'll have temporary expenditures totaling around $8,000 annually and permanent expenditures of about $600 annually even if he doesn't draw a tag.

In addition to the traditional drawings, which award bighorn tags for specific date ranges and regions within each state, several states conduct an annual raffle for a single bighorn tag that carries special privileges such as an extended season and/or an expanded region. In Arizona, for example, you can buy as many raffle tickets as you want at $25 apiece for a bighorn tag that's valid for the entire year. The odds of drawing a sheep tag with a single raffle ticket in Arizona are astronomically low— about .019 percent. Yet if you've got zero bonus points and a limited life expectancy, you might be better off investing your entire bighorn budget in Arizona raffle tickets rather than in the Arizona lottery draw. You might do even better yet by putting your budget into Colorado's raffle. There, an expenditure of $625 (tickets are $25 apiece, with a maximum purchase of 25) will earn you a better than 1 percent chance of hitting a tag that's good for all legal sheep units across the entire state.

While all of this information might make the pursuit of a bighorn tag seem absurd, it should also be taken as evidence of the mysterious appeal of bighorn sheep. It brings to mind a story told by Chris Denham, the publisher of *Western Hunter* and *Elk Hunter* magazines. He used to run a consulting service that helped hunters apply for big game lottery draws. One time, a potential client who had earned millions of dollars as a financial planner approached him about sheep tag applications. Because of this client's apparent fiscal prudence, Denham felt compelled to explain the high costs and long odds of the endeavor. After breaking it all down for the client, Denham said, "You see, it's ridiculous." The financial planner looked everything over and agreed. "You're right," he said. "It is ridiculous. But still, put me in for every state."

Denham knows the world of bighorn tags as well as anyone, and he's got a lot of well-thought advice for people who want to hunt a bighorn. When he considers the amount of money that you can spend over the course of a long and unsuccessful bid to win a tag, he wonders if a better strategy is to put your annual lottery budget into an investment plan and wait until that account builds up enough money to pay for a guided sheep hunt or to buy an auction tag. Outfitters in Mexico and Alberta are able to sell bighorn tags (bundled with their guiding services) for anywhere from around $30,000 to $50,000. In the United States, there are a number of auctions for big-

horn tags as well. The Apache tribe in Arizona auctions one bighorn tag every year for a hunt on their reservation. This typically sells for around $20,000 to $30,000—the relatively low price is due to the smallish size of the bighorn rams on that reservation. If you want to buy an auction tag for an area that produces bigger rams, you should consider the governor's tags that are auctioned by various Canadian provinces and western states in order to generate money for bighorn conservation projects such as habitat improvement, research, and battling the transmission of domestic livestock diseases into bighorn herds. At the most recent auction, which is held every year in Reno, Nevada, the Washington state bighorn tag went for $64,000. Oregon's went for $135,000, Idaho's for $150,000, and British Columbia's for $275,000. The high bidder for the permit in Montana paid $480,000.

If that kind of money is beyond your reach—and it most certainly is—do not lose faith in the application process. Garth Carter, the owner of a subscription service called *The Huntin' Fool: A Guide to Western Big Game Hunting*, has crunched the numbers again and again, and he believes that time and bonus points make the best plan for getting a bighorn tag. If you get into the sheep tag application business in your twenties, he says, and you stay with it, you're likely to win two or three bighorn sheep tags by the time you die.

JAY SCOTT AND DARR COLBURN, OF COLBURN AND SCOTT OUTFITTERS, WEIGH IN ON JUDGING BIGHORN RAMS

Darr Colburn (left) and Jay Scott (right) with a client's nine-year-old ram that was the largest desert bighorn killed in Arizona in 2012.

"You can't eat an animal's horns, but you can definitely appreciate them. For many hunters, a set of bighorn curls is the greatest and most potent symbol of America's high-country wilderness. If you get lucky and draw a bighorn tag, you'll want to make sure to harvest a large representation of the species that'll look great on your wall or book shelves. Chances are, it'll be the only one you ever kill. What's more, targeting the largest rams is a sound conservation practice. These animals tend to be past their prime as breeders and are nearing the end of their lives. We've used the following field judging tips while guiding many Arizona hunters who've won sheep tags through the state's lottery and raffle drawings.

"**1.** Remember, bighorn rams always look big! Often hunters get excited too quickly and end up shooting a young, small ram. Try to look at as many rams in your area as possible in order to get a relative idea of what's out there. It's especially helpful to have several rams together in order to get a good perspective of body and horn size. Once you identify the biggest one, try to shoot it!

"**2.** Harvesting older rams is a custom that serious sheep hunters have upheld in order to leave more virile sheep on the mountain. Try to count the growth rings on a ram's horn to determine its age. A nine-year-old bighorn ram is getting up there in years. Broomed horns and scarred noses are other indicators of old age. (*Broomed* means not sharp or pointed at the tips; rams will broom their horns while feeding, fighting, and rubbing up against their rough terrain.)

"**3.** The frontal view is usually the best when you're trying to judge a ram. This allows you to see how far the bottoms of the horns drop below the jaw, and how far up the tips extend. The second-best angle would be from the side, so you can determine the size and depth of the curl. Quartering angles are not nearly as valuable.

"**4.** Mass, or the circumference of the horns, is hugely important when selecting a good ram. Make sure that a ram maintains close to its base mass into the second and third quarters of its overall length. But be careful, as the horns of a truly massive ram will sometimes appear short to the untrained eye. That's why it's vital to compare the size of multiple rams before selecting your target."

Serious bighorn sheep hunters like to see a ram next to other rams so that they can compare the animals and get a relative idea of the selected animal's size.

BLACK BEAR
SCIENTIFIC NAME: *Ursus americanus*
A.K.A.: Blacky, bruin.

Famed hunter and explorer Daniel Boone once killed 155 black bears in a single year. He brined and smoked the meat and sold it as "bear bacon." Today, most American hunters who do hunt bears will kill only one or two in their lifetimes. For them, bears are regarded as a novelty species, something to break up the monotony of a lifetime of whitetail deer hunting. For some hunters, though, black bear hunting becomes a highly anticipated annual event. What's great about hunting bears is that you can typically chase them during the spring of the year, when all other big game besides tur-

keys is off-limits. What's more, bear flesh can be a welcome deviation from the meat of hoofed animals such as deer and elk. It's often described as a hybrid between beef and pork, and works well as a smoked meat. The fat of a black bear can be rendered into high-quality oil that fluctuates between a solid and liquid at room temperature. It works incredibly well in pie crusts and can be used as a frying medium as well. And when the meat and oil of a bear are long gone, you'll still have a wonderful trophy. Unlike the hollow hair of ungulates such as deer and elk, bears have beautiful and luxurious fur. The tanned hides can be made into floor rugs, wall hangings, and even comforters for your bed. This animal should be regarded as a worthy quarry for any serious hunter.

BARROOM BANTER: In many areas, black bears have surprisingly small home ranges for an animal of their size. Some black bears will spend their entire lives within 5 miles of where they were born, and will spend an entire summer on a single square mile of ground. Despite their homebody nature, black bears have tremendous navigational skills. On many occasions, black bears that have been trapped and relocated have traveled well over 100 miles across unfamiliar terrain, including urban centers, to return to their home turf. They have also been known to swim long distances, sometimes traveling back and forth on a regular basis from islands that are beyond sight from the mainland.

PHYSICAL CHARACTERISTICS: Mostly black in the eastern United States. In the West, colors range from black to blond. It seems that color phases are linked to annual precipitation. Wet areas, particularly in coastal environments, tend to have primarily black-phase black bears; dryer inland climates have far greater percentages of blond-phase and brown-phase bears. Interestingly, there's a population of blue-phase black bears near Yakutat Bay, Alaska, and a population of white-phase bears on Gribbell Island, British Columbia. Males achieve weights in excess of 500 pounds and body lengths in excess of 6 feet in areas with abundant food and a mild climate. Females are typically much smaller.

DIET: Omnivores, black bears are opportunistic feeders with a wildly varied diet. Favorite food items vary according to location and time of year and are almost too numerous to list. Common staples include hard mast such as acorns, beechnuts, and hazelnuts; pine nuts; fruit such as cranberry, huckleberry, bearberry, salmonberry, buffalo berry, and wild strawberry; insects and insect larvae such as yellow jackets, bees, ants, and beetles; meats such as winter-killed ungulates, anadromous fish, beached sea mammals, and newborn calves and fawns of deer, elk, and moose; grasses and forbs; buds and shoots from trees and shrubs; and agricultural products such as corn, peaches, apples, alfalfa, and honey.

LIFE AND DEATH: Black bears are the primary natural predator of black bears. Boars, or males, will practice infanticide on the cubs of their own species, probably in order to make the sows, or females, receptive to breeding. Where the black bear's range overlaps with that of the grizzly bear, grizzlies will readily kill black bears.

BREEDING AND REPRODUCTION: Although breeding occurs in June and July, implantation is delayed about four months. Young are usually born between January and March. Litters range from one to five cubs, with two cubs being the norm. Females give birth every two years at most.

HABITAT: Forests and wooded swamps in the East. In the West, forests and timbered mountain ranges.

TELLTALE SIGN: Evidence of feeding includes shredded stumps and rotten logs, overturned rocks, pawed-up ground, discarded fish carcasses along spawning streams, and the scattered remains and crushed bones of carrion. Territorial markings include trees that are scarred with tooth and claw marks, often about head-high on a human. Also rubbing marks on tree trunks, along with clumps of hair stuck to bark.

EDIBILITY: Varies according to the animal's diet. Bears that have been feeding on hard mast or berries have superb flesh that is reminiscent of beef brisket when cooked; the meat from these bears can be used for most applications that are suitable to pork, such as sausages and a wide variety of smoked and slow-cooked preparations. The flesh of bears that have been feeding on rotten carrion or dead fish can reek so strongly that it's nearly unapproachable.

HUNTING OPPORTUNITIES: Black bears are increasing in population throughout the United States. Residents of black bear states will find getting tags fairly easy, through either lottery draws or over-the-counter sales. Nonresident black bear tags are abundant and easily gotten as well. States differ widely on seasons (spring or fall or both) and the allowable methods for hunting bears. In some states, dogs and bait may not be used. In other states, these hunting methods are permissible. Refer to each state's regulations booklet for details.

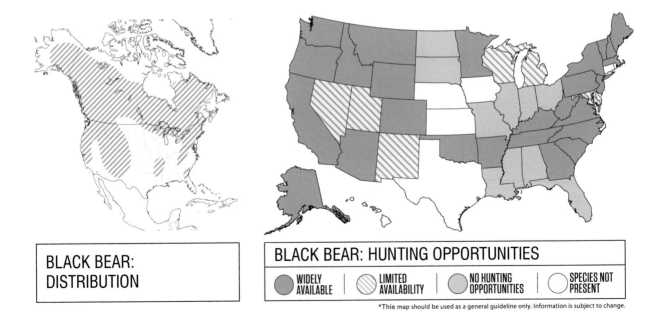

BLACK BEAR: DISTRIBUTION

BLACK BEAR: HUNTING OPPORTUNITIES

WIDELY AVAILABLE | LIMITED AVAILABILITY | NO HUNTING OPPORTUNITIES | SPECIES NOT PRESENT

*This map should be used as a general guideline only. Information is subject to change.

HUNTING METHODS: In the words of the late great hunting writer Duncan Gilchrist, "The walking [bear] hunter seldom gets his trophy." Gilchrist was an expert at spot-and-stalk bear hunting, with many years of guiding under his belt, and he implored his readers to avoid blundering through a bear's bedding and feeding areas. Human odor and disturbances, he found, will clear bears out of the country much more quickly and completely than they will affect species such as deer.

Gilchrist's findings are hardly controversial, as expert bear hunters are in almost universal agreement that bears are best hunted by patiently watching their feeding areas from a position where the bear is unlikely to detect your presence. These feeding areas can come in many forms: apple orchards, dead livestock, berry patches, salmon streams, moose gut piles, avalanche slides in the spring of the year, and man-made bait stations placed by hunters with the deliberate purpose of attracting bears. (For our purposes here, we'll discuss natural food sources in reference to spot-and-stalk hunting, and save artificial bait stations for the later discussion of ambush hunting.) The key to finding bears is locating their feeding areas. In coastal areas during the late summer, this might be as easy as locating a productive salmon spawning stream. But in other places at other times of the year, particularly in places with low concentrations of bears, finding active feeding areas can be frustrating. The upside is that bears tend to use the same areas from one year to the next. If you locate a food source that multiple bears are using in mid-May of one year, there's a high probability that there'll be bears using it again the next year.

In the West and Alaska, where most spot-and-stalk bear hunting takes place, the animals typically emerge from hibernation between mid-April and mid-May, with larger boars emerging before the sows. (This is just a generalization; there's tremendous variability between animals and regions.) When the bears leave their dens, they find a world that is still somewhat winterlike. Northerly and westerly exposures are often still shrouded in snow, as are shaded, low-lying areas. This is a prime time to locate bears, because their feeding options are limited to those snow-free areas that have been able to absorb enough of the sun's energy to promote new plant growth. In steep country, one of the best places to find these conditions is on exposed south-facing slopes, particularly those that have been cleared of snow by slides and avalanches. These slopes often produce an abundance of preferred black bear foods—glacier lily, skunk cabbage, clovers, grasses, and various other herbaceous plants—while many square miles of the surrounding country are still locked beneath a blanket of snow. Locate one of these productive slopes, and you might see multiple bears per day while other hunters are sitting at home because "it's still too early" to chase bears.

In coastal areas, such as southeast Alaska and British Columbia, the earliest emerging plant growth is commonly found on the grass flats that form on the alluvial fans at the outlets of streams and rivers. Watch areas with beach rye grass, horsetail, and skunk cabbage, especially near the timbered edges of grass flats, where bears are most likely to feel comfortable. While it's very common to glass spring bears in the Rockies during the late morning and early afternoon, coastal bears seem to prefer feeding in the open during the last hour or so of daylight. A notable exception is during low tide, when bears will work the exposed shorelines to graze on beds of blue mussels and flip over rocks in search of small crabs.

In the fall, berry patches are the most reliable places to glass for bears. In alpine areas, particularly in the mountain ranges of south-central Alaska, it's sometimes possible to glass berry "patches" that cover entire mountains. A hunter might sit at the base of one of these mountains on a September day and see a dozen or more bears during an hour or so of glassing—all of them standing in knee-high growth of blueberry, crowberry, bearberry, and cranberry, without a single tree within hundreds of yards. This type of bear hunting can seem almost too easy, at least until you start climbing the mountain toward a particular bear. It's a mystery why more would-be hunt-

Mussels are a favorite food of coastal black bears. Watch mussel beds at low tide, especially when a low tide coincides with the low light of an early morning or late evening.

ers don't try it. It's an inexpensive hunt that can be done without a guide, and the meat and fat of these berry-fed bears is absolutely phenomenal. At the same time of year, concentrations of black bears can be found where salmon are spawning. A common postcard image shows bears feeding on fresh, still wriggling salmon that would look great in a fisherman's cooler. But bears are just as likely to feed on rotten fish that have achieved the consistency of pudding. These salmon stream bears are best avoided, as their flesh can be useless: bears that feed on rotten salmon will taste like rotten salmon.

In the lower forty-eight, berry patches tend to be a bit more dispersed and often occur on ridgetop and hillside mosaics of mixed timber and brush. Here, the spot-and-stalk hunter wants to get into a high position where he can see as many of these patches as possible. It's common to get only glimpses of a bear as it works from one patch to the next, but keep in mind that a feeding bear will often stick to one area for a day or more. If he vanishes for an hour or two, it's quite likely that he simply lay down for a rest. (When glassing, you'll sometimes notice bears that are curled up in a patch of blueberries, sound asleep.) Once you've identified a general area where a bear is actively feeding, pack up your gear and try to get within shooting range of that location. Then hunker down and wait for the bear to reemerge while you continue to glass other areas for more bears. And before shooting at any bear, make sure to assess the quality of its hide. In the late spring, black bears will often rub their rumps and flanks against tree trunks or rocks. A "rubbed" hide, with bald patches, makes for a lame bear rug.

Whenever you're hunting bears, you should constantly keep in mind that bears are opportunistic feeders; they're going to show up at the richest, most productive food sources that are available in their area at a given time, whatever those happen to be. Bears in one area of the country will feed on things that bears in other areas have never seen. In dryer

Learning to properly judge the size of black bears can take years of study. A few hints: Small bears (left) have pointy ears that sit high on top of the head; they look "leggy," with long, thin appendages; and they have an overall gangly appearance and an awkward gait. Large black bears (right) have proportionately smaller ears that sit off toward the side of the head; their belly seems to sag, giving their legs a shorter appearance; they have thick rumps and shoulders and heavy legs. They seem to have an overall powerful appearance and a ponderous gait.

portions of the Rockies, fall black bears can sometimes be glassed while they feed on pine nuts in subalpine parklands. White bark pine and pinyon pine are favorites. They might also turn up in old apple orchards, stands of live oak, and near mountain ash trees when the berries are ripe. In the Southwest, hunters often glass hillsides of prickly pear cactus in anticipation of bears coming out to feed on the blossoms. Another thing to watch for are big game gut piles left by other hunters, including bear gut piles left by your hunting partners. In fact, a big gut pile is so attractive to bears that it's a good idea to keep an eye on a fresh gut pile even if a bear has yet to find it. Once a bear locates the pile, it will not last long.

Ambush hunting over artificial bait stations is the most common black bear hunting strategy in virtually every state and Canadian province where the practice is allowed. From an outsider's perspective it seems simple enough:

NEVER
SHOOT A SOW
WITH CUBS

dump some bait in the woods, then shoot the bears as they come rolling in. In actuality, bear hunting over bait requires significant know-how—especially if you want to consistently kill mature bears. One of the primary considerations is that you need to establish your bait station not only in an area where bears will find it but also where they'll feel secure enough to visit the station during daylight hours. This means placing the bait station along a frequently used bear trail or in the vicinity of naturally occurring food sources. Make sure that the bait is near dense cover where bears feel secure, but not so dense that you can't see the bear clearly in order to determine its size, the quality of its hide, and whether or not it has cubs.

A wide variety of baits can be used; specifics are usually determined by the budget of the hunter. Some hunters use dog food with molasses poured over the top, which can be very expensive. Others use beaver and muskrat carcasses salvaged from fur trappers. Some use rough fish such as carp and sucker harvested with a bowfishing rig. One of the easiest and most economical baits is expired bakery goods from grocery stores and donut shops. When choosing a bait, keep in mind that you'll be eating the animal. A bear fattened on old donuts will taste much better than a bear fattened on maggot-ridden carp. Some hunters will simply dump their bait on the ground, or place it in a hole. Others prefer to place baits in such a way that they are harder to get at. This keeps birds and small scavengers from eating it all, and it forces bears to linger for longer periods of time rather than just running in and grabbing a piece of bait on the fly. Baits can be placed in burlap sacks that are hung from trees, or put inside barrels with access holes that allow the bears to get their paws in there to scoop out food. Another strategy is to build a covered pen out of downed logs with an access point that helps put the bear in a broadside position relative to your blind.

Once a bait is getting hit on a regular basis, it should be replenished as quickly as the bears are eating it so that they don't lose interest. The bear or bears will use regular trails when coming into the bait, and you should stay clear of these routes in order to avoid spooking the bear with too much human odor. Place your stand in a downwind direction of the bait, keeping in mind that you need to be well concealed but still within reasonable shooting distance. Don't let your fear of bears dictate your stand placement. Get close enough so that you can see the bear clearly and make a lethal shot.

SHINGDADDY, AN APPALACHIA BEAR HUNTER, WEIGHS IN ON BEAR BAITS

"The thing you have to remember with a bear is they operate almost entirely off smell. If you can get to their nose, you can get them to you. I don't personally like to use a barrel because I don't want the scent of the bait contained at all. The best thing I've found to draw them is used cooking oil from Long John Silvers. I get corn or some kind of food that has enough consistency to it that I can pour that oil all over it. I also throw it in the trees and pour it on logs and branches. Bears will really eat anything. In the early spring they like foods with a higher protein base. Old meat, fish, or chicken seems to do really well. About the time summer hits they start wanting those carbs to cake that fat on. Anything you put out that is sweet, be it doughnuts or pastries, works great. A few years back I dumped an old outdated jug of molasses all over a stump. I returned the following evening to find that the stump had been totally destroyed in my absence. They seem to love white bread. If you can dump several loaves of white bread or old biscuits, that will keep them close. The only thing that will deter a bear from returning to your bait is the coming of white oak acorns. When they start maturing toward the end of August, you might as well give up for a month. Then start baiting again and they will gradually start returning back to your baits. After you get a bear coming in regularly, I recommend putting logs and limbs over and across your bait to help keep it out of the mouths of raccoons, foxes, and coyotes."

JEROD FINK, A WISCONSIN BEAR HUNTER, WEIGHS IN ON ARCHERY STAND PLACEMENT NEAR BEAR BAITS

"With bears, you need to be careful with stand placement, but there are certainly differences from deer hunting. A good rule for bowhunters to follow is that you  should place your tree stand no greater than a foot high for every yard you are from the bait. Twenty yards away and 20 feet up is a good bet. This will ensure a proper placement of the arrow through both lungs. The stand, however, must be concealed very well. Bears, despite having relatively poor eyesight, notice movement very well. But wind is much more important than anything. In my area, you want to place the stand on the southeast side of the bait. This allows you to hunt when the wind is blowing from the north, west, or northwest, which is typical. Do not hunt a bait if the wind is blowing from your stand toward the bait, or toward the animal's avenue of approach; you will spook it. It's best to set a bait in an area with a natural barrier, such as an open field or beaver pond, on the southeast side of the bait. This will keep the older and wiser bears from being able to circle downwind."

CHAD BAART, AN IDAHO BEAR HUNTER, WEIGHS IN ON RIFLE STAND PLACEMENT NEAR BEAR BAITS

"If I am hunting with a rifle, I will sit as far away as I can while still feeling like it's a slam dunk shot—maybe 50–75 yards, depending on the type of cover. Pay close attention to the prevailing winds and set up crosswind. Upwind will spread your scent to the bait. Downwind will make it so you are between the bear and the bait, as they almost always approach from downwind in order to scent-check for other bears on the bait— and for hunters if they've had past experience with hunters at baits. Be ready to adapt if you have a bear that won't commit. It may help to have an alternative stand set up downwind from the bait to be ready for the big dude that likes to stop short and have a look without committing."

Black bears can be called effectively with predator calls that mimic the sounds of panicked fawns and calves. However, it's difficult to draw bears in from great distances with a call; in that respect, they are unlike coyotes, which think nothing of covering a mile or more to investigate a sound. Many bear hunters rely on predator calls to locate bears that might have been "lost" during a stalk. If you're in a situation where you think a bear is within a few hundred yards but you can't find it, try letting out a few faint fawn bleats. Sometimes a bear will come racing toward you. But if nothing happens, increase in volume and intensity after ten minutes. Then increase again after ten more minutes. If you get desperate and feel as though the bear is gone, go berserk with your calls. Sometimes a bear will show up after you've been wailing on the call for a half hour or more.

BLACKTAIL DEER

SCIENTIFIC NAME: *Odocoileus hemionus columbianus* and *Odocoileus hemionus sitkensis*

A blacktail deer's greatest defense strategy is its own home. When faced with even the slightest hunting pressure, blacktail deer simply vanish into the thick coniferous rain forests of their coastal habitats. There, these small deer are protected by seemingly impenetrable vegetation, copious amounts of rain, and fog banks that are capable of persisting for days on end. Hunters often refer to the deer as ghosts of the forest, and for good reason. The smart ones emerge from hiding only in the last moments of shooting light and return to their haunts within minutes of daybreak. But blacktail deer are not without vulnerability. They are homebodies and will often live their entire lives in an area of just a few square miles. When you've identified the whereabouts of a blacktail buck, hunting for him should be a quiet, touch-

and-go pursuit; the word *delicate* does not overemphasize the point. To glimpse one of these bucks at close range as he navigates his dark world of ferns, moss, and giant timber is a privilege you will want to remember. And if you're skillful and lucky enough to kill him, you'll be thankful to have a freezer full of steaks and roasts to serve as vivid reminders.

There are two recognized forms of blacktail deer, Columbia blacktail and Sitka blacktail. The transition zone between the two varieties occurs in British Columbia, with Columbia blacktails to the south and Sitka blacktails to the north. Both are considered to be mule deer subspecies, though blacktail deer are genetically much older than mule deer. (Mule deer developed as a hybridized species between blacktail deer and whitetail deer, probably on the Rocky Mountain front.)

BARROOM BANTER: Across much of their range, but particularly in the north, blacktail deer are reliant on mixed old-growth forests for wintering habitat. Not only does an old-growth canopy trap snow that would otherwise bury winter feed, it also lets through enough sunlight to enable the growth of a mixed and vibrant understory of edible plants. While clear-cuts from logging operations do create good blacktail feeding grounds during early succession, they are ultimately detrimental to blacktail deer. When a clear-cut reaches a successional phase known as the closed canopy exclusion phase, in which sunlight can no

longer penetrate to the forest floor, understory growth is greatly inhibited. Unless there are newer clear-cuts for the deer to migrate to, the animals face an increased risk of malnourishment and predation. There's almost certainly a correlation between malnourishment and predation, as starving animals are easier for predators to catch. But another factor is at play as well: former clear-cuts seem to encourage higher than usual concentrations of black bears, and black bears are a primary predator of blacktail fawns.

PHYSICAL CHARACTERISTICS: Coloration ranges from reddish brown in summer to grayish brown in winter. In comparison with mule deer, blacktail deer have less white on their rumps, display more black on their tails, and have shorter ears. There are noticeable physical differences between Columbia blacktail deer and Sitka blacktail deer. For one thing, Columbia blacktail deer achieve larger sizes than Sitka blacktail deer; a big Columbia blacktail buck can weigh well over 150 pounds, while a Sitka blacktail buck will seldom achieve this stature. Another difference is physical shape. Sitka blacktails have a strong physical resemblance to whitetail deer, while Columbia blacktails have an appearance that seems more aligned with mule deer. The antlers of Columbia blacktail bucks are bifurcated, meaning the tines fork rather than grow singly off a main beam. Sitka blacktail bucks have antler growth that is more similar to that of whitetail

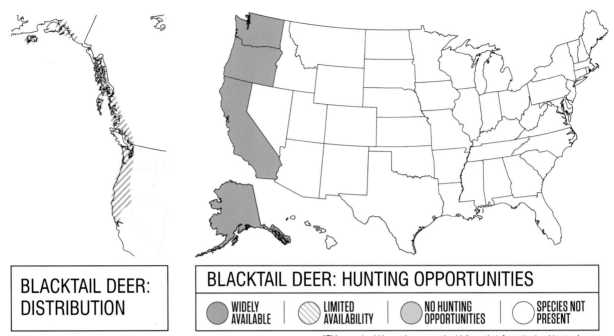

BLACKTAIL DEER: DISTRIBUTION

BLACKTAIL DEER: HUNTING OPPORTUNITIES

- WIDELY AVAILABLE
- LIMITED AVAILABILITY
- NO HUNTING OPPORTUNITIES
- SPECIES NOT PRESENT

*This map should be used as a general guideline only. Information is subject to change.

bucks, with unforked tines extending from a main beam.

DIET: Blacktail deer eat a great variety of grasses, forbs, lichens, shrubs, and trees, including salal, western red cedar, willow, salmonberry, red alder, and even poison oak.

LIFE AND DEATH: Primary predators include black bears, coyotes, wolves, and mountain lions. Blacktail deer can live up to ten years in the wild but seldom make it past six years of age.

BREEDING AND REPRODUCTION: Blacktail deer rut in November and early December. Their gestation period is 180 to 200 days. Does drop their fawns, typically one or two, in May or June.

HABITAT: Blacktails are common to coastal areas with wet, temperate climates. They frequent edge habitats where stands of heavy timber meet meadows, clearings, shorelines, clear-cuts, and brushy slopes. Unlike mule deer, which are prone to long seasonal migrations, blacktail deer make only relatively minor shifts in elevation to avoid heavy accumulations of snow.

TELLTALE SIGN: Blacktail deer sign resembles sign left by whitetail deer in similar heavily forested habitats. Besides tracks and scat, look for narrow trails as well as rubs and beds. The beds are about 2 feet wide and 3 feet long, sometimes consisting of little more than an area of matted ferns and mosses on finger ridges or just below the crests of primary ridges.

EDIBILITY: Excellent and mild, one of the best big game species. Suitable for all red meat applications.

HUNTING OPPORTUNITIES: Because of low hunter success rates and relatively limited hunter interest (due in large part to the thick, wet environments frequented by blacktail deer), tags are fairly easy to acquire in those states that have blacktails. Alaska has some outstanding blacktail opportunities, including many areas where you can legally harvest more than one buck.

HUNTING METHODS: Spot-and-stalk hunting for blacktail deer might sound like an impossible dream for hunters living in western Washington and Oregon, where thick timber, underbrush, and overgrown clear-cuts rule out the possibility of seeing animals at any appreciable distance. But in other portions of the animal's range, particularly in northern California and coastal Alaska, spot-and-stalk is one of the primary strategies used by successful blacktail hunters. In Alaska, it's particularly effective for late August and September hunts, when blacktail deer tend to congregate and feed in the subalpine and alpine zones above 2,000 feet. These altitudes can be reached in a matter of hours by physically fit hunters starting out at sea level. Thanks to the reddish color of the deer's hair at this time of year, the animals can be ridiculously easy to locate when feeding out in the open against a backdrop of knee-high, vibrant green vegetation.

Your best bet in such circumstances is to watch for fresh tracks and trails as you enter the alpine. Once you've established that animals are using the area, find a good vantage point. Ideally you'll be looking down into areas of mixed timber and alpine muskeg and also up toward surrounding peaks and slopes with brushy avalanche slides and grassy basins. Once you locate a deer that you want, you should take extra time to mark the animal's location and draw as many navigational references as possible from surrounding features.

Rather than charging directly toward a deer you've located, it's smart to head to a secondary vantage point that lies downwind of the deer's general location and within rifle range. Once you arrive at that point, make sure that you can see the general area where the deer was hanging out, and verify that it's within reasonable shooting distance. If your vantage point is good, one of two things will happen: either you'll see the deer and make your shot, or you won't see the deer and you'll hunker down for the waiting game. If the latter happens, don't rush it. Blacktail deer will hang around a particular spot for days on end if they're undisturbed. It's better to pull back and try again the next day rather than bust into the deer's home area and spook it out of the country. For archery hunters, a secondary vantage point should be used in order to fine-tune your plans for a final stalk that will deliver you into bow range.

Spot-and-stalk situations in California are a bit different, as you're usually not hunting alpine zones. Rather, you're looking at country comprising open grasslands and agricultural areas interspersed with tight brushy draws and timbered slopes. But the same principles still apply. Once you've verified the presence of deer through scouting, it's best to hang back and watch for the animals from afar rather than disturb them by trying to violate their sanctuaries. Concentrate your glassing efforts on edge and fringe habitats, where multiple features such as feeding areas and bedding areas come together. Be particularly vigilant about glassing during the first and last minutes of daylight, as pressured blacktails are notorious for going nocturnal when faced with the extra disturbances that come with hunting season. During midday, it's wise to use your optics to pick apart the slopes used by bedding deer. During cold weather, the deer will stick to slopes that get sun; during hot weather, they'll use shaded slopes. Glass beneath every tree and into every little nook and cranny where you can see through the overhead canopy. When an animal is located, take the necessary time to identify potential shooting positions where you can sneak into range without crowding the deer and alerting it. Remember, blacktail deer tend to be homebodies. Take advantage of that fact. If things aren't perfect, back out and try again another time.

In areas where glassing long distances is out of the question due to thick vegetation, still-hunting for blacktail deer is often the most productive strategy. Many hunters focus almost exclusively on still-hunting along gated or otherwise inactive logging roads that wind their way through networks of early-succession clear-cuts that provide an abundance of young browse plants that are favored by blacktails. The advantage to this is the relative silence (and easy walking) afforded by having a wide trail that's clear of clothes-snagging brush and snapping twigs that might otherwise send these animals heading toward thick cover. You want to approach each opening and clear-cut slowly and carefully and give them a thorough examination with binoculars before you enter. In good country, you should seldom find yourself taking more than ten steps without raising your binoculars to study the surrounding areas. Because blacktail deer are masters at hiding, keep in mind that you're not just looking for deer that are 100 yards away; you're also looking for deer that might be watching you pass by from a distance of 20 yards.

In high-pressure areas, particularly near large urban centers, productive clear-cuts get so hammered by competition that serious hunters ignore them altogether in favor of still-hunting in heavily timbered areas that are hard for other hunters to access because of a lack of roads, difficult terrain, or questionable property boundaries. Here, the trick is to move slowly and silently along deer trails that show evidence of recent use, particularly in the form of fresh tracks and scat. The most productive times are those when deer are naturally on the move, as the animals will be close to their trails and they'll be expecting to see and hear movements from other animals as well. The first couple of hours of the day and the last couple of hours are the best. It's even better during periods of drizzle and heavy cloud cover, or in the wake of a heavy rain. While still-hunting, behave as though you're actively stalking a deer rather than walking in the woods. The most important thing is to obey the wind. Hunt into the wind, or perpendicular to it. Swap out your heavy hiking boots for softer-soled trail runners or stalking slippers to increase your level of stealth. And keep your upper body movements to a minimum. When passing through areas where noise is unavoidable, do so quickly and then hunker down to wait and watch before you begin moving again. Direct your travel so that you pass through likely feeding areas such as forest openings, small meadows, and, in the north, muskegs. Hug the edges of these openings rather than trudging right through the middle of them. When you stop, which should be often, do so in places where the surrounding vegetation works to mask your outline. To make this system work, you do have to stop often and sometimes for lengthy periods of time to study your surroundings. Look carefully and listen carefully. Don't be afraid to pause for ten or fifteen minutes when you reach an area that seems like prime feeding habitat. And remember, you're not necessarily looking for a whole deer. Rather, you're more likely to see just a portion of a deer: an ear, an antler, a patch of hair, a leg. A cautious, alert hunter will sometimes hear a deer before the deer hears him. Or the hunter will catch a glimpse of movement from a deer before the deer sees him. But more often than not, the still-hunter will encounter deer that are aware of his presence though not totally sure about it. The animal will be waiting and watching for a telltale noise or smell that says "human." If you're careful and a bit lucky, the deer will not get this verification until it's too late. And when that verification does come, it should come in the form of a well-placed shot.

Ambush hunting is not associated with blacktail deer in the minds of many hunters, but some of the best blacktail hunters in the country swear by it. One of the greatest advantages to this strategy is that you're likely to get closer and longer looks at a species of deer that seems almost magical in its ability to escape our attention. Blacktails are best ambushed from tree stands. Rather than using the agricultural fields that are so familiar to hunters who target whitetail deer from tree stands in the East, blacktail hunters along the West Coast typically hunt near well-used deer trails in terrain that is often brushy or heavily timbered. The best trails are those connecting bedding areas and feeding areas. Because blacktail deer travel relatively short distances between their bedding and feeding areas, ideal ambush sites are quite close to bedding areas—sometimes just 100 or so yards away. At greater distances from bedding areas, the trails often branch out and grow diffuse. And because of the blacktail deer's habit of becoming nocturnal during hunting season, these more distant portions of trails might not see any buck activity at all until well after dark. In areas that appear at first glance to lack heavily traveled and clearly identifiable trails, or that lack easily identifiable bedding and feeding areas, try searching for trails near topographical features that might serve to funnel the movements of deer. Such natural funnels might include primary ridgelines that divide

A hunter in southeast Alaska blows a handmade fawn bleat on a hunt for blacktail deer.

drainages, finger ridges that branch off from primary ridges and drop down into canyons or valleys, and even passages between rock outcroppings or along the bases of cliff faces. Such simple features might be all that it takes to concentrate deer traffic in a predictable way.

Keep in mind, too, that stand placement is crucial with blacktail deer, particularly for archery hunters. Don't necessarily worry about placing your stand where you can see the maximum amount of surrounding country. Blacktails tend to be loyal to their trail systems; unless they're spooked, they will generally stick to the easy traveling. It's better to have a clear view of a well-used trail, with multiple possible shooting lanes, than a view of a bunch of areas that lie outside of your comfortable shooting range. When the wind is unfavorable, either blowing the wrong direction or swirling unpredictably, move your stand or go hunt in an altogether different location. It's not worth spooking a deer and ruining a good location just to spend an unproductive evening in your stand. In other words, think long-term instead of short-term.

Fawn bleats can be very effective for calling blacktail deer, particularly Sitka blacktails. The calls will excite and attract does year-round, but during the November rut, the annual breeding frenzy, they can be deadly against bucks as well. Typically, fawn bleat calls are employed by hunters using still-hunting strategies. Basically, a hunter will make a few calls from a likely position and then wait for a response. If nothing happens, he'll move along quietly toward a new position a few hundred yards away and try again. Often a call will do little more than cause nearby deer to stand up at attention, but even this limited response gives the hunter a huge advantage in the typically thick cover of blacktail country, where it's possible to pass within yards of a deer without seeing it. At other times, the response from a deer can be dramatic and sudden. During the rut, bucks sometimes come in aggressively to the calls, stomping and circling and providing multiple shot opportunities. As with most animal calls, blacktail fawn bleats work best on deer that have not yet heard artificially produced calls. This helps explain why the calls are so much more effective on Sitka blacktails than Columbia blacktails. In southeast Alaska, where the calls work especially well, there are literally hundreds of mountains—and even entire islands—that commonly go years or even decades without being visited by a hunter. There are deer in these places that have never laid eyes or ears on a human and never will.

HOW A SITKA BLACKTAIL IN COASTAL ALASKA USES A MOUNTAIN, AND WHAT IT MEANS FOR A HUNTER

1. At the opening of the August and September hunting seasons blacktail deer are typically found at or above the tree line, in elevations ranging upward from 1,800 feet. They've been here since late June or early July, following the upward retreat of the snowpack while feeding on the lush summer growth of herbaceous plants. 2. Once the high-altitude frosts of late September begin to kill off the summer's growth of alpine plants, the deer begin a gradual shift downward toward the upper elevation forests. They'll stay at this elevation for another month or so. 3. During the blacktail rut, from late October to late November, deer are widely scattered, though seldom above 1,500 feet. They are utilizing old-growth forest and can also be found in muskegs and forest openings. 4. Following the rut, accumulations of snow continue to push deer toward lower elevations. Hunters in late November and early December will typically find animals below 1,000 feet. The deer will remain at these elevations until May and June, when they start following the retreating snowpack toward higher elevations. 5. During years of extreme snowfall, blacktail deer will be forced down to the tide line in search of food. When these conditions arrive in December, before the close of the hunting season, the deer become easy pickings for opportunistic hunters operating from boats. In these situations, personal restraint by hunters is important for deer conservation.

Modern buffalo hunting is a nostalgic pursuit. Hunters who get an opportunity to chase these giants find it impossible to do so without pondering the historical significance of this animal in the lives of the Plains Indians and the Euro-American explorers who first traveled the American West. Just as it's difficult to comprehend the past abundance of these animals—hunters reported massive herds that took days to pass, numbering in the hundreds of thousands—it's difficult to comprehend how quickly they vanished. An estimated fifteen million buffalo lived on the Great Plains at the end of the Civil War; thirty years later, there were fewer than a thousand left in all of the United States and Canada. Today, we have a healthy and growing population of approximately half a million buffalo on the continent. The vast majority of these buffalo are semi-domesticated animals living on private property. On many large ranches, these animals can be purchased and then "hunted." While such activities might certainly give a hunter an idea of what it was like when our ancestors tangled with these massive beasts, the lack of challenge is noteworthy. (Most hunts for private herds offer guaranteed success.) Thankfully, there are fair-chase, public-land buffalo hunting opportunities in a handful of states, including Alaska, Arizona, Montana, Utah, and Wyoming, all of which award their tags through lottery drawings. By showing interest in these hunts, the hunter is actually helping buffalo conservation. The primary impediment to buffalo recovery is a lack of political will, and nothing shapes politics quite like economic incentive.

While it is commonly held that there are two genetically distinct subspecies of buffalo, the plains buffalo of the American West and the wood buffalo of Canada's boreal forests, modern work in genetics has not supported this view. While there are obvious physical differences between the two varieties, these differences are far less significant than the differences between various breeds of cattle.

BARROOM BANTER: Accidental deaths such as those caused by forest fires, falling, and drowning claim between 3 and 9 percent of North America's buffalo population annually. Assuming that these rates were similar at the time of European contact, when there were thirty-two million buffalo in North America, somewhere between one million and three million of the animals were dying by accident every year. Judging from historical accounts, drowning was clearly the leading cause of accidental death. In 1795, a fur trader along the Qu'Appelle River in Canada counted the carcasses of 7,360 drowned buffalo in a single day. Another traveler along Canada's Saskatchewan River estimated a total of 10,000 drowned buffalo near a ford. A traveler along the Missouri River observed several massive groupings of drowned buffalo carcasses in sloughs, some numbering close to 2,000 animals. Today, biologists believe that the near extinction of the buffalo in the late 1800s helped bring about a collapse in grizzly bear populations on the Great Plains. The bears relied on the spring "runs" of drowned buffalo just as Alaska's bears rely on salmon today.

PHYSICAL CHARACTERISTICS: The largest native land animal in North America. Chocolate-brown body with a shaggy mane and head. Long tail. Both sexes have curved, sharp-pointed horns that appear glossy black. Heads are blocky and massive. Big bulls stand 6 feet high at the shoulder and can weigh over 2,000 pounds. Cows can weigh over 1,000 pounds.

DIET: Grasses, sedges, forbs.

LIFE AND DEATH: Wolves are the only truly effective predator of adult buffalo, though buffalo calves are often killed by coyotes, black bears, and grizzly bears. Both sexes can live up to twenty-five years in the wild, though females tend to live longer. While many buffalo live in captivity, the primary long-term threat to wild, free-ranging buffalo is a lack of human tolerance for these great, powerful beasts.

BREEDING AND REPRODUCTION: Buffalo typically breed during June and July and drop their calves in the early spring after a nine-month gestation period.

HABITAT: Primarily open grasslands, though historically there were buffalo ranging from the boreal forests of northern Canada south to the deserts of Mexico, and from the mountain peaks of Utah east to the coastal piedmont of North Carolina.

TELLTALE SIGN: Look for well-used rubs, or scratching surfaces, including large trees on which the lower 3 to 4 feet of bark has been

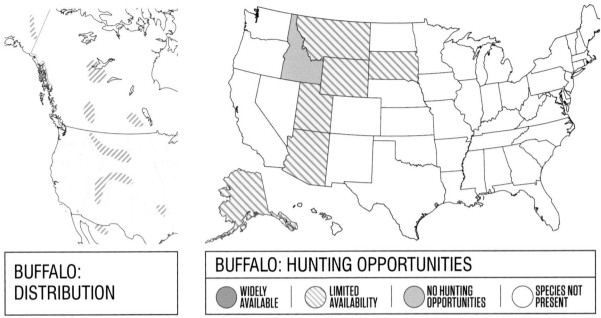

BUFFALO: DISTRIBUTION

BUFFALO: HUNTING OPPORTUNITIES
WIDELY AVAILABLE | LIMITED AVAILABILITY | NO HUNTING OPPORTUNITIES | SPECIES NOT PRESENT

*This map should be used as a general guideline only. Information is subject to change.

rubbed smooth. Large clumps of shed hair can be found hanging from brush along well-used trails and stuck to the bark of rubbing trees. Buffalo wallows can be over 10 feet wide, and deep enough that they'll fill with water in the spring and support amphibian life. Buffalo trails can be as wide as bike paths.

EDIBILITY: Superb, especially cows and young bulls. The flesh of older bulls is well flavored but sometimes exceptionally tough. The fat of buffalo is similar to beef fat and can be eaten as such; it does not need to be trimmed away. Suitable for all red meat applications.

HUNTING OPPORTUNITIES: Some hunters spend a lifetime applying in multiple states for a tag to hunt a wild, free-ranging buffalo without ever hitting the jackpot. But many people do get lucky every year. Next year it might be you.

HUNTING METHODS: The historical record is full of buffalo hunting accounts that demonstrate a wide variety of suitable tactics. Buffalo hunters on the Texas Panhandle ambushed buffalo along rivers and watering holes, Indian hunters on the northern Great Plains organized drives to push the animals over cliff edges, Kentucky hunters such as Daniel Boone still-hunted buffalo in cane brakes, and there are accounts of Indian hunters draping themselves in the hides of buffalo calves in order to decoy cows. Today, however, buffalo hunting is mostly a spot-and-stalk endeavor. With the exception of the winter migration hunts for the Yellowstone herd in southwest Montana, the handful of locations that offer truly free-ranging buffalo hunts share in common a lot of land and a small scattering of animals. Rather than being a slam-dunk, these hunts can be excruciatingly tough. Some of the most cherished buffalo tags in the country—the north rim of the Grand Canyon, Utah's Henry Mountains, Alaska's Copper River—have success rates that are often well below 50 percent. In these places, small buffalo herds might migrate as much as 20 miles or more in a matter of days, seemingly vanishing out from under hunters who are pursuing them. Some guys put in multiple days on these hunts, and sometimes multiple *trips*, without ever seeing an animal.

Hunters who've been successful on free-ranging buffalo hunts usually share in common an ability to cover a lot of ground. This requires both physical stamina and a solid plan for moving a load of meat and hide that could possibly total 1,000 pounds—a subject that will be addressed in a short while. Thankfully, buffalo are a somewhat difficult thing for the landscape to hide. While the animals can certainly vanish into timber or brush, especially during hot weather, they habitually seek out open grazing grounds during the morning and evening hours. When trying to locate a herd, it's wise for a hunter to be vigilant about positioning himself in prime glassing areas during these times. The selection of such glassing areas is hardly a random process. Buffalo leave an immense amount of sign wherever they go, and this sign can be readily identifiable even when it's a year or more old. The trick is to make sure that you're glassing areas with sign that demonstrates recent or current use by a herd. There are many indicators of fresh buffalo sign, including wet, sloppy droppings and also tracks that were laid down in the wake of a recent rainfall or snowfall. But one of the best ways to determine the presence of buffalo is to use your nose. More than any other North American game animal, buffalo have a way of stinking a place up. Some of the odor—it's reminiscent of a cattle or barnyard odor, though somehow cleaner-smelling—has a residual quality and can linger for days or even weeks in the absence of rain. But the odor of a recently passed herd is really hard to mistake. It smells distinctly warm and full of life, like the scent you get from pressing your nose to the neck of a horse. When you smell this, trust that you're in the vicinity of a herd. Get into a position where you can glass as much of the surrounding terrain as possible and watch for the movement of animals.

You often hear people say that buffalo are dumb, which is a dumb thing to say. Surely this sentiment comes from people whose exposure to the animals is limited to national parks and ranches, where they do not face hunting pressure. When the animals do face hunting pressure, they can become incredibly wary. Their primary defense is their sense of smell; a whiff of human odor will sometimes send them running—possibly for miles. For this reason, the spot-and-stalk hunter should plan his approach according to the wind.

Sound isn't nearly so important, as buffalo herds make a lot of noise and the animals aren't really sensitive to it.

Buffalo are huge and therefore tough to bring down. Good shot placement is essential. For this reason, you want to avoid shots that are too close or too far away. Close shots are less than perfect because they can quickly turn into rushed shots if the animal detects your presence and starts to fidget or bolt. Long shots are less than ideal because of imprecise shot placement and also because of the buffalo's tendency to herd up in tight balls. Not only do you need a clear view of the animal you're aiming at, you need to see what might be standing behind it. Do not risk having a pass-through shot that will injure a second animal. There are widely divergent views on the subjects of ballistics and shot placement regarding heavy animals like buffalo, but a safe bet is to use a hard-hitting caliber at least as powerful as a .300 Win Mag pushing 180-grain bullets. Shots to the upper portion of the shoulder might very well drop the animal in its tracks, but this point of aim is somewhat risky for novice shooters who have an imperfect understanding of anatomy. Put your shot about a third of the way up the buffalo's body, tucked as tightly as possible behind the shoulder, and you're virtually guaranteed to have a dead buffalo on the ground in a matter of minutes even if you fudge the shot by a few inches in either direction. And no matter what you hear from so-called experts, never attempt a head shot on a wild buffalo. It's a recipe for disaster.

There's a cliché about buffalo hunting that's often applied to elk and moose as well: the real work begins after the animal is down. This is absolutely true. Someone who's never dealt with a 1,000-plus-pound carcass is going to be in for a shock when they approach a buffalo. Unless the animal has fallen on smooth, level ground, a single person is not going to budge it. You might have to begin skinning whatever part of the carcass is facing the sky, and then remove whatever meat you can expose in order to lighten the animal up. Once you skin and quarter the upward-facing half, you can remove the entrails by cutting away the animal's paunch and slipping them through the opening. Then you can maybe roll the animal and work on the downward-facing half. Put simply, it's advisable to let the animal's position dictate your skinning and butchering process rather than trying to follow through with preconceived ideas of how you'll get the job done.

With buffalo, there is little that you'll want to leave in the field. The hides make great rugs and blankets when tanned, the skulls are beautiful wall ornaments, and the femurs and portions of the forearms can be processed into marrow bones; the fat can be rendered for pemmican, the edible organs make superb eating, and the meat, of course, is fantastic. Getting this all out can be a grueling task if

TRADITIONAL USES OF BUFFALO

Tongue: boiled and eaten. **Hooves:** rattles, spoons. **Horns:** charcoal carriers, ladles, head ornaments, bow laminates, powder horns, arrowheads, and decorative flourishes on headwear. **Untanned skins:** buckets, mortars, war shields, drums, splints, cinches, lariats, packing straps, knife sheaves, saddles, blankets, stirrups, masks, ornaments, quirts, snowshoes, boats, and moccasin soles. **Tanned hides:** moccasin uppers, blankets, beds, winter coats, shirts, leggings, dresses, belts, bridles, quivers, backrests, bags, tapestries, sweat lodge covers, tipi covers, and tipi liners. **Skin** from the hind leg could be taken directly off a freshly killed buffalo and used as emergency footwear. **Buffalo hair** (particularly from the forehead): stuffing pillows, dolls, sleeping pads, and medicine balls; insulating moccasins. **Buffalo hair:** ropes, which can be turned into headdresses, bracelets, hairpieces, bridles, and halters. **Tailbone** and its covering: flyswatters, whips, decorations, and children's toys. **Beard:** decoration. **Shoulder blades:** boat paddles; gardening implements such as shovels and hoes. **Other bones:** fleshing tools, smoking pipes, arrowheads, sled runners, saddle frames, war clubs, scrapers, awls, paintbrushes, sewing needles, gaming dice, knives and knife handles, forks and spoons. **Teeth:** ornaments for clothing. **Brains and livers:** to treat leather. **Stomach:** kettle, a washing basin, a water bucket, or as packaging material for meat. **Scrotum:** rattles. **Bladders:** balloons, flotation devices, waterproof pouches, storage for marrow or fat. **Fat:** hair treatment, base for medicine or cosmetics, cooking oil, food item, waterproofing agent. **Hooves and noses:** cooked down into glue. **Tendons and sinews:** bowstring and cords. The best sinews came from alongside the spine. These could be split into fine, strong threads for sewing clothes. **Buffalo heads:** many uses, but mostly of a spiritual or metaphysical nature. A skull represented a form of rebirth to many tribes.

the animal is in a place that's inaccessible to vehicles and you don't have friends with horses. A cow buffalo might require eight trips carrying 100 pounds; a bull might require a dozen or more. It can take an experienced and physically fit hunter a total of 3 days to move a cow buffalo a distance of three miles across rough terrain. So keep this reality in mind at all times when hunting buffalo or any other large-bodied game. Much of our history with this iconic mammal involves catastrophic waste and mismanagement. We owe it to the animal, and ourselves, to use it thoroughly and with utmost respect.

The actual task of hunting a caribou is not that hard. Instead, the challenge of pursuing these animals is reaching an area that holds caribou and then trying to maintain your comfort and sanity when faced with everything that arctic and subarctic environments can throw your way: bush planes delayed for days on end by unflyable weather, tents and gear soaked by horizontally driven rain, late summer blizzards, persistent fog, waist-deep rivers, hordes of mosquitoes and blackflies, ankle-busting tussocks, and the ever-present threat of grizzly bears claiming your hard-won meat. Enduring these conditions for a week or so can feel like a great achievement in itself,

and successful caribou hunters never come away from the experience lamenting the fact that the hunt wasn't challenging—even in situations where the herds seemed intent on stampeding the camp. What's more, caribou hunters get to witness a landscape that most Americans will never experience. The northern tundra is our last true wilderness, a place where you can be 100 or more miles from the nearest road. When a hunter walks these landscapes, he cannot help but feel a deep and immediate connection to his ancient, primal self.

All caribou and reindeer throughout the world are considered by taxonomists to be one species. A total of seven varieties, or subspecies, are recognized worldwide. Of these, Alaska has barren-ground and woodland caribou. Canada has barren-ground, woodland, and Peary.

BARROOM BANTER: Caribou milk has the highest fat content of any member of the deer family. And caribou have the highest ratio of antler weight to body weight of any animal worldwide. Caribou are also the only members of the deer family in which the females have antlers. While male caribou usually shed their antlers in December or January, females retain theirs through the winter and well into spring. It seems that this adaptation allows the females to effectively defend limited food resources against larger but unarmed males during a time of nutritional stress.

PHYSICAL CHARACTERISTICS: Brown, with whitish or grayish neck, rump patch, and sometimes flanks. During the rut, bulls develop a beautiful mane of whitish hair as well as a pronounced dewlap. Mature males can weigh well over 400 pounds; females are around half that size.

DIET: Primarily lichens, but also grasses, sedges, mushrooms, and twigs from birch and willow.

LIFE AND DEATH: Wolves are the chief predator of caribou, and the two species can often be found in close proximity. Grizzly bears and wolverines will kill caribou as well, particularly the young or injured. The life expectancy for caribou hasn't been studied as closely as other species of deer, but four to seven years seems to be typical, with some animals living to be older than ten.

BREEDING AND REPRODUCTION: Caribou breed in October and November. Females drop their calves, usually one or two, between mid-May and early June.

HABITAT: Tundra and taiga ecosystems, and also mountainous regions with coniferous forests and plenty of lichens.

TELLTALE SIGN: Heavily used trails along migratory routes. From the air, the trails often appear in tightly packed, crisscross patterns, especially in places where migrating animals are funneled by mountain passes, river crossings, and large bodies of water.

EDIBILITY: Not the greatest of the deer species, but still quite good. Caribou flesh is tender, though some folks complain of dryness. A careful cook who keeps the idiosyncrasies of his ingredients in mind will find nothing wrong with this meat. Suitable for most red meat applications.

HUNTING OPPORTUNITIES: Heading to Alaska or Canada will be required for the caribou hunter. Once there, acquiring tags is easy. In most places, several caribou may be taken because of healthy herd numbers.

HUNTING METHODS: Spot-and-stalk is the best way to hunt for caribou. You're pursuing a far-ranging and fast-moving animal on vast tracts of land, so maintaining a level

CARIBOU:
DISTRIBUTION

CARIBOU: HUNTING OPPORTUNITIES

WIDELY AVAILABLE | LIMITED AVAILABILITY | NO HUNTING OPPORTUNITIES | SPECIES NOT PRESENT

*This map should be used as a general guideline only. Information is subject to change.

of mobility is key. Most hunters who travel to caribou country are using services such as bush pilots or jet boat operators to reach their hunting grounds. These transporters are usually aware of the whereabouts of the herds, and they usually do a good job of putting you into the general vicinity of the animals. If you get dropped into an area that reportedly has caribou and you're not seeing any, you should spend your time traveling across the tundra or from valley to valley and ridge to ridge in search of the animals. It's quite possible to be in a situation where your particular area is empty of caribou while dozens and dozens are passing through just a couple of miles away.

Caribou do not like hot weather. If you're hunting during a period of warm weather, particularly in the mountains, it's wise to glass around snow patches and glaciers during the warmest part of the day. Caribou will lie directly on the snow or ice and stay there for hours. They also hate biting insects. Caribou can often be found in the vicinity of large lakes and at the feet of glaciers when bugs are bad, presumably to take advantage of the breezes generated by these features. When a stiff enough breeze kicks up to keep the insects down altogether, caribou will often stop to feed in lower pockets of land and along the fringes of tundra ponds. The hunter who was watching traveling animals at a distance might suddenly not see any movement at all. When this happens, wait for the breeze to die. When it does, you might see the land suddenly boil over with caribou as the animals start trotting along in a mad effort to escape the onslaught of insects.

If you see a group of caribou traveling in the distance, make a note of the exact route they traveled. Other groups will usually come along, and they'll have a tendency to follow that exact same route. Sometimes you can hunt for a few days and then realize that every single caribou you've seen has come into view at the same point along the skyline. If they are traveling on more general routes and are not confined to a particular trail or valley bottom, then position yourself near natural funnels. Isthmuses between lakes work well, as do river crossing locations and saddles along high ridges. Caribou travel farther and more often than any other species of North American big game; they've certainly learned how to travel smart, and they move across the landscape in predictable and efficient ways. Once you identify the land features that are directing their travel, it might be a good idea to move your camp closer to these features so that you can glass right from home. When bugs are bad, it's a tremendous relief when you can remove the rain fly from your tent and then glass from inside the mosquito netting.

Despite their wandering ways, feeding caribou will sometimes stay put for days on end. If you glass a way-off bull that's feeding in one location for an hour or so, it's worthwhile to head in his direction, even if that means a 2- or 3-mile walk. It's quite possible that he'll still be there when you arrive, or you might run into more caribou while you're walking in his direction. When it comes to caribou that are on the move, don't make the mistake of

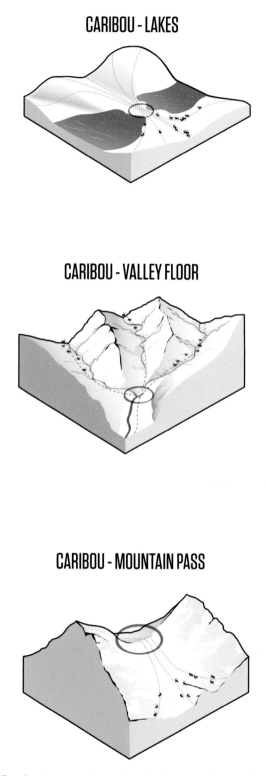

CARIBOU - LAKES

CARIBOU - VALLEY FLOOR

CARIBOU - MOUNTAIN PASS

When hunting migrating caribou, look for natural funnels that will guide the animals toward a predictable location.

[MALE]   [FEMALE]

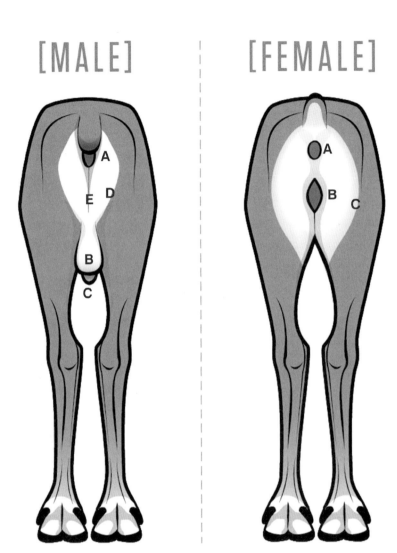

The presence of antlers cannot be regarded as definitive proof of sex on caribou, as both sexes have antlers. (The antlers of young bulls and mature cows are very similar.) There are other reliable indicators, including the direction of urination. Bulls urinate forward of the penis sheath, while females urinate behind the rear legs. Also look for these sexual indicators.

MALE:

A. Anal opening

B. Testicles

C. Penis sheath

D. Narrow rump patch

E. Lack of dark vulva patch

FEMALE:

A. Anal opening

B. Vulva

C. Wide white rump patch

thinking that you'll catch animals that are walking away from you. Caribou can move ridiculously fast on the tundra, and a human traveling across tussocks is no match for them. Instead, you want to concentrate your efforts on caribou that are moving toward you. When you get out in front of a herd, you don't need to take too many precautions. Just hunker down into the vegetation and hold still. As often as not, they'll actually veer from their course in order to satisfy their curiosity about that strange shape on the tundra. Sometimes cows and young bulls that walk past you will then double back and approach you within 100 yards from behind.

Even though caribou aren't easily spooked, don't be lazy or stupid when you're stalking them. One caribou might let you crawl within bow range across open ground, while the next might decide to run over the next three ridges at the sight of your head poking up above the horizon a couple of hundred yards away. But don't let your worries about concealment keep you from making a quick approach. If you're after a feeding bull and he seems a little restless due to bugs, then don't be afraid to expose yourself from a few hundred yards out. And if your presence starts to make him nervous, try getting on your hands and knees. He might just get curious and close the distance for you.

Finally, when it comes to shooting, caribou are not that hard to bring down. And because of the openness of the country, you don't have to worry about losing an animal that might run off 100 yards before dying. For this reason, it's a good idea to aim 3 or 4 inches back from the front shoulder in order to avoid ruining any meat. As long as you punch a hole in a lung, either with an arrow or with a bullet, the animal will be down on the ground in a hurry.

There is no such thing as an easy Dall sheep hunt. Every time you head into the northern mountains for these white sheep, you are in for a grueling high-country adventure. Sheep hunting tests all of your skills: camping, orienteering, alpine trekking, stalking, and, above all else, physical endurance. Sheep hunting also tests your gear. If you spend ten days backpacking after these elusive and high-climbing ghosts, you'll find yourself full of fresh opinions about backpacks, tents, footwear, and apparel. Because there's an undeniable link between gear performance and personal performance when you're living in such an abusive environment, Dall sheep hunters are among the least apologetic gear freaks in the world. No wonder that there's a dedicated industry of manufacturers who make "sheep gear," basically ultralight, extremely durable hunting products. Some hunters look at the cost of this stuff and come away feeling that sheep hunting is nothing but a rich man's game. Don't make this mistake. If you've got the necessary drive and devotion, you can head into sheep country with your usual hunting kit supplemented by a few items that can easily be found used on Craigslist or eBay. And if the costs of a sheep tag or a guided hunt are beyond your means, consider joining up with another hunter on his adventure. By the end of the trip, neither of you will care who actually pulled the trigger. When two sheep hunters come off the mountain with one animal, there's no such thing as "my sheep." It's "our sheep."

At the southern extreme of the Dall sheep's range, the animals are colored grayish brown. These are commonly known as stone sheep, though taxonomically speaking they are still *Ovis dalli*. Fannin sheep are another color phase of *Ovis dalli*. They occupy the middle ground (both in color and in geographical distribution) between the white-phase Dall sheep and the gray-phase stone sheep.

BARROOM BANTER: Dall sheep and bighorn sheep both share a common genetic ancestor that migrated from Siberia to Alaska sometime during a glacial epoch when sea levels were low enough to expose the Bering Land Bridge. It's likely that at one time a single species of mountain sheep ranged all the way from northwest Russia eastward and southward through Alaska and into the Rocky Mountains of the lower forty-eight. Eventually, a number of barriers arose that blocked genetic exchange among these populations and allowed for the development of three distinct species: Siberian snow sheep, Dall sheep, and bighorn sheep. It seems likely that massive glacial ice sheets were responsible for the separation between bighorn and Dall sheep. Today, the gap between the ranges of these two species is still mostly consistent with the placement of ice sheets during the last glacial epoch.

PHYSICAL CHARACTERISTICS: White, with sometimes yellow or "dirty" casting. Males carry magnificent and highly conspicuous curved horns that measure up to 40 inches long. The horns of ewes, or females, resemble a barnyard goat's. Males can weigh well over 200 pounds, females about half that.

DIET: Primarily grasses, sedges, and forbs, with fescue and saxifrage being among their favorites. Dall sheep will also eat horsetail and the shoots and buds of willow.

LIFE AND DEATH: Wolves kill a lot of Dall sheep. The sheep are also preyed upon by wolverines, lynx, bears, and golden eagles.

The latter can catch the lambs by simply nabbing them or toppling them over cliff faces. Avalanches are another common killer of Dall sheep. As for life expectancy, a twelve-year-old ram is quite old. Very few females live beyond fourteen years.

BREEDING AND REPRODUCTION: Dall sheep rut in late October and November. Ewes will drop one lamb in May.

HABITAT: Rocky, precipitous terrain, usually above tree line. Frequently found in glaciated terrain toward the heads of river drainages.

EDIBILITY: Superb, one of the absolute best. Suitable for all red meat applications.

HUNTING OPPORTUNITIES: Unless you're a resident of Alaska, British Columbia, the Yukon, or the Northwest Territories or have an immediate family member in one of those places, you'll have to hire a guide to go Dall sheep hunting. Bargain prices start at $12,000, but most hunts will cost you closer to $20,000 and the top end easily approaches $30,000. For many people, the best way to experience a Dall sheep hunt is to join another hunter as a packer and helper. It's cheap, and just as much fun as being the guy who pulls the trigger.

HUNTING METHODS When you're traveling in good sheep country, it's common to see at least some Dall sheep every day. However, finding a ram that's large enough to be legally harvested can be extremely challenging. In

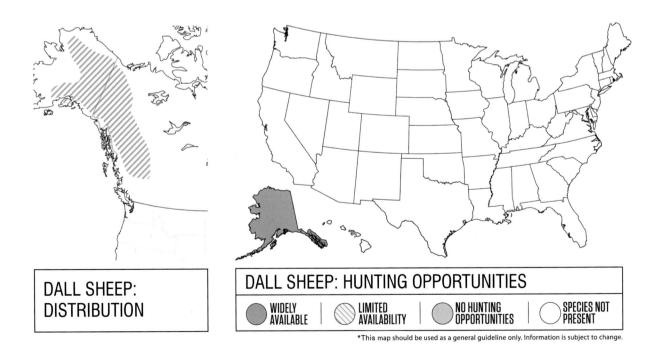

DALL SHEEP: DISTRIBUTION

DALL SHEEP: HUNTING OPPORTUNITIES

WIDELY AVAILABLE | LIMITED AVAILABILITY | NO HUNTING OPPORTUNITIES | SPECIES NOT PRESENT

*This map should be used as a general guideline only. Information is subject to change.

some areas, legal rams account for less than 10 percent of the total sheep population. These legal rams can be the hardest to find, too, because they like to hang out in the highest, least hospitable, and most difficult-to-reach portions of their mountain homes. Many hunters return from ten-day sheep hunts having seen dozens of rams but not a single "full curler."

DEFINING A LEGAL RAM

The three rams above were all killed with the assistance of Rick French, a master Alaska sheep guide. (A) Full-curl ram. (B) Double-broomed ram. (C) The ram's horns are neither full curl nor broomed, yet the ram is legal because it has at least eight annuli. Here, eight of the most obvious annuli are highlighted. There are four more that are difficult to see. This ram was documented by the Alaska Department of Fish and Game as twelve years old.

To seriously hunt Dall sheep, you need to be willing to cover massive amounts of ground in search of legal rams. Eight miles a day isn't unusual, and twice as many miles a day isn't unheard of. And sheep country is hardly flat. You're likely to gain and lose thousands of feet of elevation every day. Multiply these distances and elevation changes by the 7 to 10 days you plan on hunting, then add on the additional 5 or 10 miles that it takes to reach sheep country from lower-altitude landing strips used by bush planes, and you'll begin to see the

In this image, the X's mark actual places where Dall rams like to bed down. Learn to identify similar areas and glass them carefully.

importance of being in rock-hard physical condition before you commit to a Dall hunt.

What enables sheep hunters to travel so widely, beyond being in good shape, is that Dall sheep are fairly easy to see. The title of Alaskan outfitter Rick French's Dall sheep hunting video, *Black Shale, White Sheep*, really says it all. Thanks to their color, you can typically rule out the presence of the animals in those areas where you don't see them after an initial inspection. Thus it's possible that you might glass 6 or 7 miles of a drainage in a single day, along with the basins of as many tributaries, without feeling that you overlooked something obvious. (Compare this with whitetail deer hunting, where you can stare at the same patch of brush for five days and still not see half the deer that are hiding in it.) When you wake up in the morning on a sheep hunt, you're not thinking about backtracking for a second look. You're thinking about what lies over the next ridge.

Don't take this to mean that you can be lazy about glassing. You still need to give the landscape a careful looking over. Rams are often found in the large cirques or bowl-like basins at the absolute heads of drainages. They like to bed in areas where they've got escape cover to their backs, often in the form of steep and broken cliff faces. When the sun's behind them, these cliffs cast shadows that are difficult to penetrate with optics at a long distance. Make sure to check them carefully. Rams also like to bed along the crests of finger ridges just below their junction with the primary ridgeline. Large boulders and jumbles of rock can obscure these sheep. Pick these areas apart with great care. And keep in mind that you might just see a white leg poking out in the sunshine from behind a shaded rock, or a curved section of horn jutting out from the side of a rock jumble. If you do get into a situation where you can't rule out the presence of a ram, it's a good idea to glass the area in the evening. The rams will get up then and move around. Should it snow, your job just got tough. Dall sheep have a yellowish or "dirty" cast that makes them stand out against the snow a little bit, but not too much. Rather than just looking for sheep in the snow, you want to look for sets of tracks as well. These appear at a distance as lines that seem to be etched into the mountainsides or running up the crests of finger ridges. Follow these lines both ways. Sometimes the tracks will mysteriously vanish. As you try to figure out where the animal went to next, you'll realize that the trail ended simply because you're looking at the sheep that made it.

Try not to get bogged down with a fixed campsite when hunting Dall sheep. Remember, mobility and flexibility are key. Countless Dall sheep have been killed by hunters who ended up 20 or more miles as the crow flies from where the bush plane dropped them off. Carry what you need, and only what you need. Sleep wherever you happen to be when the day is done. And when you do stop for the night, pick a place where you can see a lot of the surrounding country. Dall sheep are typically hunted in late August and September. You can't possibly hunt from dawn to dusk during the early season, because at those latitudes there are only a few hours of dark. It's nice if you can keep glassing while you cook and do whatever chores need to be done before you start hoofing it up and down the mountains the next day. After all, it's next to impossible to enjoy all the climbing that a Dall sheep hunt involves. But the sights that you'll see in sheep country make all the blisters and strained ligaments seem like a very small price to pay.

RICK FRENCH, AN ALASKA SHEEP GUIDE, WEIGHS IN ON THE DOS AND DON'TS OF HUNTING DALL SHEEP

DO:

• "Do stay out of sight. If you can't see them, they can't see you. If possible, it's okay to occasionally check on the sheep to ensure that circumstances haven't changed. Then get back out of sight and continue on.

• "Do take the high road. Sheep tend to look down rather than up. Get above them and you have turned the tables in your favor.

• "Do cover your face and hands with a head net and gloves when within shooting range or when you're peeking over a ridge. Human skin reflects a lot of light, especially when it's oily and sweaty. By covering up you are much less likely to cause alarm if a sheep happens to spot you at close range.

• "Do pay attention to wind, and think ahead to what thermals will be doing later in the day. For example, if you're above a ram in the morning and you have to descend the mountain for a shot, let the thermals change to their uphill direction before you start your stalk.

- "Do use the best optics you can afford. Determining that a ram on the next mountain is actually sublegal could save you a day of pointless hiking and thereby earn you a day of looking for legal rams.

  DON'T:
- "Don't let them see you first. If they do, it's typically game over.
- "Don't stalk them from below if you can prevent it. Most times, coming from below will put the odds in the sheep's favor.
- "Don't worry too much about kicking a rock or two lose. Sheep are accustomed to rocks falling. Simply stand still for a few minutes and then quietly begin your stalk again.
- "Don't be lazy. You may think about taking a shortcut where a ram may see you crossing open country in order to save a couple of hours of walking, but don't do it. Always go the long way, if that's where you'll find cover. A little extra hard work will pay big dividends.
- "Don't go on a sheep hunt without a SPOT emergency locator or a satellite phone. These tools can literally save lives if you or your partner gets injured."

While we now regard elk as a western species found primarily in the Rocky Mountains, at the time of European contact they were found across virtually all of the lower forty-eight, with particularly impressive herds on the Great Plains. Habitat loss and commercial hunting almost wiped the species from the map, though modern conservation practices have led to a dramatic rebound of the animals. Every year, elk make their way onto new lands where they've been absent for over a century, bringing with them renewed elk hunting opportunities. Today, we have limited elk seasons in a half dozen states lying east of the Mississippi River—up from zero states during much of the twentieth century. These expanding herds are certain to gradually shift our perception of elk country away from the rugged western landscapes, but for now it's still fair to say that elk live in some of the wildest, wooliest terrain that this nation has to offer. Venturing into such landscapes in search of this toughest and most graceful member of the deer family should be regarded as an essential pilgrimage in the life of any American hunter.

BARROOM BANTER: The two smooth and

loose-fitting toothlike structures in an elk's upper jaw are commonly known among hunters as ivories. Rather than being teeth, these are actually vestigial remnants of tusks that once adorned—and defended—the ancient genetic ancestors of the species.

PHYSICAL CHARACTERISTICS: Coat is copper brown in summer; light tan in fall, winter, and spring. Rump patch is light beige. Mane and legs are considerably darker than the body. Males sport antlers, which are shed in the late winter and then sprouted anew in the spring; the antlers of a mature bull can measure well over 4 feet in length, with six tines per antler and a tip-to-tip spread of over 3 feet. Bulls stand 5 feet at the shoulder and weigh around 700 pounds, with some specimens pushing well over 1,000 pounds. Females, or cows, typically weigh between 300 and 600 pounds.

HABITAT: Elk live in a variety of habitats, from coastal rain forests to Rocky Mountain alpine to the grassland and forest mosaics of the central and eastern United States. In mountainous regions, elk migrate into higher altitudes in the spring and in the opposite direction in the fall, retreating from the deepening snow.

DIET: Elk are primarily grazers, with a strong preference for native bunch grasses. Will also consume forbs, woody browse such as willow and aspen, and a variety of common agricultural crops.

LIFE AND DEATH: It is common for elk to reach ten years of age, rarely fifteen. Predators include wolves, mountain lions, grizzly bears, black bears, and coyotes. Habitat loss is the primary long-term threat to elk.

BREEDING AND REPRODUCTION: Elk breed from mid-August through mid-October; females drop one or two calves in late May and early June. Calves weight about 35 pounds.

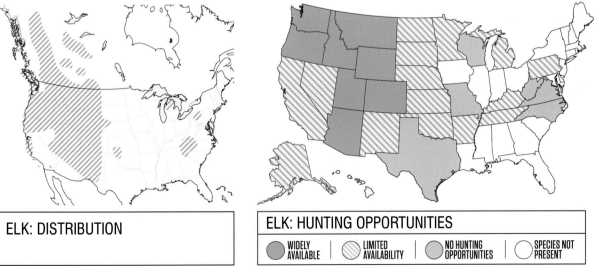

ELK: DISTRIBUTION

ELK: HUNTING OPPORTUNITIES

WIDELY AVAILABLE | LIMITED AVAILABILITY | NO HUNTING OPPORTUNITIES | SPECIES NOT PRESENT

*This map should be used as a general guideline only. Information is subject to change.

EDIBILITY: Many hunters accept as fact that elk is the finest game meat in existence, and it is commonly regarded as being far superior to beef. Suitable for all red meat applications.

HUNTING OPPORTUNITIES: Residents of western states enjoy liberal tag allocations; in some states two elk can be killed annually. In most states, nonresident elk hunters have to apply for tags through a lottery system in the spring application period. Many of these lotteries offer nearly 100 percent success rates to applicants, particularly for archery hunters. Colorado and Idaho offer over-the-counter options for nonresidents; tags can be bought until the night before the season opens. As for the eastern elk herds, tags are very limited and tough to draw.

AN ELK'S YEAR

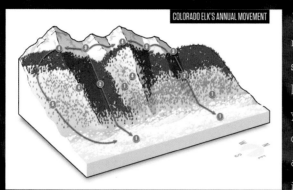

COLORADO ELK'S ANNUAL MOVEMENT

1. *Winter range.* Elk are commonly found on lower-elevation south-facing slopes as well as low-elevation sagebrush and pinyon or juniper habitat. At this time of year they consume a significant amount of woody browse, including sagebrush, aspen bark, and mountain mahogany.

2. *Spring migration.* Elk follow the receding snows up into the high country as they feed on emerging vegetation. Elk will make it to their calving grounds by mid-May and into the high subalpine basins by June. In years with high snowpack, it might take until late July.

3. *Calving and summer range.* The protein-rich grasses of the high country put fat on young calves and old bulls alike. The higher elevations offer cooler temperatures and fewer biting insects.

4. *Rut.* During the rut, elk will be the most spread out. Some will remain in the high country, while others will begin their gradual descent to lower country.

5. *Fall/winter migration.* With the onset of winter snow accumulation, all but the wiliest of bulls will bail off the mountain toward low-elevation winter range. Eventually, even the toughest bulls will follow.

HUNTING METHODS: Elk are movers. Be it from hunting pressure or weather, great numbers of them will cover great distances with mind-boggling speed. But an elk's toughness goes beyond its ability to climb 1,000-foot inclines in times measured in seconds rather than minutes. When hunters hear these massive animals coming through a forest of lodgepole pine, they often draw comparisons to the sound of trains. And there's no other animal, save perhaps moose, that can withstand a poorly placed arrow or bullet as hardily as an elk. Even after absorbing a well-placed shot, elk have been known to just stand there as they try to determine the source of the loud booms.

Long walks are the norm with elk hunting, and your legs and lungs are almost guaranteed to suffer the effects of massive and constant elevation change. One well-regarded outfitter likes to describe elk hunting as "up the hill, down the hill." You should be in peak physical shape before undertaking a Rocky Mountain elk hunt, though your discipline will be rewarded with amazing vistas and, if you're lucky, a freezer full of the finest game meat in the world.

If there's an easy way out for the elk hunter, it's private land. Whether you pay for access or are lucky enough to have friends or family with a western ranch, elk hunting on private ground generally requires a lot less perseverance on the part of the hunter. Vehicles can be used to access ranchland, and dead elk can be retrieved with a lot less hassle and sore muscles. Plus, limited access usually equates to limited pressure, meaning that the elk can be much more forgiving if you screw up during a stalk. By no means is this meant to discredit the private land elk hunter, for many of them work incredibly hard, but if there weren't sig-

nificant advantages to hunting private land, then it wouldn't cost so much money to do so. But one thing that can't be bought is the immense sense of satisfaction that comes from bagging an elk on publicly owned ground.

Elk are highly vocal, which makes them the most exciting big game animal to hunt using calling strategies. Most first-time elk hunters are simply blown away by how vocal and loud a group of elk can be. While the animals will talk year-round, it's the rut, or fall breeding season (typically early September to mid-October), that turns a herd of elk into a beehive-like mass of vocal energy as the cows try to maintain herd cohesion while the bulls engage in a game of bugling one-upmanship. Since the rut typically coincides with archery season in most western states, calling strategies are best suited for bowhunters. (By no means do they not work for rifle hunters in places with firearm rut seasons; it's just that tags for such seasons are very limited.)

To become a competent elk caller, you must study the language of elk. It's very helpful to get into the woods and listen to the elk themselves. But if you happen to live in an area that doesn't have any elk within easy driving distance (which is true for most Americans), there are CDs and digital downloads on the market that feature audio recordings of every elk sound imaginable. Once you learn the language of elk and how it is used, you must commit to hours and hours of practice as you develop the necessary skills required to mimic them through the use of game calls.

Perhaps the most easily distinguished game call that you'll hear in the mountains is the high-pitched bugle of a bull elk. Bulls will bugle for a variety of reasons. Early in the rut, they bugle to other bulls as they struggle to determine a hierarchy among themselves. This can save them from the trouble of serious fighting, which can lead to exhaustion and death. Later on, bulls will bugle directly at cows as they attempt to collect and maintain harems and then protect those harems against the

A hunter sends a locating bugle across an alpine bowl in Colorado.

incursions of other bulls. (This leaves very little time for feeding, and a mature bull can lose 20 percent of his body weight during this period of constant action.) Bulls often follow their high-pitched bugles with a series of grunts known as "chuckling." This sound is often heard on its own as well. Bulls will also emit a more guttural tending sound known as "glunking." When you're watching a glunking bull, you'll actually see its belly bounce up and down in a very dramatic way as it emits a deep *glunk, glunk, glunk.* During sparring, bulls will make a whiny squeak that is easily mistaken for an excited cow call. Finally, bulls (as well as cows) will make an alarm bark when something is amiss and they can't quite make sense of it. It sounds like a loud, wheezy, high-pitched bark-grunt without the *b*. It's a raspy and piercing *ark!* Very rarely are multiple barks made in a row. It's one note and then silence as the elk continues to assess the danger. If you hear this bark while hunting, you can be sure that you've been had or something else has buggered the elk. In any case, the elk you were hunting are now in an alert state and it's best to back out.

The primary reason to mimic the bugle of a bull elk is to locate distant animals. Hunters create bugles by using commercially produced reed-type calls fitted onto the end of a tube for amplification, and also by blowing diaphragm calls into a tube. A locator bugle is usually loud and long, and done from a high point

Top: Bugle or grunt tube. Bottom, left to right: Diaphragm pouch; diaphragms from Phelps and Bugling Bull; Primos internal reed call; external reed calls from Bugling Bull, Carlton's, and Phelps.

where the sound will travel and, equally important, where you will be able to hear a response and pinpoint its direction. Once that's accomplished, you can move toward the elk and then make your next move according to whatever situation you find when you get there. Once you get close to a bull, a bugle can be used to challenge the animal and potentially draw him closer, but this should be attempted only in dire situations when nothing else is working. Bugles have been grossly overused by hunters and now work better at repelling bulls than drawing them in. What's more, even if your bugle dupes the bull, he may just gather

up his cows and leave the area rather than risk losing them to a bigger, badder animal. But if a bull is keeping his distance and will not approach your cow calls, and there's no way to get closer, a soft bugle might just give him the impression that another bull has joined the group. And if you're lucky, his sense of jealousy might bring him in a precious few yards closer—and right into shooting range.

Besides the alarm bark mentioned above, cows use a wide array of sounds to communicate with herd members. These range from short chirps of contentment (a half-second-long *ee-oh*) to medium-length locating mews (a one-second-long *eeee-oh*) and the elongated, excited whines (one to two seconds long, sometimes two separate notes changing in pitch at the front of the call: *eeeee-eeeee-oh*) associated with estrus. It is the caller's personal preference whether to end the cow sound with *oh*, *ah*, or *eh*. All three will work and will add variation to the caller's elk dialect. All of these calls can be produced using external reed calls as well as diaphragm mouth calls. Whatever type of call you prefer using, it's best to stick to the chirps and soft mews of the cows once you've worked into close range of elk, especially in the first few moments. Sometimes, these softer mews are just what a rutting bull wants to hear: he's looking for cows, and there they are! Nearby elk might also be enticed to come your way for the simple reason that elk are gregarious and they want to engage with other elk that happen to be nearby.

Under the right circumstances, louder cow mews can be used to say more than just "I'm over here." This call has a direct, succinct nature. A cow might mew because she's gotten separated from her group and feels lonely, or a lead cow might mew to communicate that the herd should get moving or change direction. During the rut, cows that are nearing or in estrus (meaning breeding will happen soon) start to call very intently, almost pleading for attention. These mews are louder, drawn out, and very nasal-sounding; they could be called whiny. Some cows will sound raspy and have

a sort of buzz to their mew when they make these calls. Such sounds can be very effective at bringing in bulls, but use them with restraint. You want to avoid making sounds that don't correlate well with the real situation that's happening on the ground. Remember, *bomb* is a frequently used word in the English language, but you don't want to say it when you're going through TSA security screening at the airport.

Obviously, there's a lot more to calling elk than just making the proper noises. Let's take a moment to walk through a typical morning of elk calling and hunting in order to see the sorts of real-time decisions that need to be made. Say it's early in the morning and you have reason to think that elk are in the area, but you don't know exactly where they are. So you start with a locator call—either a bugle or a hefty cow call. If you don't get an answer, you continue to cover country. Many elk hunters refer to this as "prospecting." Basically, you're walking and calling as you search for animals.

Once you do get a response from a bull, or you hear a bull that just happens to be bugling independent of your calling, you need to determine how far away the elk is and in what direction—if any—it's traveling. You can do this by listening to the elk's subsequent bugles, and you can prompt him to make more noise by repeating the same type of locator call that got him talking in the first place. If

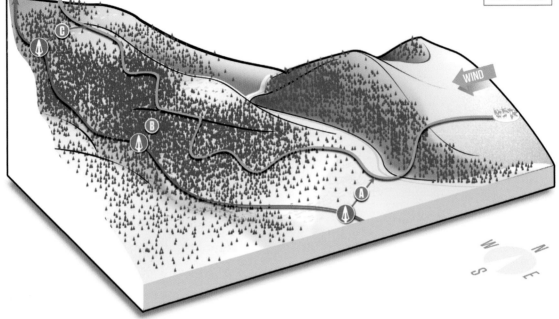

In a strategy sometimes known as "T-boning," a hunter can parallel a herd of elk in a downwind direction and wait for the perfect set of circumstances to get in close and call. Calling is not always necessary, as this tactic can result in a quick ambush as well.

he's making noise, you want to take advantage of that by closing the distance as much as possible while you have a beacon of sorts to guide you. Elk will rarely come to a call 300 yards away, let alone a mile away, so closing the gap is your responsibility. Do it quickly but quietly.

As you move in, you're more or less employing a spot-and-stalk strategy, or rather a listen-and-stalk strategy. You want to get as close as possible without spooking the elk, because proximity is directly tied to a bull's willingness to investigate the source of your calling. You might have to shadow the herd from a downwind position for hours until you

finally have an opportunity to slip in close enough to make an actual attempt on the elk. A hundred yards or less is a great distance to call from, so long as the elk are unaware of your presence. At this distance, you're in the bull's comfort zone and you'll be putting pressure on him to physically react to your call. Either he comes to herd you back into the harem, thinking you're a loose cow, or he comes to open a can of whoop-ass, thinking you're an accosting young bull.

Before delivering your call, identify the most likely routes that the animal will use in getting to you, and make sure you've got shooting lanes. A range finder is helpful in determining

HUNTING ELK WITH A CALLING PARTNER

Although this hillside might seem too open for a calling setup, the rolling edge of the bench provides just enough screen. With a rising thermal, the elk has no choice but to look onto the bench to identify the source of the calls. At that point he will be in range of the shooter (), who will have to rely on the sparse vegetation for a concealing backdrop.

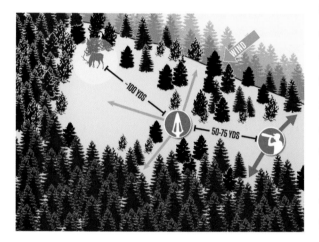

This bull might approach the caller () by coming through the timber in order to stay within the cover or by coming through the meadow in an attempt to get downwind of the caller. The shooter () is positioned so that he can move freely to either location.

distances to likely shooting lanes, and doing this now will save you from doing it under pressure when a bull comes charging in with all of his senses on high alert. When you start calling, try using short, sweet sounds before you progress to louder and more intense sounds. If you find something that the bull likes, stick to it. And if you're hearing cows calling around you as well, listen to what they sound like and mimic their tone and length of call.

If a bull keeps pushing his cows away from your setups, try making a sweeping loop and get out in front of the moving herd. As with any calling, the animals being called to are more apt to come to the call if it is in the general direction of their travel. Remember, it's easiest to call animals in a direction that they naturally want to go. Since the moving elk are making plenty of their own noises, don't be afraid to hustle and neglect stealth for a minute as you make a move. Even after several failed attempts, do not get lax about your strategy. Treat each attempt the same way you treated the first. Stay ready, stay focused. When it all gels and that snorting, eye-bulging, 800-pound monster finally decides to come, it happens fast and often when you least expect it. Be prepared with your arrow nocked or your rifle ready—and your head clear!

A BUNCH OF THINGS TO KEEP IN MIND WHEN CALLING ELK

- By adding an elk decoy to a calling setup, your realism factor soars. If you can fool the elk's eyes as well as its ears, you're going to be getting some action. But try to get out ahead of your decoy, so you're between it and the approaching elk. The elk is likely to hang up at a safe distance even after it sees the decoy; if you're out front, you might be in range when it does.

- Hunters often progress too quickly to cow calls that are too long and too whiny. Elk make chirps and mews more than other sounds. So should you.

- If the woods are quiet but you know elk are in the vicinity, try blind calling. This is often done at the edge of a patch of evergreens that might be a bedding area. Set up as if there are elk within 200 yards and start with a couple of chirps. Escalate your calling through a sequence of sounds as you try to kindle interest from the animals. On some occasions you'll move on, but often you'll receive a response of one kind or another and find yourself "in elk." It's good to remember that bulls are often trailing cows, so communicating with the lead cow and calling her in can result in the bull being in range as well.

- Calling works for more than just bringing elk to you. Loud cow calls can bring a whole herd to a stop, offering an opportunity for a shot. This works at close range for a bow shot and at long distances for rifles. And don't stop calling after the shot. Even with loud, startling rifle shots, both wounded and healthy elk can be calmed down and stopped. Commanding cow calls can even bring the herd back to you. This tactic not only can afford second opportunities but also can shorten tracking on wounded animals.

- When hunting with a partner, the caller should usually stay around 50 to 100 yards behind the shooter. Think of it as calling the elk past the shooter as it approaches the call. The caller should stay mobile, as his position dictates where the oncoming elk goes. If a bugling bull gets hung up and absolutely refuses to come closer, the caller should try walking away from the action while calling. The thought of the cow leaving is often enough to entice a few more steps.

- Manufacturers are trying to sell calls. Instead of buying the latest and greatest "Sexy Seducer" elk calling gimmick, spend a few more hours on your diaphragm and external reed calls and learn to mew consistently like an elk. Most serious elk hunters will head into the mountains with just a diaphragm or two, an external reed call, and perhaps a grunt tube for making bugles.

- A bull elk who's busy destroying a sapling with his antlers is often blind to his surroundings. If you're fortunate enough to encounter one and have weapon in hand, abort previous plans and walk quickly toward the bull, approaching from downwind (and from his backside, if possible). Often, you can get into range without being noticed.

- While listening to elk vocalizations, take notice of the nonvocal noises that elk produce. Elk are big animals, and as they go about their daily business they snap sticks, run through brush or bushes, pull leaves off trees, clunk hooves on logs and rocks, splash water, and thrash trees, grass, and mud with their antlers. Elk hear these sounds daily, and if you can learn to mimic them effectively and integrate them with your bugles and mews, your calling will gain authenticity.

- In general, calling in open spaces has poor success on elk. You need to make sure that your calling setup is realistic—and that refers both to what is there and to what isn't. When choosing your location, be sure that there is vegetation around you or behind you that could be hiding the elk that you are supposed to be. When an elk is coming to a call, it knows exactly where the source of the call is. When it does not see the supposed elk, it gets suspicious. Give oncoming elk plenty of places to expect the supposed elk to be.

- Always pay absolute attention to the wind. Elk will often circle downwind of the caller to confirm the presence of a real elk. The hunter should be set up to cut off such an attempt by the elk.

The elk's long legs and outsized lungs seem to compel it to travel almost constantly, and a hunter's desire for elk meat seems to compel him to follow. No matter where or how an elk hunter is hunting, he or she is almost surely going to end up using some aspect of the spot-and-stalk strategy.

Thanks to their size and two-tone appearance (tan body, chocolate mane), elk can be much easier to spot at long distances than other mountain game. When glassing for the animals, a hunter can move fairly quickly with his optics, especially in the morning and evening hours when the elk are most likely to be up on their feet feeding. When hunting in the snow, you can glass for elk sign as readily as you can glass for the animals themselves. Feeding areas, where elk have pawed through the snow to reach the grass below, show up at great distances through binoculars and spotting scopes. So do elk beds. And if you're lucky to be hunting in snow that's less than twenty-four hours old, you can get especially excited about the discovery of elk feeding areas. Make sure to be watching that area again at dusk and again at dawn—there's a good chance that the elk will be back.

When glassing for elk, you sometimes need to ask yourself whether you want to spook an elk now or kill an elk later. The importance of patience is something that all experienced spot-and-stalk elk hunters will agree on. Quite simply, it's not always best to just start chasing after a herd of elk as soon as you see them. Sure, if it seems like the elk are calmly feeding and you've got plenty of daylight left, or that a bull has a group of cows balled up and he's rutting them enthusiastically, then it might be advisable to check the wind and start after them. But if the elk are in single file and moving, it might be best to sit back and see what the herd is up to and where it's headed. Often, elk that are unapproachable due to their location and general attitude will move into a location that's much more conducive to a stalk. Or you might even decide to wait until the next day, when you can use what you learn from your observations in order to plan the perfect approach.

But when you do decide to go, go quickly. If you lose sight of your herd and then dillydally for several hours in the bottom of a canyon, you might not ever find them again. For this reason, hunting elk requires peak physical condition. Most hunters who fail physically on an elk hunt do so after they've already spotted the animals. They can see the prize, but they just can't reach it.

While patience is important to spot-and-stalk elk hunting, it's essential to ambush elk hunting. Elk hunters with detailed knowledge of their hunting grounds can be very successful utilizing an ambush strategy if they keep in mind the wide-ranging and seemingly willy-nilly habits of the animals. Elk do in fact have patterns and preferences, but those occur over large landscapes. An elk's feeding grounds might cover many square miles within multiple drainages, and it might travel for hours just to get a drink of water. If someone tells you that elk frequent a certain south-facing hillside, this might mean that elk show up there three or four times a month rather than three or four times a week. Thus, ambushing elk can turn into a waiting game that favors the patient hunter.

Typically, an ambush hunter will set up on one of two types of locations for elk. Travel route ambush sites are positioned along well-used trails, pinch points such as ridgeline saddles, major migration corridors, and historically used escape routes. The last is where experience in a certain area pays off especially well. Let's say you know that a herd of elk gets spooked off Green Mountain every year on the opening day of the season. And you know that when they are, they spill off the east side of the mountain and then wrap around the neighboring hill on the lowest game trail before crossing Sentinel Creek near the main fork . . . well, you get the point. You can put that kind of information to use when elk hunting, because elk are that kind of animal. You can trust them to behave in the same general ways, year in and year out.

The second type of site is where elk go for feed and water. These are places such as meadows, hayfields, watering holes, and wallows. When contemplating an ambush setup near food or water, check for plenty of fresh sign, and not just elk tracks but also fresh scat and beds. Elk leave tracks everywhere, but scat and beds are found mostly where they are spending a considerable amount of time. Beds

are usually associated with thick cover, but elk actually bed down during the night to chew their cud in the meadow they are feeding in. Fresh scat will have a moist appearance, and fresh beds will look crisp, with the grass matted down flat. Don't be afraid to use your nose; the more pungent the bed, the less time has elapsed since the animal left it. These signs point to recent activity, making for a good ambush location.

Wallows can be trickier to set up on, because it might only be a single animal that's using it—and he may visit only periodically. But still, wallows are great places to sit during the middle of hot days, when there might not be anything else going on. Quite often a bull will sneak away from his midday bed to have a splash in his favorite mud hole, which might be located at a small seep or along a stream or even at a cattle stock tank. Bulls will literally crawl into the mud and cover themselves with it—it could do any number of things for them, from repelling biting insects to distributing his glandular odor to cooling him off to making him look mean and scary in the presence of other bulls. In the Southwest, some hunters will even pour jugs of water into dried-up and abandoned wallows in hopes of drawing the bull back to his preferred cooling-off spot. While pop-up blinds and blinds built from natural materials are commonly used at wallows, tree stands are another great option because they keep your scent up off the ground.

Speaking of scent, mountain thermals are yet another consideration for the ambush hunter. In steep terrain, the swirling afternoon winds will usually give way to a constant downhill thermal in the evening. Sometimes this happens two hours before dark, and sometimes it happens just twenty minutes before dark. Regardless, an ultracautious hunter might use these thermals as protection when sneaking into an evening ambush location—particularly when hunting elk that are approaching an evening feeding area from an uphill direction.

Thermals are also useful to the still-hunter, whose goal is to spot an elk before he's detected by the animal. The eyes of an elk might let you get away with a fast movement, and its ears will forgive the thud of your boot on a log, but let your scent enter the elk's nostrils and you can bid it farewell. For this reason, a still-hunter has to constantly monitor the wind and do everything in his power to keep it in his face. Despite the challenges, still-hunting works well enough under most circumstances and remains a trusted elk-hunting strategy for many rifle hunters. (Generally, still-hunting does not produce close enough shots for archery hunting. An archer's still-hunt will often morph into a stalking situation when he locates an elk and then moves in for a shot.)

Most hunters who are good at still-hunting insist on going alone, in order to minimize disturbance. If you have the luxury of time, it's best to save your still-hunting efforts until immediately before or after a storm. Elk tend to be on their feet and feeding in preparation for coming weather and again on its heels, and it's typically easier to creep within range of feeding elk than bedded elk. Another benefit of waiting for bad weather is that it leaves fresh snow on the ground, which is a great aid for muffling your footsteps and also for revealing the whereabouts of elk through the presence of fresh tracks. Around these weather events, expansive groves of aspens provide a near perfect medium for the still-hunting elk hunter. These groves hold elk by providing security as well as an abundance of bunch grass (a favorite elk food) whose long blades poke up through the snow. The vertical lines of the aspen forest work well at breaking up your outline, and the aspen's lack of lower limbs (elk eat those, too) allows for clear shooting from a kneeling position.

Still-hunting through bedding areas and along well-used trails through thick timber can be a productive way to hunt, though you should refrain from doing it during the early season because you're likely to spook elk clear of your hunting area. But if the clock is winding down and you're running out of options, it's worth considering. Keeping quiet is not the challenge here, as these trails often look and feel as if someone has recently run a tiller through the soil. But in the dark evergreen timber, it can be very difficult to spot elk—especially bedded elk—before they're jumping out of their beds and storming up the mountainside in retreat. Not only do you need to use your binoculars to pry apart the timber and examine every shadow, but you need to be ready for quick shots as well. And those shots will need to be accurate. Elk are undoubtedly the toughest critters in North America. They can take a punishing bullet or arrow and still run up mountains that you could hardly climb at a slow crawl. But if you do your job right and put your shot where it needs to go, an elk will tip right over or drop within a few steps. At that point, you're free to start planning a year's worth of the finest eating that you'll ever enjoy.

JAVELINA

SCIENTIFIC NAME: *Tayassu tajacu*

A.K.A.: Collared peccary, skunk pigs

Most big game animals have plenty of fanatics. These are guys who devote themselves entirely to the studying and hunting of a particular species, often to the exclusion of all other game animals. Javelina are a notable exception. While there are certainly a handful of hunters out there who regard themselves as javelina geeks, the species does not inspire widespread devotion. Most hunters who live in javelina country regard the animals as something of a novelty species that's unworthy of serious consideration. They say that javelina are small, they are not particularly hard to hunt, they are not particularly great to eat, and they don't have awesome-

looking horns or antlers that you can hang on a wall. But the hunter who turns up his nose at javelina is missing out on one of the most thrilling and unusual hunting opportunities that North America has to offer. Thanks to the poor sensory perception of javelina compared with critters such as deer, it's possible for a careful hunter to literally merge with a group of the animals and get an insider's perspective on herd behavior before selecting a particular animal for harvest. Crawling along just yards away from six or seven javelina is a rush, particularly as you listen to their grunts and snarls and smell the fecund stink of their glands. It's about as up close and personal as you can get as a hunter, and the intensity only grows when you pull out a javelina distress call and blow a few notes. As these critters expose their tusks and come rampaging your way, you'll experience an unusual sensation that you don't often get when hunting such critters as deer or elk: it's called fright.

Javelina are one of three peccaries in the New World. The white-lipped peccary ranges widely from southern Mexico into northern South America. The Chacoan peccary ranges only in the Gran Chaco region of Argentina, Bolivia, and Paraguay.

BARROOM BANTER: In the United States, javelina can only be found in portions of Arizona, New Mexico, and Texas. It seems that the animals are relatively new arrivals to these areas. Prior to A.D. 1700, they are conspicuously absent from the archaeological record in many areas that now have stable populations. At archaeological sites that are newer than A.D. 1700, however, the bones are much more prevalent. While this could be taken as evidence of a change in dietary habits among Southwest Indian tribes, it should be noted that javelina are also absent from older-dating pictographs and petroglyphs, which include depictions of many other species that are not commonly eaten. As a species that experienced a sudden northward extension of its range during the last few hundred years, the javelina is not alone. Raccoons and opossums are two other species that made significant northward movements over the past few hundred years.

PHYSICAL CHARACTERISTICS: Javelina have a strong resemblance to pigs, including a piglike snout, though they are only distant relatives of pigs. (According to scientific understanding, the genetic split between peccaries and pigs occurred some thirty million years ago.) Javelina are grizzled gray or black, with a prominent "collar" of lighter-colored hair that sits like a yoke between their neck and shoulders. Mature javelina typically weigh between 40 and 60 pounds.

DIET: Javelina are classed as omnivores, meaning they will eat both plant and animal matter. While they do occasionally eat bird eggs, grubs, insects, and reptiles, their primary food sources are desert plants. Favorites include prickly pear cactus, mesquite beans, sotol, agave, various tubers, and acorns from scrub oak.

LIFE AND DEATH: Mountain lions, jaguars, and black bears all prey upon javelina. Smaller predators such as coyotes and bobcats generally steer clear of them, perhaps because of the javelina's incredibly sharp tusks and fighting spirit.

BREEDING AND REPRODUCTION: Javelina can and will breed year-round, though most litters are dropped in the summer. Litter sizes vary from two to six offspring, with twins being most common.

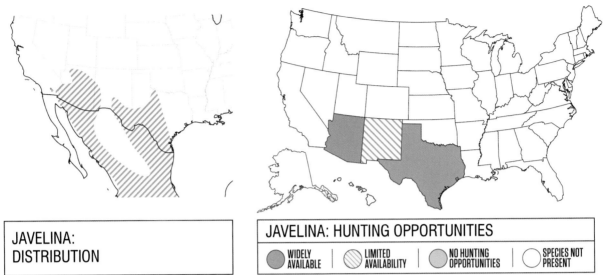

**JAVELINA:
DISTRIBUTION**

JAVELINA: HUNTING OPPORTUNITIES

WIDELY AVAILABLE | LIMITED AVAILABILITY | NO HUNTING OPPORTUNITIES | SPECIES NOT PRESENT

*This map should be used as a general guideline only. Information is subject to change.

HABITAT: Desert country, ranging from rocky desert scrub to desert grassland.

TELLTALE SIGN: Evidence from feeding includes chewed paddles of prickly pear cactus, shredded sotol and agave plants, rooted-up ground, and overturned cow pies. Bedding locations can often be found beneath rocky overhangs or in thick brush that provides shade. Javelina can also be detected by their powerful, musky odor.

EDIBILITY: Probably the least regarded of all North American big game animals. Javelina have a potent scent gland on their lower back; contamination from this gland can give the meat a nasty taste. With careful field care, though, javelina meat is quite passable. It is best used for the kind of slow-cooked and/or heavily seasoned preparations that one might use on an old wild boar. Think chorizo, shredded BBQ, and brined and smoked hams.

HUNTING OPPORTUNITIES: Arizona offers the best opportunity for public-land javelina hunting. Nonresidents and residents alike have to apply for javelina tags, but leftover tags are available every year. There, javelina are hunted in the spring. While West Texas has a great many javelina and readily available tags, it is short on public land.

HUNTING METHODS: In terrain that affords you a vantage point with clear views, spot-and-stalk hunting will provide the most javelina hunting action. When looking for javelina, pay close attention to the weather. Javelina are poorly insulated, as they do not have guard hairs. On cold mornings that are near or below the freezing point, you might not see any movement until well into the morning, as the animals will be huddled up for warmth. When they do emerge, they will likely choose areas that receive direct sunlight. During hot days,

on the other hand, their daylight movements might be restricted to the first and last few minutes of the day. The animals will also avoid the heat by hanging around in the bottoms of deep, shaded canyons, where they can be difficult to locate by a spot-and-stalk hunter who's perched up on a high vantage point.

Javelina are fairly predictable in their patterns. Left undisturbed, a herd of the animals might spend days or weeks within a small area that can be glassed from one position. If you spend all day looking and only catch a glimpse of a distant javelina, don't disregard the sighting as a fluke. There were probably multiple animals with the one you saw, and you will probably find them again if you keep hanging around the area. If necessary, move closer to where you saw the javelina and concentrate your efforts on likely habitats within that zone.

When glassing, keep in mind that javelina are small, dark, and low to the ground. Hillsides covered in prickly pear are great areas to find them, but don't expect to see an animal rising obviously above the cactus palms. Instead, you're looking for a critter that can be difficult to spot when it's holding still. Nine times out of ten, you'll spot a herd because you detected movement. But don't rule out the possibility of seeing javelina that are either bedded or standing still. Take time to examine any strange shapes or dark patches. If a shape can't be ruled out as a potential javelina, watch the area around it for the movement of other animals. Javelina are seldom alone; when six or seven of them are lounging around together, one of them is bound to fidget or scratch or get up to take a piss before too long.

When you find a group, you can go after them pretty hard as long as you stay downwind and don't approach within a couple of hundred yards before switching to stalk mode. Their vision is not great, but don't mistake them for stupid. If you startle them, they will scatter and clear out. Javelina have low sexual dimorphism, which means that the males and females are similar in form. It's difficult for an inexperienced javelina hunter to look at a herd and pick out the males. Since javelina can breed year-round, make sure that your targeted animal does not have offspring. The youngsters will usually stay quite close to their mother, often traveling directly in her wake. For the maximum chance of getting a mature, large-bodied animal, try to compare the body sizes

of the various herd members to get a relative idea about each animal's body size. Pick the biggest one and go for it.

It's hard to do spot-and-stalk hunting in flat desert country with thick vegetation. You just can't see enough ground to make it worthwhile. In these areas, the best option is to slowly cover ground on foot in search of javelina and javelina sign. The animals can be pretty much anywhere, but it's good to concentrate your efforts around canyon bottoms and dry washes where tracks from the animals can be most readily identified. By locating fresh tracks, you can "shrink" the desert down to a few likely areas and then concentrate your efforts in more probable locations. It's especially advantageous if you can hunt after a rain, when all of the old tracks have been washed away. This way, if you hit some very fresh tracks, you can slowly follow the animals and will likely catch up to them as long as they continue to travel on soft surfaces that will reveal tracks.

At all times, pay attention to your nose and ears as much as your eyes. Javelina have a unique odor, and you might just smell them before you see them. They are also quite vocal; on occasion, the location of a herd is betrayed by the sound of grunts and snorts coming up from the bottom of a canyon. It's also possible for a javelina's location to be given away by the sound of its chewing. When three or four of the animals are ripping into prickly pear, it makes a lot of racket. Finally, make sure that your binoculars get a lot of use. Because ja- velina are so difficult to spot in thick scrub, you should be vigilant about dissecting the surrounding cover with your binoculars as you creep along. An alarmed javelina will often freeze in its tracks and watch for the source of a disturbance. If you can identify them before they identify you, you might be able to make a quick shot before they take off. But when shooting in thick cover, make sure to carefully verify your target and ascertain whether or not another javelina is standing behind the one you're aiming at. A bullet can easily pass through one javelina into another, killing both. There is no need to make a hasty shot; if the herd spooks, you should be able to find it again over the next couple of days if you're diligent about looking.

Under the right circumstances, javelina will respond more dramatically to a game call than any other species of big game. Appropriate javelina calls mimic the sound of a distressed and frantically struggling javelina. (An excel- lent javelina call is the J-13 Javelina Call, by Arizona Predator Calls.) Such calls will not bring in javelina from great distances, but they can be extremely effective if blown within 75 yards or so of a herd of javelina. In some re- spects they work almost too well, as many hunters are so dumbfounded by the sight of a charging herd of javelina that they fail to make a shot before the javelina spook and vanish. The most effective use of a javelina call is to locate a herd of javelina and then stalk to within 75 yards of the animals without alerting them to your presence. Then, before blowing the call, you should get your bow or firearm ready for action. Start out with a short burst of frantic calls lasting about five seconds. If the javelina are going to respond, they will likely do so immediately. Sometimes the an- imals will charge right past you while clacking their teeth and whoofing; if you don't get a shot, you might bring them around for a sec- ond pass with continued calling. If you blow your initial call and the herd spooks immedi- ately in the opposite direction, stop calling. They may have been "educated" by a previous hunter using a similar call. If so, let the herd calm down and return to normal before you attempt another stalk. Javelina calls can also be used to turn around a bad situation. If you accidentally stumble into a herd and send the animals clattering off into the brush, a quick sequence of calls might bring herd members who are unsure about the source of the trouble charging back in your direction. There's a very good chance that the call will not work in this situation, but it's worth a try since the animals were already spooked in the first place.

REMOVING JAVELINA SCENT GLANDS

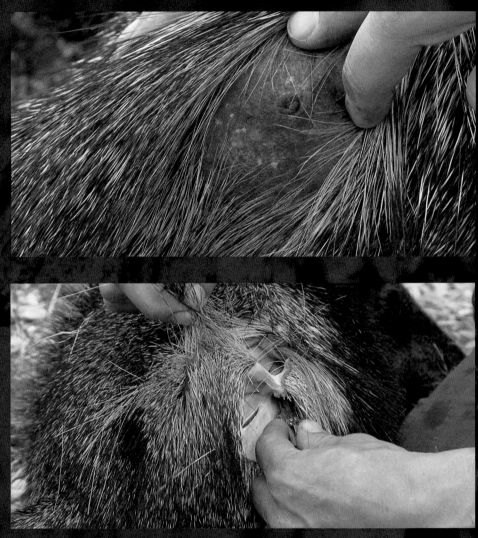

Centered on the lower back of the animal, a javelina's scent gland bears a strange resemblance to a human breast. Musk from the gland can contaminate the taste and smell of the animal's meat, so it should be removed before you begin the butchering process. After cutting a circle around the gland that goes all the way through the hide, you can simply skin the gland away and discard it. Rinse your hands and cutlery before continuing with the butchering process.

MOOSE
SCIENTIFIC NAME: *Alces alces*

Moose are huge and excellent to eat. Once you put a moose on the ground, you've earned yourself a year's worth of wild game meals that are unsurpassed in quality. For many hunters who live in moose country, where the animal is associated with abundance and good living, the fall hunting season is incomplete without putting a moose in the freezer. Moose have fantastic trophy value as well. A big bull moose can carry more pounds of antler than any other antlered game in the world; sets of antlers spreading out to widths of 5 feet are not uncommon. When you hang a set of these antlers over your garage door, you've got a permanent reminder of a difficult task that was undertaken and accomplished. And *difficult* is the perfect word to describe a moose hunt. Traveling in moose country can be extremely tough due to thick vegetation and abundant water. Moose can also be frustrating to find. While their size would suggest an animal that's easy to locate, they are good at vanishing into thicket timber and brush where you can't see more than 20 or 30 yards ahead of you. And because they often like to feed in these same thickets, they can stay hidden for days on end. But the really tough thing about moose hunting is dealing with the animal once it's down. The carcasses are massive and hard to maneuver. Butchering a moose can be a daunting task for the uninitiated, and packing it out can be even worse. Many hunters have suffered sprained joints and torn ligaments from trying to pack moose meat in wet, boggy country. Before heading out on any moose hunt, ask yourself if you and your companions are committed to seeing it through to the end, no matter what. If the answer is yes, you're in for a rewarding adventure.

There is only one species of North American moose, though hunters typically recognize either three or four varieties. The largest is the Alaskan or Yukon variety that occurs in Alaska, the western Yukon, and northwestern British Columbia. The second-largest variety is the Canadian moose, which some divide further into the northwestern and eastern varieties. The northwestern variety occurs across the northern portions of Minnesota, Wisconsin, and Michigan as well as the bulk of Canada, excluding central Ontario and the Maritime Provinces. The eastern moose is found in the northeastern United States as well as the Maritime Provinces westward to central Ontario. The smallest variety is the Shiras moose, which occurs only in the mountain states of the western United States as well as in small portions of southeastern British Columbia and southwestern Alberta.

BARROOM BANTER: While the classic postcard image of a moose shows the animal feeding on marsh plants in knee-deep water, this hardly does justice to the moose's aquatic abilities. A moose can swim for a couple of hours at a constant speed over 6 mph. It's perfectly

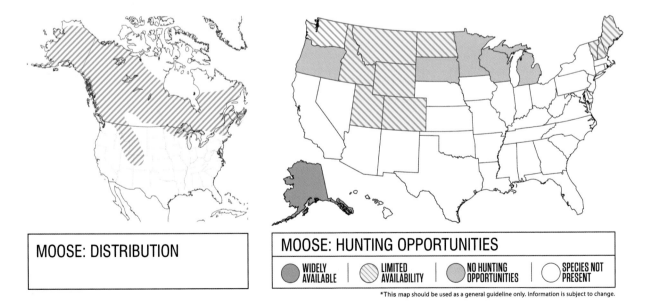

MOOSE: DISTRIBUTION

MOOSE: HUNTING OPPORTUNITIES

WIDELY AVAILABLE | LIMITED AVAILABILITY | NO HUNTING OPPORTUNITIES | SPECIES NOT PRESENT

*This map should be used as a general guideline only. Information is subject to change.

common for them to undertake long-distance swims covering more than 8 miles. A moose can almost completely submerge itself and keep its head underwater for several seconds when retrieving desired plant species in deep water. They will also submerge themselves with nothing but their nostrils exposed in order to escape hordes of biting insects. But don't pigeonhole the moose as a lowland creature. The animals are frequently found feeding on willows in alpine zones far above the timberline and miles away from any significant body of water.

PHYSICAL CHARACTERISTICS: Dark brown hair, humped shoulders, a huge muzzle, and a prominent dewlap under the chin. Legs are long and slender. Moose are the biggest cervids in the world. They are horse-sized, with some specimens standing over 7 feet tall. A big Yukon bull can weigh up to 1,500 pounds. Females, which are antlerless, sometimes tip the scales at over 1,000 pounds.

DIET: Willow is a staple element in the diets of most moose. They will also eat aquatic vegetation as well as the buds, twigs, and bark of a variety of trees and shrubs, including aspen, dogwood, and maple.

LIFE AND DEATH: Wolves are their predator, though black bears and grizzly bears will readily kill calves. It is not uncommon for moose to live up to twenty-five years in the wild. Their primary long-term threats are infectious disease, expanding populations of predators, and higher annual temperature averages.

BREEDING AND REPRODUCTION: Moose typically rut in mid-September, sometimes extending into mid-October. Females drop one or two calves in late May or early June.

HABITAT: Forested areas, including taiga and subalpine zones, with abundant lakes, bogs, and rivers. Access to browse species such as willow, birch, and aspen is key.

TELLTALE SIGN: Along with scat and tracks, look for wide, well-traveled trails along the edges of rivers and lakes or at the borders between heavy timber and forest openings. Also browsed willow and other shrubs, some gnawed down to stubs as thick as a human finger. Moose create large circular wallows in muddy areas that are heavily tracked and reek of urine. Bulls also thrash trees and shrubs with their antlers, leaving behind impressive amounts of destruction.

EDIBILITY: Beeflike and excellent. Suitable for all red meat applications.

HUNTING OPPORTUNITIES: Besides Alaska, all other states harboring moose will require you to submit an application into a tag lottery for the chance to buy a moose tag. In Alaska, some units have over-the-counter tags, while tags for other units are awarded through a lottery draw. Alaska also enforces strict antler size restrictions (see page 250), which mostly limit the harvest to mature bulls. Other states are much more lenient, usually designating either antlered or antlerless animal.

HUNTING METHODS: In the mountainous

country of the Rockies, western Canada, and Alaska, spot-and-stalk hunting is one of the primary methods of taking moose. The best glassing positions are those that overlook large expanses of willow. In the absence of willow, watch younger stands of birch and aspen. Hillsides or brushy draws where the willow is shorter than a moose can often be glassed effectively from a position at the base of a slope. But when it comes to glassing brushy creek beds and large braided river flats, a little elevation is almost mandatory. This way you can peer down into the willows from above and potentially see moose that would be nearly impossible to locate from the animal's own elevation. Hills and knobs are the best glassing platforms, but in the absence of topography you can scale a tree to have a look around. Some hunters even construct glassing platforms with lashed poles in order to get up above the willows. Just 8 or 10 feet of elevation might be all that it takes to start seeing distant animals.

If you glimpse a moose but then lose track of it, keep hunting the area. Unless the moose is spooked, it's unlikely to wander too far. Bulls will typically travel only very short distances each day. They travel very little at night, which means that if you find a bull in the evening, he's likely to be in that same area at dawn. Likewise, if you see fresh sign, chances are the moose is in the area and you'll eventually cross paths with it if you're careful about controlling your odor and keep disturbances to a minimum. During peak rut, bulls are not such reliable homebodies. They will travel several miles per day in search of cows. This makes them less predictable, but it also opens up good opportunities for a spot-and-stalk hunter who's in a prime glassing position. If a lot of moose are up and traveling around, he's likely to see more of them. But still, many successful moose hunters will hunt just one small feeding area that they know from past experience to hold moose. They think nothing of waiting three or four days for the moose to eventually show up.

In many areas, moose harvests are limited to bulls only. If a hunter is hunting for a bull during the rut, he should still pay very close attention to any cows that he finds while glassing. Rather than staying glued to a cow for days on end, a bull is just as likely to drift in and out of her presence. Remember, just because she's not accompanied by a bull in the morning doesn't mean she won't be accompanied by one at night. When you find a cow, always come back around to glass her location a second, third, or even fourth time.

Moose are not difficult to stalk, at least when compared with highly cautious species such as whitetails, elk, and Dall sheep. Once you locate a bull and memorize the details of its location, you can approach rather aggressively as long as you're careful about wind direction. Moose are used to hearing the sounds of snapping brush and breaking twigs, so don't worry if you're making a bit of noise. Just be sure to avoid unnatural sounds, such as metal on metal, as well as rhythmic footsteps that sound nothing like an animal. Moose are notoriously hard to bring down, even with well-placed shots, so make sure to stalk into a position where you can make a quick follow-up shot in the event that your moose keeps his feet after the initial round is fired. You don't want him running off and dying in the water. And remember, wounded moose have been known to charge and trounce hunters.

A lot of moose country is flat, and the best way to still-hunt it is by moving slowly and carefully through likely moose hangouts during the morning and evening hours when moose are most active. Wind is the key element to consider; moose might tolerate some noise and mysterious shapes, but there's a high probability that the smell of a human is going to send them busting away through the brush. If you keep the wind to your face, you might very well approach within easy shooting distance of a moose, even though the animal is looking directly at you. An advantage of still-hunting for moose is that moose country has a lot of moose trails. These are often wide and cleared of leaves and twigs; a hunter wearing clothes of wool or soft fleece can move fairly quietly along a moose trail while he glasses the surrounding terrain for the ears, antlers, or legs of hidden moose.

When still-hunting through head-high willows, take advantage of any land features that let you get up to see over the tops of the surrounding brush. Even something like the overturned root wad of a spruce can give you an advantage. Also pay careful attention to tracks. If you see a fresh track in the snow, or a track that wasn't there the day before, the moose might be very close. Use topographical maps and Google Earth to locate bodies of water in your hunting area. Cows and calves will often hang around water sources, and bulls will come looking for them during the rut. Areas with beaver ponds are another good bet. By using a pair of hip boots or lightweight waders, a still-hunter can move easily through wet, marshy areas that might be avoided by his competition.

Another great way to still-hunt is by paddling or drifting along watercourses in a canoe or raft. As you come around each bend, check ahead for moose feeding or traveling along gravel bars or shorelines. Check topographical maps and Google Earth ahead of time in order to identify willow flats or networks of meadows and beaver ponds within easy walking distance of the water. Beach the boat in order to check these places out. And if you encounter any high bluffs or climbable trees that rise above the river valley, use them in order to glass the areas where you've already been and the areas where you're headed. Remember, it's possible to pass within easy shooting distance of a moose without ever knowing it's there.

One disadvantage of still-hunting is that your moose encounters might be rushed and the animal might be partially obscured by brush. This is especially troublesome in places with legal antler restrictions, where only bulls of a certain size are legal quarry.

GAUGING THE LEGALITY OF MOOSE

In much of Alaska, nonresident hunters are limited to taking bulls that have either a 50-inch antler spread or at least four brow tines on one antler. It's all too common for inexperienced hunters to see midsized bulls and be absolutely blown away by how huge they are. They'll think, "That thing just has to be legal!" Don't make this mistake. All bull moose look big, regardless of whether or not they are legal. It's the hunter's responsibility to carefully assess a moose's legality and not rely on something as fallible as gut instinct.

There are a lot of tricks to gauging antler spread. Some hunters figure that the average moose skull is 10 inches wide above the eyes, so they use that as a way to guess antler spread. Or they figure that the average distance between the tips of a bull's ears is 28 to 30 inches, and they use that as a gauge. Another trick holds that if a broadside moose stops to look at you, it's possible to judge his antler spread based on where his antler tip falls in relation to his shoulder hump. While there is

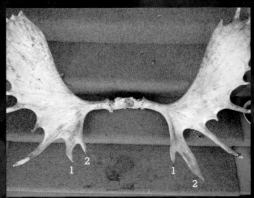

This bull has a 48-inch spread with two brow tines on each antler; it was killed in a hunting unit with no antler restrictions and would *not* be a legal bull in a unit that requires a bull to have a 50-inch spread or four brow tines.

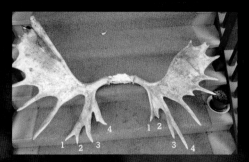

This bull has a 53-inch spread and four brow tines on both the left and right antlers.

This bull has a 46-inch spread and four brow tines on the left antler (three on the right)—legal in areas that require a bull to have a 50-inch spread or four brow tines.

validity to these methods, they should be left to experienced moose hunters who have handled many moose racks and spent many hours observing bull moose in the field. For everyone else, stick to the brow tines. These are easy to count on a bull that's facing you, and making a legal determination doesn't require guesswork. It either has four brow tines or it doesn't. And if you're worried about passing up all kinds of 50-inch bulls that don't happen to have four brow tines, keep in mind that most bulls with a legal spread also have the legal number of brow tines.

Moose are very vocal during the rut, which seems to be an adaptation that helps the animals cope with low population densities. By making a lot of noise before and during the breeding season, bulls and cows are better able to find each other. Moose hunters can use these vocalizations to their benefit, either as a single strategy or as a component to spot-and-stalk or still-hunting. Hunters typically use four calls, alone or in unison, depending on the progress of the rut. Opinions on this subject vary widely, but here's a basic rundown.

During pre-rut conditions, say around early September, bulls are not yet fighting. Instead, many bulls are still bound together in loosely affiliated social groups. Bulls can be called in a couple of ways at this time of year: one is by mimicking the noise of a bull thrashing brush and scraping trees with its antlers, and

Moose are huge animals; butchering and packing the meat of a moose is physically demanding and sometimes downright painful. Be realistic about how much abuse you can take, and never kill a moose that will require more packing than you're able to handle.

the other is by mimicking the nonthreatening *gluck* sound that bulls use to communicate with other moose. Often, a *gluck* will elicit a response from a bull but not draw it in. In that case, you can start easing your way toward the moose from a downwind direction. Since moose antlers are so large and unwieldy, many hunters make thrashing and rubbing noises with a moose scapula or even a gallon-sized plastic milk jug. The sound from these tools is very convincing. *Gluck* sounds can be made without the aid of a call, though most hunters use megaphone-like devices of birch bark or plastic to amplify their sounds.

In mid-September, when the rut begins, bulls start to be adversarial. When you see and hear evidence suggesting they've begun to fight, you can lure bulls with a challenge call that sounds like *mu-whah*. You have to make the sound from deep within your gut, and stack three or four of these calls in a sequence. It's especially effective for bulls that do not yet have cows, as they will be coming to see about the prospect of stealing your cows away from you. Also around this time, and extending throughout the rut, cow calls can be particularly effective. Like other moose calls, most hunters typically make their cow calls naturally, without the aid of reed or diaphragm calls. It's a very nasally *moooooo-ah* sound that plays out over a couple of seconds and begins and ends with a high pitch.

When calling moose, do not expect instantaneous results. Moose are slow, relaxed movers. While some might approach within minutes, others may take a couple of hours or even a day to finally come over to investigate the source of the noise. Be patient and do not overcall. Moose have excellent hearing. If they're out there, they will hear you. And hopefully they will come.

DANNY RINELLA, AN ALASKAN HUNTER, WEIGHS IN ON HUNTING THE HIGH COUNTRY FOR MOOSE

"Set up camp near a hill or knob that gives you good visibility over a huge area, and plan to spend a lot of time up there glassing. In alpine country it's not unusual to spot moose several miles away. Needless to say, good 'nocs and a spotting scope are a must. If you're in an area with other hunters, set your camp at least a couple of miles away. Alpine moose hunting takes place over huge areas—if you don't give other hunters enough space, you'll be competing for the same animals.

"In mountainous terrain, it often becomes apparent that most moose are occupying a specific elevation band. If this is the case, spend some extra effort scrutinizing this band. Other places worth extra scrutiny are willow-lined gullies and creeks, alluvial fans, flat benches, and ponds. Do some calling around your camp after dark, before first light, and sporadically during the day. Thrashing brush, cow calls, and bull grunts all have their place, but don't overdo it. Sometimes bulls respond instantly, but more often they make a mental note and then check out the source of the sound at their own leisure.

"Don't shoot a moose that's in water or likely to wind up there. They're too heavy to drag, so you'll be stuck butchering a floating moose—this is misery for the hunter and bad for the meat. And bear in mind that moving a moose requires about eight man-trips with a very heavy pack. Brush, tussocks, and steep terrain all add to the difficulty. Be realistic about the amount of work involved and come to an up-front agreement with your hunting partners regarding how far you're willing to pack a moose."

MOUNTAIN GOAT
SCIENTIFIC NAME: *Oreamnos americanus*

Mountain goat hunting is arguably the most dangerous form of North American big game hunting. The rugged terrain and the extraordinary climbing abilities of this animal conspire to put you into tough situations where you have to weigh your own safety against your desire to be successful. Almost every year, a mountain goat hunter will die in the high country of the Rockies, Canada, and Alaska. Slip-and-falls kill some; hypothermia and exposure kill others. As any mountain goat hunter will tell you, there is no such thing as an uneventful mountain goat hunt. Goats live in the alpine zone beyond the reach of vehicles, and usually beyond the reach of pack animals. You have to climb to them on foot, usually sleeping on the mountain for multiple nights in conditions that can be wet, cold, and sometimes icy. Under these circumstances, hunting can become a torturous exercise in problem solving. So when planning a mountain goat hunt, make sure to allow adequate time. You don't want to be rushed when you're hunting such dangerous country. Despite all the hardships, or perhaps thanks to them, there remains an undying interest in mountain goat hunting among seasoned backcountry hunters. It is one of the ultimate hunting challenges.

Mountain goats are not actually goats. They belong to a bovid subfamily called Caprinae, which is populated by many horned mountain dwellers. The mountain goat's closest living relatives include the serows and gorals of Asia, as well as the chamois of Eurasia.

BARROOM BANTER: Mountain goats are probably the least understood of all North American big game. For a long time, it was assumed by biologists that mountain goats could withstand harvest rates similar to species such as deer and elk—sometimes as high as 20 to 30 percent. In reality, mountain goats have very low reproductive rates as well as significant mortality rates from predation, starvation, and accidental death from avalanches and rock slides. Typical big game harvest rates can lead to declining populations and even localized extinctions. Thankfully, state game agencies now set their mountain goat harvest goals as low as 3 or 4 percent. This helps ensure a viable resource of mountain goats that will benefit future generations of hunters.

PHYSICAL CHARACTERISTICS: Stocky and heavily shouldered, with stout, muscular legs. Whitish fur, often stained a dirty yellow; it is short in summer and long in winter. Both males and females are armed with small, stiletto-like horns. Males can weigh close to 200 pounds, females up to around 160.

DIET: A wide variety of alpine plants, including grasses, sedges, forbs, lichens, and moss. Also limbs and leaves from low-growing shrubs and conifers at or near the timberline.

LIFE AND DEATH: Mountain goat predators include wolves, wolverines, and golden eagles, though avalanches and rockslides probably kill more mountain goats than all natural predators combined. Mountain goats can live into their teens. Habitat disturbance is the greatest long-term threat to this shy species.

BREEDING AND REPRODUCTION: Mountain goats rut in November and December. Females drop one or two kids, though sometimes three, between mid-May and mid-June.

HABITAT: Precipitous and rocky country at or above the timberline.

TELLTALE SIGN: Besides tracks and scat, look for shed wool collected on shrubs near trails and bedding areas. Bedding areas are often marked by shallow depressions excavated into soft ground on ledges and near the bases of cliffs. These depressions are usually bordered by an abundance of droppings.

EDIBILITY: Excellent-tasting, though older animals can be almost unchewably tough. When dealing with a tough mountain goat, use slow-cook methods such as braising. Goat meat is also well suited for corning, grinding, and sausage making.

HUNTING OPPORTUNITIES: Unless you're a resident of Alaska, British Columbia, the Yukon, or the Northwest Territories, or have an immediate family member in one of those places, you'll have to hire a guide if you want to hunt mountain goats on a regular basis. Most western states do offer mountain goat tags through permit lotteries, but the odds of drawing one are slim. It's best to team up with a bunch of friends and make a deal: if one of you draws a mountain goat tag, you all go along and share the experience, costs, and meat.

HUNTING METHODS: Like most alpine hunting, mountain goat hunting is a spot-and-stalk venture. The goat's habit of hanging around steep cliff faces and along knife-edge ridgelines makes it a fairly easy animal to find once you get into the appropriate terrain. Because of the extreme steepness of goat country, the animals are often glassed from below. Getting up to the highest point of land requires too much effort and entails too many risks.

Thanks to their coloration and the openness of high mountain country, it's possible to spot mountain goats at greater distances than probably any other big game animal. An exception is when mountain goats are at lower elevations at or near the timberline. This is especially common in coastal British Columbia and southeast Alaska, where goats inhabit lower elevations than they do on inland mountain ranges, and also during late-season hunts elsewhere, as winterlike conditions in the high country push goats downward toward shelter and less snow. But even goats that are bedding in timber will still keep steep cliffs to their back as escape cover. During morning and evening hours, they will move up to the cliff faces, or out to open bowls, basins, and timber-free ledges where they can find their preferred foods. If you're hunting goats in such a situa-

MOUNTAIN GOAT:
DISTRIBUTION

MOUNTAIN GOAT: HUNTING OPPORTUNITIES

WIDELY AVAILABLE | LIMITED AVAILABILITY | NO HUNTING OPPORTUNITIES | SPECIES NOT PRESENT

*This map should be used as a general guideline only. Information is subject to change.

Goat hunting can be a scary business, but the right attitude can help you overcome any hardship. This Alaska hunter killed a large billy while six months pregnant.

tion, make sure that you're glassing during the early and late hours of the day, when otherwise hidden goats are visible.

When mountain goats are up in the alpine zone, above all traces of timber, they may be easy to find, but that doesn't mean you can reach them. Mountain goats can climb to places where no predator besides a golden eagle has even a prayer of touching them. There are many goats out there that simply cannot be hunted thanks to the inaccessibility of where they hang out. It's common for mountain goat hunters to watch a particular goat for a couple of days before the animal moves into a stalkable position—if it ever does. You need to be patient and vigilant when hunting goats in tough country like this. Sometimes your only chance comes when a

goat crosses a ridgeline that separates its bedding and feeding areas, or when it crosses a gulley or wash that bisects an otherwise unclimbable face. If you notice that a goat crosses a piece of vulnerable terrain like this, make note of when it happens. Left undisturbed, mountain goats tend to follow the same patterns from one day to the next. Put yourself in the proper position at the right time the next day, and you have a good chance of getting your goat as it passes through a reachable area.

Of course, not all mountain goats are in such difficult places to reach. Often a mountain goat can be stalked in a fairly straightforward manner. If you're a competent marksman who can handle shots of around 300 yards, goats can be approached from directly below if there's adequate cover to conceal your movements. But since the animals are sensitive to threats coming from below, there's a good chance that they'll spot you before too long. When they do, they'll head for the cliffs if they've been experiencing any hunting pressure. A better bet is to use a gulley that lies off to one side or another of the goat you're after. You can scramble up the bottom of the gulley until you're even with the goat and then move laterally to a point where you can make your shot. If you get into a situation where you can approach from above, the goats might not even think to look up. But if they see you above them, they'll likely panic. They are very shy

A mountain goat hunter should bring along whatever climbing equipment he or she is comfortable using. A rope and carabiners can come in handy for retrieving a downed animal in a difficult spot, or for securing an animal that might go over an edge during the butchering process. During late-season hunts, when conditions get icy, crampons and ice axes can make mountain travel much easier.

about threats from above and will probably make a hasty retreat by moving along the face below you to a safe position. No matter the direction of your approach—uphill, sidehill, from above—keep this in mind: if a mountain goat sees you, he isn't going to forget about you just because you duck behind some boulders. When you vanish from sight, he's going to get nervous about where you went and will probably leave much more quickly than if you stayed out in the open and attempted a slow, direct approach.

Retrieval of the animal is perhaps the number one thing that should be on a mountain goat hunter's mind. You should never shoot at a mountain goat unless you are sure that

[BILLY SIDE]

[BILLY FRONT]

[NANNY SIDE]

[NANNY FRONT]

Horn size and configuration can be used to determine the sex of mature mountain goats, but it is often difficult for novice goat hunters to make the call without having extra information. The animal's urination posture and visible genitalia can also be used to distinguish between billies and nannies. During urination, billies stand up with their hind legs stretched backward and splayed to the side, while nannies squat with their rump close to the ground. The scrotum can be clearly visible on a billy in a short summer coat, and the dark patch of the vulva can be visible on a nanny when her tail is raised.

ADULT BILLY:
1. Larger horn base—usually wider than the eye. 2. Bases are closer together. 3. Horn is heavy throughout its length. 4. Horn has gradual curve.

ADULT NANNY:
1. Wider space between horns. 2. Horn is thin throughout its length. 3. Horn is straighter with most of the curve near the end. 4. Smaller horn base—equal to or smaller than the eye.

you're going to be able to reach the animal's carcass. It isn't enough to plan on the animal dropping right in its tracks, either. Mountain goats can take a hit quite well and will often travel a few steps before tipping over from even a well-placed shot. Those few steps are all that it takes for a goat to reach a precipice and plummet into oblivion. And if a mountain goat does

This mountain goat has thick horn bases wider than its eyes and a narrow gap between its horns, signifying a male. A side view is still needed to inspect the curvature of the horn. A billy's horns will sweep back in a steady, fairly constant curve. A nanny's horns will be straighter toward the base with a sharp curve near the tips.

keep its feet after the initial shot, fire another round immediately. You want to anchor the animal as quickly as possible. Even downed goats are capable of traveling tremendous distances, as their barrel-shaped bodies and short legs seem custom designed for rolling down hills. So you need to account for plenty of after-shot movement, both walking and rolling, when assessing whether a goat is in an appropriate location to shoot.

Finally, goat hunters have an obligation to the species to learn the difference between billies and nannies. Because it's so hard for inexperienced hunters to distinguish between sexes, game managers aren't able to mandate male-only harvests with mountain goats. But if hunters did a better job and limited their harvest to billies, it's fair to say that we would see increases in the number of mountain goat tags available to hunters throughout the range of the species. This isn't to say that there's anything wrong with harvesting female specimens of big game in general; in fact, doing so is often necessary for sound management. Instead, this is something that is specific to mountain goats, which have fairly low fecundity and relatively small population sizes. By killing a billy, you remove just one animal. By killing a nanny, you're removing three or four. If possible, shoot a billy. If it's not possible, you can always apply for another tag in the future.

MULE DEER

SCIENTIFIC NAME: *Odocoileus hemionus*

A.K.A.: Muley.

After its big ears, the second thing most new mule deer hunters notice is the deer's fleeing gate, known as "stotting." Stotting has been described as bounding, hopping, even pogoing. At first it's a funny sight, until you realize that this goofy-looking jump puts a mountain of steep, obstacle-filled terrain between hunter and hunted in a hurry. Luckily for you, after the mule deer reaches relative safety, it will often stop and take a look at its pursuer, sometimes providing a shot opportunity. Just don't expect this behavior from the big bucks of the species; with old age, they commonly adopt a trick used by their whitetail cousins, which is to get clear of trouble in a hurry by heading immediately for escape cover without looking back.

Hunters are often drawn to mule deer hunting because it's a great western experience that can be done on the cheap—at least relative to other western big game. Even novice hunters can expect to see loads of mule deer if they do an adequate job of research before the hunt. And the smaller body size of mule deer means that one hunter can manage packing the carcass out of a backcountry location without needing to enlist pack stock or an army of buddies. And mule deer hunting is action-packed. On an average whitetail hunt, you spend day upon day in suspended animation in a blind or tree stand. But when it comes to mule deer, you can do as much roaming as you'd like.

BARROOM BANTER: The end of the Pleistocene epoch ushered in mass extinctions of large-bodied North American mammals, such as woolly mammoths, short-faced bears, giant ground sloths, and the American camel, but it wasn't all bad news for big game. Around that time, the mule deer began to evolve along the Rocky Mountain Front as a hybridized species created by female whitetail deer from the East being bred by male blacktail deer from the West. Thus, mule deer are one of the "newest" species on the continent—a truly North American creation.

PHYSICAL CHARACTERISTICS: Brownish gray in color, with white rump patch and a small white tail that is tipped black. Large, mulelike ears. Mule deer antlers are bifurcated, meaning they fork as they grow. Mule deer

stand about 3½ to 4½ feet tall at the shoulder. Mature bucks weigh up to 300 pounds; does average around 150.

HABITAT: Mule deer occupy many types of habitats in the western United States, Canada, and Mexico, including grasslands, forests, deserts, and mountainous terrain ranging from foothills to the alpine zone.

TELLTALE SIGN: Rubs, trails, beds.

DIET: Primarily browsers of woody vegetation and forbs, with preferences varying according to location and season. They typically eat relatively little grass, though they are often drawn to crop fields where available.

LIFE AND DEATH: Typical life span of nine to eleven years. The mule deer's top predators are wolves and mountain lions. Bobcats, coyotes, wolverines, black bears, grizzlies, and golden eagles all prey on mule deer as well, usually targeting fawns. Loss of habitat, particularly wintering grounds, and blockage of migratory routes by highways and game fences are the leading long-term threats to mule deer.

BREEDING AND REPRODUCTION: Mule deer mate from late November to mid-December. Birthing occurs in May or June. It is common for does to drop twin fawns.

EDIBILITY: Due to the animal's preference for shrubs, including sage, mule deer meat is often condemned as being sagey or gamy. On the flip side, this flavor can be described as highly aromatic and herbal. Good for any red meat application.

MULE DEER:
DISTRIBUTION

MULE DEER: HUNTING OPPORTUNITIES

⬤ WIDELY
AVAILABLE | ◍ LIMITED
AVAILABILITY | ◉ NO HUNTING
OPPORTUNITIES | ◯ SPECIES NOT
PRESENT

*This map should be used as a general guideline only. Information is subject to change.

HUNTING OPPORTUNITIES: Sixteen western states have made deer seasons. Almost all mule deer tags are distributed through some kind of a lottery that must be applied for. This is especially true for nonresidents. Still, tags are widely available for those who are willing to file their applications on time.

HUNTING METHODS: Spot-and-stalk hunting is one of the most productive and thrilling ways to pursue mule deer. Whether you're spotting from a hard-to-reach mountain peak or a pickup truck parked along a ranch road, plan on treating your binoculars as though they are glued to your face. Mule deer can be hard to pick out from their surroundings, and good optics are an invaluable tool for finding them. In snow-free terrain, you'll often locate mule deer by seeing their whitish rumps. With snow on the ground, you'll find them by looking for their brown bodies. In intermediate conditions, when you've got dry ground intermixed with patches of snow, finding the deer can be extremely difficult. This is when having a well-trained game eye really comes in handy.

Mule deer love brushy hillsides because that is where their preferred foods are found, so focus much of your glassing attention on areas with willows, shrubs, and other browse. Muleys tend to bed not far from a food source, so after a quick scan, make sure to give every hillside a second pass, this time telling your brain to look for only the heads and necks of bedded deer. Without the bright white rump showing, a whole herd of bedded deer can easily disappear in sagebrush no more than 2 feet tall.

As much as mule deer are associated with

Alpine basins like this one are ideal summer habitat for mule deer.

sagebrush habitat, in the early season they are often found up in high-country basins, where they can enjoy cooler temperatures and high-nutrition feed. Most of the high-country hunts are offered early in the season and are reserved for bowhunting. (Rifle opportunities do exist for these hunts, though the best units require a few bonus points in order to draw them.) A typical high-country archery strategy is to use glassing techniques to find the deer in the morning while they are feeding in meadows and on open avalanche slides. Then you watch the deer to see where they're going to bed down in the late morning. Once they've settled in, it's time to plan your stalk and make an attempt.

Bowhunters who insist on approaching from above execute a high percentage of the successful high-country archery stalks. There are several good reasons for this. First off, deer naturally face downhill when they bed. And although they might turn their heads and scan uphill every so often, the majority of the time the deer's heads and eyes are pointed down or across the hill. By starting the stalk above the deer, the hunter is at a huge advantage for this reason alone. Second, high-country basins have a fairly predictable mid- to late morning thermal that causes the wind to move up the hillsides. So after the hunter has watched the deer bed, he typically has a two-to-four-hour window to perform a stalk with the wind in his face. However, clouds and incoming weather will quickly kill a sustained wind direction. If major weather is imminent, it's best to back out and wait for a better scenario.

Since the bedded deer are blind to their backside and can't smell what's above them, they will often bed with a rock, cliff, or clump of vegetation to their backs. This bit of protection can serve to give the hunter a much-needed bit of cover to use while approaching the deer on the final leg of a stalk. Beware, though, because the deer will be highly sensitive to any noise that comes from its blind side. Serious bowhunters will shed their boots on the final portion of an archery stalk and proceed in stocking feet or wearing a pair of soft-soled stalking slippers.

If the morning plan doesn't pan out, you can set up an afternoon ambush near the same food source that the deer was using in the morning. Or you can wait for the next morning in order to make another attempt. Either way, use extreme caution when hunting high-country basins. If you spook deer from these hideouts—especially mature bucks—they are likely to move into entirely new country.

STEVEN REID, A COLORADO HUNTER AND GUIDE, WEIGHS IN ON GLASSING FOR MULE DEER

"Spending time behind your optics can greatly increase your odds of harvesting a buck. There are three main factors that I focus on to maximize my glassing efforts: good vantage points, good optics, and patience.

"Whether I'm hunting sage-covered hills or high alpine basins, I always find a vantage point clear of vegetation, where I can efficiently glass the surrounding landscape. It's simple: the more country you can look over, the more deer you are going to find. Ideally, I like to be on a high ridge glassing across a valley or sage flat to areas where I think I will find deer. Within my hunting area I'll have three or four of these lookouts that I can use to find a decent buck. Once I find a promising buck, I start looking at how I am going to hunt him. The same vantage point that I use to find the deer will also serve as a vantage from which to study the buck's habits as well as the terrain he is using.

"When I'm glassing, I insist on getting set up well before first light. I don't want to miss any deer movement during peak activity. And when I'm glassing a large area, I break it up into smaller sections by using landmarks such as distinct logs or rocks to set the boundaries. This ensures that I take my time and study every square inch of the terrain, and it helps me to avoid spending too much time looking at the same exact patch of ground. As I examine each small section, my glassing movement resembles that of a typewriter. I will scan horizontally across the top of a section, drop down to the next level, and scan horizontally again. I repeat this until I have finished scanning the whole section. When I do spot deer, I switch to my spotting scope to identify the presence of a decent buck. If I am having trouble finding deer with my binoculars, I will use the same methods with my spotting scope. All the while, I keep the weather in mind. If the sun is out, I focus my glassing on the shady pockets of trees, rocks, bushes, et cetera. If it is windy or there is precipitation, I glass the areas where deer can limit their exposure to these elements.

"As for patience, it kills! When picking apart mule deer country, you cannot be in a rush. Sometimes I will glass a particular area all day, constantly reminding myself to take my time. This is a must if I'm going to spot an ear twitching or an antler shining in the sun. I also take a little break now and then to rest my eyes and keep my brain focused on slow, steady glassing.

"In short, finding mule deer comes down to sitting high, glassing with purpose, and exercising patience."

Without a doubt, the greatest time to hunt mule deer is during the rut—or as close to the rut as your particular state allows you to hunt. You might sit on a glassing knob on October 20 and see two bucks, then return on November 20, during the peak rut, and see twenty.

At this time of year, the tactic is fairly straightforward: find the does and wait. Cruising bucks wander between groups of does, so sitting on one group of does two days in a row can produce two or more different bucks. It's smart to glass large expanses of sagebrush at this time of year, especially in areas where the sagebrush is bordered by aspens. These places can become mule deer magnets. And don't limit your hunting times to the standard dawn and dusk routines. During the rut, mule deer tend to stay active until very late into the morning, and they are often up and moving in the early afternoon. If you're looking for a mule deer buck, especially a big one, it's highly advisable to hunt all day long during the rut. And when you find what you're after, don't be afraid to pull off an aggressive stalk. Mule deer, particularly rut-crazed bucks, are not that hard to approach. If you can stay downwind and not get too close to the deer—preferably you will never get closer than 200 yards—you have a strong chance of securing the animal as long as it doesn't wander off.

REMI WARREN, A NEVADA AND MONTANA HUNTER, WEIGHS IN WITH TEN MULE DEER HUNTING TIPS

1. "The key to mule deer hunting is covering ground. Out west we have a saying, 'Let your eyes do the walking.' This does not mean you won't have to put in some footwork, but the most successful mule deer hunters are the ones who know how to glass. When looking for mule deer, I get steady and do an initial scan for the ones that stand out. I am generally looking for white butts. This is the easiest thing for the eye to pick up. After that I look closer, picking the hill apart for anything that looks out of place. This is where I am searching for just a piece of the deer: the lateral shape of the back, an ear, a tine, or the gray of their coat.

2. "Look for magpies. Mule deer and magpies have an interesting relationship. Often you will see magpies landing on mule deer in order to pick ticks and deer lice off them. When hunting tall sagebrush I will focus in on areas where I see a congregation of magpies. They will often sit on the tops of the sage, jump down to pick food from a bedded deer, and then jump back up. I have found a lot of deer that I would have otherwise missed by homing in on these highly visible birds.

3. "Mule deer have extremely acute hearing. Their large ears allow them to pick up sounds that other species of big game would miss. This means that you have to be extra quiet. Unnatural noise is like an air raid siren to mule deer. Wear quiet clothes and refrain from talking above a whisper. If you plan on sneaking into bow range, it is best to stalk in socks or barefoot. Mule deer can pick up even the slightest sound of your foot hitting the ground.

4. "Mule deer live in broken terrain. After spotting one, you have to be able to navigate to the exact place where the deer was. This can be tricky for many people, because as you get closer everything looks different. Before you leave from where you spotted the deer, pick out four unique landmarks and consciously go over them in your head. I also like to pull out my digital camera and take a picture of my view from where I spotted the deer, in order to use it as a reference while I stalk in.

5. "During the rut mule deer can be grunted and even rattled like a whitetail. Although they are less responsive than other deer species, it still works! I have used this trick when visibility is low or the cover is heavy. Another great trick is using a fawn bleat or even a distress call. This one works best on does, but I have had bucks literally come sprinting in to see what was going on.

6. "Just because you blew a stalk does not mean the game is over. Veteran mule deer hunters are always ready to give a fleeing buck a loud whistle or grunt. This often piques their curiosity and gets them to stop just long enough for a shot.

7. "Before you squeeze the trigger or release an arrow, try to anticipate if the deer is going to move. If so, wait. Mule deer often flick their tails right before making a movement or taking a step. In open country, where long shots are the norm, a single step can mean the difference between a perfect shot and a miss or a nonlethal wound.

8. "Just because a mule deer sees you does not mean the gig is up. Lie down or hold perfectly still. They might stare you down and burn holes through you, but if you don't move they will often go back to their regular business. One time I had a deer stare me down for well over an hour. I lay there, unmoving, until it finally decided to walk off and bed down. I then gave it some time before stalking in for a shot. That day I killed the biggest buck of my life.

9. "You can fool their eyes, you may fool their ears, but you will never fool a mule deer's nose. The most important factor in planning a mule deer stalk is keeping the wind right. Always be mobile, and never be afraid to put in a little extra effort to keep the wind in your favor. Scent control products rarely work in this type of hunting because you are always hiking and constantly sweating. You need to play the wind, or else stay home!

10. "Mule deer are pocket animals, meaning 80 percent of the deer live on about 10 percent of the land. Find where the deer like to be and focus on those areas."

The curious nature of the mule deer makes them a near-perfect animal for still-hunting. Mule deer are much more likely than white-

What we all hope for: a pause and a look from a four-point buck before he crests the ridge.

tails to pause for a few moments after they've been alerted to your presence. And even when they bolt, there's a good chance that they'll stop before vanishing in order to assess whether or not they're being followed. So even when you feel like you completely blew an opportunity on a still-hunt, it's smart to be prepared for a shot and to quickly move toward an area where you can see in the direction that the deer was headed. Big, mature bucks are generally an exception to this rule, as they have an annoying tendency to vanish almost immediately without ever looking back.

When still-hunting mule deer, focus on

edges between bedding and feeding areas. Mule deer often bed down on the leeward side of any roll in the topography, so keep this in mind as you move across the land. Always ask yourself, "Where is the pocket of terrain that is not affected by the wind right now?" When you find this pocket, be sure to hunt it. More open bedding areas, such as coulees or ridges with sparse coverings of pine and juniper, are also good. The openness of these areas gives you a chance to see deer after you've bumped them from their beds. When hunting coulees, walk the upwind side and watch for deer that have smelled you and are sneaking or bounding away up the opposite side. The steep wall of a coulee might slow the deer down enough to make a shot. If not, try whistling or blowing a fawn bleat to get the animal to pause. Failing that, watch for that signature mule deer look-back as he crests the next ridge and pauses before vanishing.

Typical mule deer ambush locations are food patches, travel routes leading to food patches, and, in dry climates, water sources. If you find a patch of mule deer food that's attracting deer, you can set up within rifle range of the location and then wait for the animals to appear. If it's an expansive area, bowhunters should try to position themselves along the approach route to the feeding area in order that they might get within close range of the animals. Since mule deer will often bed quite close to where they feed, wind direction should be monitored when approaching your stand. You don't want to spook the deer before they even get out of their beds. For those hunters with access to western agricultural lands, setting up between crop fields and bedding cover such as creek bottoms and sagebrush hillsides can be very productive. In dry areas, setting stands near watering holes works exceptionally well. Careful scouting will tell you which water sources to focus on; when you find the right one, be patient. It might take a deer several days to return to any given water source.

Calling and driving are two tactics that aren't typically used by mule deer hunters, though there are situations when each strategy might be put to use. Mule deer are not nearly as likely as whitetails to approach the sound of rattling antlers—used to simulate the noise created by fighting bucks—but if you've lost track of a buck while stalking in thick cover, you might just make him show himself by employing this trick. As for drives, the general openness of mule deer country makes it hard to reliably predict their escape routes. But if you have intimate knowledge of how mule deer respond to threats in your particular hunting area, you might have luck posting standers along preferred escape routes and then sending pushers into bedding areas to spook the deer out. More often than not, though, you'll find that the mule deer do not cooperate with your plans as agreeably as whitetails.

BRODY HENDERSON, A COLORADO GUIDE AND HUNTER, WEIGHS IN ON THE IMPORTANCE OF MULE DEER HABITAT

"I'm fortunate to live in the epicenter of the country's best mule deer hunting. Central Colorado has high numbers of my favorite big game animal and has long been known for producing trophy-quality bucks that, despite some misinformed detractors, are very good table fare. Colorado has the perfect blend of productive alpine summer range, large aspen groves, and sage-covered winter range. As a do-it-yourself public land hunter, I believe consistently scoring on a nice mule deer buck depends more on your ability to find productive habitat than on any other factor.

"The mule deer's predictable annual migration is my key to finding large bucks. Summer finds them in alpine high country, where food is plentiful. During fall, as snow begins piling up, does lead their fawns downhill through transitional habitat to find more accessible food sources, ultimately reaching flatter sage-covered wintering areas. Mature bucks take the same downward path as the does, driven along by their breeding urge. These bucks generally lag behind the does and young bucks by a matter of days or weeks. At the time of year when I like to hunt (Colorado's third rifle season, in early November), I target these bucks by anticipating where they'll ultimately be headed and then trying to find them along their migration corridors.

"Because I don't use four-wheelers or horses and I don't have access to private ranches, I work hard to hunt areas that are underutilized by other hunters. Most publicly owned BLM or national forest land is easily identified on a map, so I look for parcels without roads that have impediments to reaching them. Many hunters drive past plenty of sweet country that they never hunt because it demands a long trek around private land or perhaps a short wade or paddle across a river. Once I'm in some country that I know will hold deer, finding them just requires a little time. At first, locating a solitary big buck may seem daunting, since mule deer move a lot throughout the fall and their preferred hangouts are constantly changing. For this reason, I don't spend a lot of time scouting much more than a week prior to my mule deer hunt. It simply doesn't do a hunter much good to pinpoint a buck three weeks before the season when he'll be in a completely different location on opening day. Due to changing food sources or heavy snow, deer may move down to a completely different habitat during the season. It can happen fast—overnight in some cases—and a smart hunter needs to react accordingly.

"In general, a good hunting strategy is to start higher than you expect to find deer and then work your way downhill until you begin to see a few does; the bucks will be nearby. I usually start the season by glassing south-facing aspen slopes but each year may find me eventually concentrating on a different habitat type that the deer are traveling through. For me, it's helpful to think of my hunting area as having zones. The lowest zone consists of the sagebrush flats where deer spend the severest part of the winter. Above that you have the travel corridors, transitional oak brush, aspen, timber, and alpine zones.

"One of my favorite types of terrain for late fall hunting are transitional zones found between the sagebrush wintering grounds and higher-elevation aspen groves. I seek out open feeding areas adjacent to thick bedding spots where shade lingers and deer stay on their feet later in the morning. Mule deer seem to gravitate toward shade. Once I'm dialed in and seeing good numbers of deer, I give an area plenty of time even if a mature buck hasn't appeared yet. If I find a lot of does and young bucks in a particular zone, I'll look a little bit higher up for larger bucks, dissecting the terrain carefully with optics. From there, it may simply be a matter of waiting for a big buck to move in; better yet, he might already be there. Last season, I glassed a group of ten does off and on all morning before I spotted a large buck that had been with them the whole time. I quickly planned my stalk based on wind direction and terrain, closed to within reasonable shooting range, and took my largest mule deer buck ever.

"For someone hunting mule deer during the early fall in Wyoming or midfall in Montana, the situation might be completely different. However, the seasonal migrations of mule deer are pretty similar throughout their range, so mule deer bucks become easier to find if hunters understand the different habitat types in their hunting area and apply that knowledge to the time of year the hunt will take place. Speaking of mule deer habitat, people who love to hunt mule deer should understand that we are losing that habitat at an astonishing pace. The loss of wintering range in particular is probably the biggest single problem facing mule deer in the Rocky Mountains. We are losing sagebrush terrain thanks to fire suppression (this allows the encroachment of pinyon and juniper into sagebrush habitat), and we are losing it to energy, residential, and commercial development. To help mule deer and other western wildlife, hunters need to become involved. For example, throughout the West, there are plenty of volunteer opportunities for hunters looking to join a habitat improvement project that will result in better mule hunting for everyone. If we put a little effort into supporting conservation groups like the Mule Deer Foundation, big ol' mule deer bucks can continue to challenge hunters throughout their range."

This Colorado hunter found a pre-rut buck in the bottom of a valley. The deer were seeking shelter from a blizzard.

Everything a mule deer needs: lots of sagebrush, a smattering of grasses and aspens, and plenty of rolling terrain broken by draws and coulees.

In this area, there is a vast amount of bedding cover among the ponderosa pines. Below the pines, mule deer will feed among the sagebrush patches.

WILD PIGS

SCIENTIFIC NAME: *Sus scrofa.* A.K.A.: wild hogs, wild boars, feral hogs, feral pigs, Eurasian wild boars, Eurasian wild hogs

There are two competing narratives about wild pigs in America. The first is from landowners who are quick to cite the growing abundance of wild pigs that are wreaking havoc on their property by causing extensive crop and landscaping damage. The second is from would-be hog hunters who can't seem to get hunting permission. When they inquire with a supposedly plagued landowner, they either get turned down outright or are asked to pay a big chunk of change for trespass permission. It's unfortunate, and it doesn't make absolute sense, but it's reality. Many farmers and ranchers are having legitimate wild pig problems, but they are also having legitimate money problems. If they can turn a nuisance into a dollar, they're not going to pass up the opportunity. Therefore, aspiring hog hunters with a limited budget need to forget the whole nuisance thing and approach permissions the same way that deer and turkey hunters have always done. Start out by working your immediate family and social connections as well as the connections of friends and coworkers. Failing that, you can offer to swap a weekend's worth of labor to a landowner for a weekend's worth of hunting privileges. The other option is to hit public land. Yes, it's extremely challenging. Hogs on public land are heavily pressured, no matter the location. They often feed exclusively at night and then bed down through daylight hours. While the private land hunter in Texas is shooting pigs from a weather-protected blind near a timer-controlled corn feeder, the public land hunter in North Carolina or California is trying to get the drop on a bedded pig by crawling silently through nearly impenetrable brush with the breeze to his nose. While the former hunter might have the advantage, the latter hunter gets to know that he took on a tough task and gave it his all. A dead pig is just icing on the cake.

BARROOM BANTER: There are eight species of pig worldwide; none is native to North or South America. The pigs that we have in the United States, whether classified as domestic, feral, or wild, all belong to the same species, *Sus scrofa*. This pig's native range extended across much of Europe, Asia, and North Africa, with island populations from Corsica and the British Isles to Japan and Sumatra. Domesticated strains of pigs were derived from this wild species on multiple occasions over thousands of years in Europe, Asia, and the Middle East, though the original wild population continues to thrive in many parts of the species's native range. (Conversely, the wild foundation species of the domestic cow, the aurochs, went extinct in A.D. 1627.) Domesticated strains of *Sus scrofa* were introduced to the United States as early as the 1500s, and many of these escaped to become feral. In the late 1800s and early 1900s, wild strains of *Sus scrofa* from the forests of Germany and Russia were introduced in New Hampshire, North Carolina, California, and perhaps elsewhere. While we still have scattered populations of these genetically pure ancestral hogs in the United States, most American wild pigs are either wild/domestic hybrids or descended from purely domestic stock. When the numbers are totaled up, we've got about eight million wild pigs spread out over thirty-five states. Both of those numbers will continue to rise in the coming decades.

PHYSICAL CHARACTERISTICS: Feral domestics have a strong resemblance to typical barnyard pigs and vary widely in color. Eurasian wild pigs are distinguished from feral domestics by a combination of attributes, including black hair, a longer snout, a straighter tail, a raised mane of bristly hair, and more prominent tusks. Large male wild pigs can weigh over 400 pounds, females over 300 pounds.

DIET: Highly opportunistic omnivores. Favorites include hard mast such as acorns and hickory nuts, tubers, roots, fruit, and bird eggs. Will also eat worms, snakes, frogs, grasses, insects, young rabbits, tree bark, various rodents, carrion, manure, and newborn livestock.

LIFE AND DEATH: Bears, coyotes, and bobcats will kill young wild pigs; older animals are generally safe from predation. They can live to be well over twenty years old. Wild pigs have no long-term threats; they are here to stay.

COMMON PHYSICAL CHARACTERISTICS OF WILD PIGS

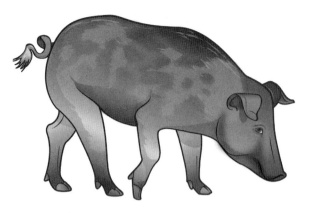

Feral Domestic   **Eurasian Wild Pig**

BREEDING AND REPRODUCTION: Can breed year-round. Litters range from three to twelve.

HABITAT: Highly variable, ranging from forested mountains to coastal swamps.

TELLTALE SIGN: Rooted-up ground, overturned cow pies, and stirred-up leaves and ground cover are all indicative of feeding activities. Also look for wallows in mud, plus rubbed and muddy tree trunks with hair stuck in the bark from the animals scratching themselves. Wild pig trails are narrow and often run straight up and down hillsides, unlike the angled trails of deer.

EDIBILITY: Usually very good, quite similar to domestic pork though much leaner. Older boars, as well as pigs that have been feeding on rotten carrion, can taste quite awful.

HUNTING OPPORTUNITIES: Roughly twenty states offer pig hunting. Acquiring a tag in those states is a fairly straightforward process requiring no special applications. In some states, including Florida, you do not even need a hunting license to hunt wild pigs. Wild pig seasons are long; in many states, they run year-round with no bag limits.

HUNTING METHODS: Spot-and-stalk tactics work great for hogs in the dry, semi-open country of California as well as in many areas of Texas, Hawaii, and elsewhere. Timing is key to spotting pigs. While they will sometimes move in the late morning or even at midday, they do the bulk of their daylight traveling during the first hour of the morning and the last hour of the evening. That's when you're likely to catch them in the open, and you absolutely *have* to be watching from a good vantage point where you're overlooking prime food sources that show recent evidence of hog activity in the forms of fresh tracks and scat. This could be rolling hills of oak, irrigated alfalfa fields, pastures full of wild oats, or even ripening stands of wild guava trees. During dry conditions, when water is limited, another great option is to set up where you can watch multiple water sources or a long stretch of valley bottom.

Once you spot pigs, you need to make a quick assessment about whether or not you should go after them. If the pigs are hundreds of yards off and traveling quickly in the opposite direction, it might be wise to let them go for the time being. It is very difficult to catch up to pigs, as you'll be forced to move at a speed that makes detection likely. As long as you leave them undisturbed, you can try locating those pigs again the next day from a more strategic vantage point. If the pigs are coming toward you or traveling perpendicular to your line of approach, it's good if you can ascertain where they are headed. A fast-traveling pig always has its destination in mind; it's going to be food, water, or bedding cover. By being knowledgeable about your hunting area, you should be able to anticipate which it is and then try to get there first and set up where you have a good command of the surrounding area. But when the animals are moping along slowly or actively feeding, you can do a more direct approach as long as you pay careful attention to the wind. A pig's nose is its primary defense against danger; if it smells you, your stalk is going to be over in a hurry. But as long as the wind is good, you can approach a pig rather aggressively until you get within a hundred or so yards. Don't take that to mean you can just run right at them. You still want to utilize available topography and cover, but it's nothing like stalking antelope or deer.

If you do spook a group of wild pigs at close range while trying to stalk them, don't lose hope. Often there will be some confusion within the group, and certain pigs might scatter while others go just a short way and then hold tight in order to assess the situation. You should try to press ahead quickly and see if you can catch up to them. If the animals go down into a creek bottom or head uphill in the bottom of a draw, try running parallel to the land feature to see if you can pass them and then get them as they come through. It's a long shot, but you might as well try it since you've already blown the situation anyway.

Still-hunting is probably the most exciting way to hunt wild pigs. You're right in there, smelling 'em and hearing 'em, and things can happen very fast. The area you should hunt depends on the time of day. In the early mornings and late evenings, focus your efforts on feeding areas. Work into the wind along active pig trails that course through oaks or any other areas that show recent evidence of rooting and feeding. If you maintain silence and use the wind to your advantage, it's possible to slip within easy bow range of a pig without the animal even knowing you're there. Dark-colored pigs blend in very well with the shadows, so keep your binoculars around your neck and use them often to examine shadows and mysterious shapes. Pigs make a lot of noise, so listen for them. You might hear grunts and squeals, or you might hear them rustling leaves as they root.

During midday periods, focus your efforts on bedding areas. Pigs will consistently use the same bedding areas again and again, though they will have multiple preferred bedding locations and might go weeks or months without visiting one. So again, it is vitally important to identify fresh sign. During hot weather you want to look for dank and thickly vegetated areas, particularly in the vicinity of mud and water. The thick brush along creek bottoms is a good bet, as are the edges of marshes and the middles of palmetto thickets. There will be well-used trails heading into these areas if they are actively used. During cold weather, pigs are more likely to bed on semi-open hillsides where they can soak up some warmth from the sun. Work into the wind when hunting bedding areas. If it's really thick, don't be afraid to get down on your hands and knees in order to peer beneath the vegetation. Look for dark shapes and shadowy blobs tucked up beneath bushes or against tree trunks or curled into shallow wallows. And use your nose. Pigs live in extended family groups called sounders, and they'll bed close together. That much pig flesh packed into a small area is going to let off an unmistakable

odor. It doesn't smell like old pig; it smells like new pig. If you catch a whiff of this, get ready for something to happen. You want to proceed very slowly and scrutinize every shape. While you might get a shot at a bedded pig, it's more likely that you'll get a shot at a pig when it stands up to see what's going on. You will not have a long time to make your shot, but you still need to take careful aim. Big boars can be difficult to bring down. They have a thick hide around their shoulder area known as a shield, and their organ placement is lower and more forward than a deer's. Rifle shots can be placed about a quarter of the way up from the bottom of the pig and just a couple of inches back from the shoulder's rear edge in order to avoid destroying a lot of the shoulder meat. The pig won't go far. Bow shots are trickier. Ideally, you want the pig quartering away from you so that you can send your arrow at a forward angle into the area behind the shoulder. On broadside shots, keep your arrow as close to the rear edge of the shoulder as possible. Quartering or broadside, aim low. A pig's heart and lungs are just a few inches up from the bottom of its brisket. When hunting pigs with dogs and a knife, a 3-inch blade is all that it takes to penetrate the hide and pierce the heart when you stab into the pig's armpit. Shot placement is especially critical because pigs do not bleed well thanks to their thick hide and layers of fat. A mortally wounded pig might leave a faint or even nonexistent blood trail if there's not significant damage to both lungs and/or the heart. Losing them is a very real threat. Remember: aim small, miss small!

Where it's legal, most wild hog hunters who use ambush strategies do so with the help of bait. Wild pigs are suckers for fermented or "soured" corn, and they have a hard time keeping away from it. Still, bait has to be placed in an area that is frequented by pigs or else they are unlikely to find it in a timely fashion. Baits are typically placed in covered holes or containers or in commercially produced feeders that prevent the pigs from getting all the bait at once. A cost-effective method is to take a 5-gallon bucket and drill a dozen ¾-inch holes through the bucket about a third of the way down from the top. Fill the bucket with soured corn and wire the lid in place, then hang it from a limb near a pig trail so that the bucket sits just 5 or 6 inches off the ground. The pigs will quickly figure out how to nudge and tip the bucket in order to spill corn. The slow release will cause them to linger much longer than if you just dump the corn on the ground.

If you're willing to work hard and do some careful scouting, you can ambush pigs from a stand position without having to rely on bait. The key is to identify features that are being actively exploited by pigs, including wallows, feeding areas, water sources, or travel routes leading into bedding areas. (Don't try to set up an ambush too close to a pig's bedding area; if you spook it badly, it's not likely to return anytime soon.) It's best to ambush pigs from a tree stand because you see more of the surrounding country and your odor is up away from the ground. But it's not essential. Pigs have poor eyesight and will easily walk into range if you're wearing muted colors and sitting against a suitable backdrop—so long as the wind is to your advantage. You have to stay downwind of the pig's avenue of approach or you're not going to have much luck. The other important factor is to be in your stand well before daylight in order to catch the early flurry of activity at first light. And make sure to be back in your stand a couple of hours before dark in order to be ready for the evening activity. During the middle of the day, you can do some still-hunting in other areas as long as you're not disturbing the same group of pigs that you're trying to ambush. And if you go a couple of days without seeing any pigs from your stand, you're probably not in the right spot, or you were in the right spot but the pigs have moved to different feeding and bedding areas. Do more scouting and get yourself on to fresh sign. Only then will you bring home the bacon.

Whitetails are America's deer. More than thirty million inhabit the United States, with a total of forty-five states having whitetail deer seasons. Every year American hunters kill approximately six million deer and consume roughly 300 million pounds of venison. Along with deer meat, we devour an encyclopedic amount of literature on the subject. For one human to try and read everything written on whitetails in a single year would be a fool's errand—it's a rich field of inquiry with literally thousands of living experts. A quick Internet search will uncover a dozen or more whitetail-specific magazines, as well as dozens of whitetail TV shows and many other media enterprises that cover the topic of whitetails within a broader hunting context. However, the bulk of these resources focus on information about hunting trophy-sized bucks. The following overview on whitetail hunting is meant to help a prospective whitetail hunter get up and running—and to fill his freezer.

BARROOM BANTER: According to the esteemed biologist Valerius Geist, whitetail deer have been in existence for somewhere around four to six million years. For the greater part of that period, whitetails scraped by, eking out an existence among many specialized herbivores and predators in an area centered around the southeastern United States. Their big break came about ten thousand years ago, when many of North America's giant mammals went extinct. With much less competition and fewer predators, the whitetail flourished. With the disappearance of America's giant herbivores, plant communities became larger, more uniform, and susceptible to wildfire. Wildfires cleaned out mature vegetation, creating vast food sources for the whitetail deer. Just as now, the whitetails of ten thousand years ago were opportunists of the highest degree. They used this dramatic change of the landscape to multiply and expand their range across much of North America.

PHYSICAL CHARACTERISTICS: Reddish brown in summer, grayish brown in winter. Males have antlers with one main beam and unbranched tines. Tail is brown with white underside. At the shoulder, whitetails stand 21–47 inches. Males, or bucks, average 140–300 pounds. Does average 90–180 pounds.

HABITAT: Common to deciduous forests, the whitetail has adapted to the open prairies of the West as well as the semi-arid grasslands of the Southwest. They are equally at home in wilderness, suburbs, and farmlands.

TELLTALE SIGN: Rubs, scrapes, trails, beds.

DIET: The whitetail's ability to adapt extends to its diet. Depending on geographic location and seasonal availability, it consumes many different varieties of grasses, forbs, mast, fruit, fungi, and woody browse materials—basically everything from corn to cactus.

LIFE AND DEATH: Wolves and mountain lions are major whitetail predators, capable of killing even healthy adults. Coyotes, bobcats, black bears, and several other midsized predators will readily kill the fawns and, on occasion, adults as well. The typical life expectancy of a whitetail deer is seven to ten years.

BREEDING AND REPRODUCTION: Breeding activity typically peaks between early and mid-November in northern states; in southern states, it can peak as late as early February. Gestation is about seven months.

EDIBILITY: Flavor varies depending on diet and location, becoming milder and fattier with closer proximity to intensive agriculture. Great for any red meat application.

HUNTING OPPORTUNITIES: Aside from a few states that manage their whitetail bucks for extreme trophy potential, whitetail hunting

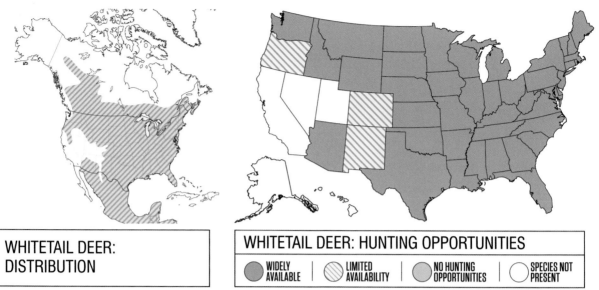

WHITETAIL DEER: DISTRIBUTION

WHITETAIL DEER: HUNTING OPPORTUNITIES

● WIDELY AVAILABLE | ⬚ LIMITED AVAILABILITY | ◯ NO HUNTING OPPORTUNITIES | ◯ SPECIES NOT PRESENT

*This map should be used as a general guideline only. Information is subject to change.

is generally wide open to both residents and nonresidents in the bulk of whitetail states. Tags can be purchased over-the-counter or online for just about all of the available seasons and methods of take. Most states allow the harvest of multiple animals; in some states, you're allowed a deer per day during whitetail seasons that last a month or more.

HUNTING METHODS: Ambush hunting is by far the most common whitetail strategy, with most whitetail hunters preferring to ambush the animals on or near agricultural land. Aside from hunting pressure, the whereabouts of whitetail deer are dictated largely by the locations of their favorite foods,

and whitetails are suckers for crops. True numbers are hard to come by, but even a conservative estimate would be that well over 50 percent of the whitetail deer that are killed every year are killed on active farmland. However, having access to such property does not negate the need to do some serious preseason whitetail scouting as you strive to put together a cohesive picture of how the local deer population happens to be using the habitat where you're hunting. Specifically, you need to know where the deer are feeding, where they are sleeping, and how and when they are moving back and forth between these locations.

CHRIS EBERHART, A MIDWEST HUNTER, WEIGHS IN ON PUBLIC ACCESS WHITETAILS

"Think you need access to private property to have great whitetail hunting? Think again. About half of the mature bucks I have killed in my life have come off public ground. Access to public hunting opportunity is what sets North America apart from the rest of the world. Some of the best whitetail hunting in the United States can be found on public land, and it is closer than you might imagine. Public land whitetail hunting is an opportunity that you just can't miss.

"There are numerous types of land that allow public hunting access. Some property is simply open to the public, like state and federal land. Other potential hunting areas include state game areas, refuges, municipal property, parks, lumber company property, and private land with state-organized access, among others. Some of these require jumping through a few hoops to gain access and you might be limited to a certain period of time or special rules, but the effort is worth it. There are abundant opportunities, and if you look hard enough you will find them. You might be surprised just how much public land is within an hour's drive of your home. The Internet is a great place to start your search.

"It is important to realize that when the land was divided, most of the public tracts were areas poorly suited for farming. This means that public ground is often swamp, marsh, rocky or hilly terrain, or areas that were just plain hard to get to. These kinds of marginal terrain are the exact kind of areas that attract deer, particularly mature bucks. Often deer will feed on surrounding farmland or managed property only to spend their days bedded on public ground. With careful hunting you can capitalize on this movement pattern. Timing your hunting to intercept this movement is an important element to success on regular public land.

"The other critical thing to recognize when you hunt public land is that you won't be alone. Areas that have easy access will have other people hunting there. With that in mind, it is important to be able to recognize both deer activity and people activity.

One of the most overlooked factors in hunting public land is figuring out what the other hunters are doing. Nothing affects deer movement more than hunting pressure. One of the keys to being successful in a situation like this is finding gaps in that pressure. This often means going into areas that other hunters avoid. Sometimes something as simple as donning a pair of waders and crossing a cattail marsh can open up unbelievably good hunting. Using a canoe to cross a lake or a float down a river can also provide good access to great hunting. Even climbing a steep ridge or just walking more than a half mile will sometimes open the door to practically unhunted deer.

"I have spent much of my life bowhunting whitetails on public ground. In my books, *Bowhunting Whitetails the Eberhart Way*, *Whitetail Access*, and *Precision Bowhunting*, I outline the steps I take for regular success in such areas. You can pull deer and mature bucks off public ground year after year, but you must be more precise and take a slightly different approach than the other guys."

Finding the deer's preferred feeding area is more complicated than just looking toward the nearest farm field. The feeding habits of deer are constantly changing throughout the year as they switch from one food source to another. In a typical fall, a deer's favorite food might shift from alfalfa to beechnuts to acorns to apples to dogwood limbs. Keeping up on the changing habits of deer requires flexibility and observation skills. Tomorrow's deer will not necessarily be found in the same place as today's, and you'll need the observation skills

necessary to anticipate the changes in a deer's dietary habits based on clues drawn from the landscape. For example, you might see deer feeding along the fairways of an irrigated golf course all August, but you'll know that the smart choice for an October hunt will be near that stand of oak trees in the neighboring state forest that's been developing a massive crop of acorns. It's impossible to address or anticipate all possible scenarios simply because whitetail deer habitats are so incredibly varied, but hopefully you get the point. Identifying deer feeding areas comes down to observing not only the animals but also their surroundings.

As for whitetail bedding areas, *thickets* is the best single word to describe them. Whitetails, especially those that see substantial hunting pressure, generally like thick vegetation that impedes the eyes and blocks the passage of their predators. Think marsh edges, briar patches, early-succession clear-cuts, young Christmas tree plantations, creek bottoms, windrows, abandoned farmsteads, and fallow fields that have become overgrown with vines and woody vegetation. There are exceptions to this, of course, particularly in hilly country. Here, deer will sometimes bed on finger ridges, which provide them with a wide-angle view of the surrounding country, or they will use hillsides to maximize their exposure to the winter sun during periods of extremely cold weather. In short, deer are likely to spend their days in the kind of cover that you'll sometimes need to get on all fours to pass through. Since bedding areas are much more consistent than feeding areas—that is, deer will continue to bed in the same location while their feeding areas go through constant changes—you need to be very careful not to disturb these locations any more than absolutely necessary. Repeatedly spooking deer from a bedding area might cause them to abandon its use altogether. If you stroll into a brushy swale on a midday walk and kick out a half dozen deer, you should congratulate yourself on a valuable discovery. But you should also promise yourself that you'll never walk through that swale again.

Once you've determined where the local deer are bedding and where they're likely to be feeding during the hunting season, it's time to figure out the travel routes that they're going to be using as they move back and forth. Often this is as simple as finding a deer trail, though deer seldom travel exclusively along one well-defined path. It's more common for them to use what we'll call travel corridors—basically areas that deer are likely to pass through as they move, often while feeding, from one location to another.

Since we're ruling out the ill-advised approach of hunting deer directly in their bedding areas, it's time to decide if you're better off targeting the animals in their feeding areas or along their travel corridors. This decision should be informed by a number of considerations: what sort of weapon you're hunting with, how expansive the feeding area is, and how well defined the travel corridors are. The first consideration—what sort of weapon you're using—will tell you how close you need to get to the deer. With a rifle, you can keep a relatively comfortable distance of 200 yards between you and the deer, a yardage that greatly reduces the chances that you'll spook the animals. In a shotgun-only zone, you'll want to at least halve that distance even if you consider yourself to be a good marksman. Same with a muzzle loader. And with a bow, you'll want to trim that distance down to 30 yards or so.

Once you know how close you need to get, you can weigh the pros and cons of hunting the feeding areas or the travel corridors. There is no fast and easy way to make this determination. First, imagine that you're hunting with a rifle and you've identified a cut cornfield measuring 300 yards across that is being used heavily by deer. There are at least three good travel corridors approaching this field from multiple directions. In this situation, the smartest move is to set up an elevated blind where you can observe the entire cornfield, knowing that you can reach any deer that materializes at the terminus of every travel corridor with a well-placed shot.

Now we'll imagine the same scenario except that you're hunting with archery equipment. If your maximum effective shooting distance is 40 yards, then there's little point in trying to cover the entire cornfield from your ambush location. Instead, you need to do some careful scouting to determine which of those three travel corridors is being used most heavily. And once that's done, you need to identify the best point along that corridor where you can expect deer to pass within range of a plausible ambush location. In the case of single game trails this is fairly easy, but in wider corridors you need to search out pinch points or funnels that serve to constrict deer traffic down to precise locations. Examples might include an old

beaver dam that deer are using to cross a stream, a skinny strip of brush connecting two larger patches of timber, a chunk of dry land between two flooded swamps, and a convergence of two or three deer trails. While searching for funnels, keep in mind that whitetails have a relatively small home range. Their bedding and feeding are often separated by very short distances or might even bleed into one another. Be careful that your chosen ambush point isn't crowding the bedding area, because this might cause you to spook deer as you get into position to hunt.

Now for another scenario, this time a large pair of parallel ridges covered in white oaks that have been dripping with ripe acorns for two weeks. The ridges are hundreds of yards long, and there's a lush understory of vegetation that prevents you from seeing more than a hundred or so yards in any given direction. Running between these ridges is a small stream that flows into a swampy wetland, and this wetland is traditionally where the deer like to bed. There's a bunch of game trails leading out of the swamp and running along either side of the stream, and these trails become more and more diffuse as they get away from the swamp—presumably because deer are peeling away from the trails in order to ascend the ridges and feed on the acorns. Since it's impossible to cover the entirety of these two ridgetop feeding areas, even with a rifle, both the bowhunter and the rifle hunter are going to focus their attention on the trails that exit the swamp and follow the creek. The difference between their strategies is that the rifle hunter would be wise to find a location where he can get a little bit of elevation on one of the hills and then overlook the entire creekbed, preferably in a place where the bottom is wide enough and open enough to allow for multiple shooting opportunities at an animal that is traveling through. The bowhunter, on the other hand, will need to get down into that creekbed and select an appropriate pinch point or funnel where a number of the deer trails converge. He'll be much more likely to spook deer, and it's certainly possible that deer will pass beyond his range, but it's the surest approach to capitalizing on a temporary food source that's drawing an abundance of deer.

They ought to put a whitetail deer next to the word *skittish* in the dictionary. These animals tend to run first and then wonder later about what spooked them. The challenge for a whitetail ambush hunter is to stay in your stand for extended periods of time while limiting any effects that your presence might have on approaching animals. One Wisconsin hunter describes what it's like to ambush whitetails by saying, "You even gotta move your eyeballs slowly."

The best way to avoid a whitetail's acute sensory perception is to use an elevated platform such as a tree stand or freestanding ladder stand. This does a few things for you:

(1) it helps keep you above a deer's field of view; (2) it helps keep your odor up higher, where it might be taken away on the wind rather than pooling around you; and (3) it gives you a more commanding view of your surroundings. But don't make the mistake of thinking that a tree stand will allow you to get sloppy. You still need to stay mindful of wind direction and camouflage when using a tree stand—just not as mindful as you need to be when using a ground blind.

When hunting from the ground, either because you can't legally hunt from an elevated platform or because the landscape isn't conducive to elevated platforms, it's vital that you take serious precautions to mitigate your sound, sight, and odor. This is especially true when hunting with a bow or muzzle loader, where you need to get nice and close to the animal in order to make a clean kill. You can construct serviceable ground blinds using native materials located around your hunting area, but it's hard to beat the manufactured tentlike structures known as pop-up blinds. Pop-ups offer unmatched visual coverage and can also help to deaden noises and prevent scent dispersal. They are a bit clumsy to transport into the field, but once they're on location you can easily move them around to adjust for changing circumstances such as wind direction and the preferred travel routes of your quarry. They are also quite helpful in protecting you from foul weather, which enables you to stay in the woods longer and therefore see more deer.

The best time to hunt whitetails is whenever you can get into the woods. With that said, there are a couple of occasions when it's an extra-good idea to be in your stand. The first is on opening day of the firearm season. In most states, opening day accounts for 50 percent or more of the entire annual whitetail harvest. Until daybreak on opening morning, deer are usually going about their typical business in a fairly predictable fashion. They haven't yet adjusted their routines to account for hunter pressure, so you've got the element of surprise on your side. Usually within minutes of the arrival of legal shooting hours, the deer will know that something is seriously amiss and they will begin moving in seemingly erratic patterns as they get bumped from one hunter to the next. This usually goes on for hours, often enabling hunters to see more deer by noon than they'll see in the entire remainder of the hunting season. Once the initial flurry of opening-day activity is over (this usually happens around 10:00 a.m. or so), don't succumb to the temptation to head back to your car or truck. Instead, you should remain in your blind and allow less-disciplined hunters to spook more deer past your stand as they leave their own ambush locations and begin bumbling through the woods. Inevitably, the midmorning silence on opening day is broken by a few shots fired from hunters who had the

wherewithal to stick it out and capitalize on the laziness of other hunters.

If you don't manage to kill a deer on opening day, don't lose faith. The majority of America's whitetail hunters spend only two days in the field. Within a week of the opener, the woods have usually quieted down enough for the deer to come out of the temporary state of odd behavior that begins with the onslaught of opening day. Once they've started to return to their normal routines, you can begin the serious—and much more rewarding—task of hunting deer that are actually behaving like deer.

The rut is the other time when it's extremely productive to be in the whitetail woods. This is when the ultracagy, sometimes nocturnal, always elusive whitetail bucks abandon their inhibitions in order to breed females. Hunters often describe the rut as occurring in three stages: pre-rut, peak rut, and post-rut. While no two serious hunters will agree on what exactly these terms mean and when exactly they happen, here's a general guideline.

Pre-rut is the period when the bucks start to establish their hierarchies and begin showing a bit of enhanced interest in the local population of does. However, their feeding and bedding activities are generally normal during pre-rut, so don't make any drastic moves in terms of stand location. And be prepared for some quiet days. In fact, many hunters call this period the "October lull." (Pre-rut can begin as late as December in the southern United States.)

Eventually, pre-rut gives way to something called peak rut, which is an approximately one-to-two-week period when the bulk of the female deer come into estrus. This usually results in massive amounts of deer activity, with bucks on the move all day as they defend their territories from other bucks and harass pretty much every doe they can find. At this time of year (early to mid-November in the North, as late as late January in the South) bucks will abandon all caution and behave in ways that might strike a person as outright stupid. Now's the time when you want to be in the woods, no matter what! Also consider moving your ambush position away from food sources and toward travel corridors in order to capitalize on the increased wanderlust and decreased appetites of the local bucks. And if you see a doe in your area that is displaying submissive postures, urinating frequently, or being hounded by bucks, pay attention. If she's in estrus, her scent could attract bucks from a mile or more away.

The post-rut period is just what it sounds like. As does cease coming into estrus, the rut winds down and comes to an end. Bucks begin the process of rehabilitating themselves after a period of self-neglect that has left them famished, exhausted, and sometimes hurting from minor injuries sustained in fights with other bucks. Post-rut is when bucks like to do a lot of resting, often hidden and alone, which can make for tough hunting. Now's the time to focus your efforts on good feeding areas.

Hunters who are interested in calling whitetail deer will have their best luck during the various phases of the rut. Pre-rut is a great time to try antler rattling, which mimics the sounds of sparring or fighting bucks. This is best done in places where deer are likely to congregate anyway, such as feeding areas, because you will often draw in deer that seem only passively curious about what's going on—they're not yet ready to be in a fight themselves, but they enjoy watching others go at it. Many products are made to imitate this sound. Rattle bags and "pack racks" do the job and are easier to carry than real antlers, but most diehards choose to carry a real set, as they are thought to have a more realistic sound. Some guys even soak their year-old rattling antlers in a five-gallon bucket of water prior to the season to give them that "alive" sound. Try short, minute-long bursts of clacking antlers at ten- or fifteen-minute intervals. Be prepared at all times, as bucks can come out of nowhere and show up fast. But don't just wait for the hard-charging monsters. Bucks of all sizes will sometimes skirt your position as they try to sneak a peek at the action.

During peak rut, when the woods have really heated up with breeding activity, you can try many different kinds of deer calls. Antler rattling will still work, sometimes very effectively.

Grunt calls also work well. Most often, bucks will grunt when trailing a doe—this is known as a tending grunt, and sounds a lot like a burp—and nearby bucks might respond to the noise in hopes of displacing their rival and snatching up the doe. Mimic these sounds with a commercially produced grunt tube. There are literally dozens of commercially made grunt tubes on the market today. Try several in order to find one that works for you, and then stick with it. Other commercially produced calls mimic what's known as a "snort-wheeze," which is a threatening noise that a dominant buck makes when agitated by other bucks who are invading his space. This type of call will bring in other bucks who are trying to either assert their dominance or relieve their curiosity. Finally, many hunters call in rutting bucks by mimicking the bleating sounds of does and fawns. Such sounds are made with manufactured internal reed calls as well as bleat cans that are operated simply by flipping the can end-for-end in your hand. These calls can also be used quite effectively to stop a rut-crazed buck that is walking too fast for a clean shot. But be sure to have your bow or gun ready before you try it, as the deer will likely look right in your direction when you make the noise. If it sees you, it's likely to bolt.

Some whitetail hunters combine calling and still-hunting strategies; they rattle or call in one place, then wait ten or fifteen minutes before moving on to their next calling location. Other still-hunters rely on absolute silence in order to walk up on whitetails that are unaware of their presence. This is best done when the forest floor is damp from rain or wet snow, which greatly diminishes the sound of crinkling leaves. Besides maintaining silence, the biggest challenge to the still-hunter is spotting deer before they've spotted you. With their gray-brown coat, whitetails have an uncanny ability to blend into a variety of backgrounds ranging from deciduous trees to evergreen forests to desert scrub. When still-hunting whitetails, go excruciatingly slowly and use your binoculars to dissect your surroundings. Look for parts rather than the whole. You're far more likely to see an ear, nose, or antler than an entire deer.

Finally, drive hunting can be an incredibly effective (and very fun) way to hunt whitetails if you've got a few buddies who don't mind hunting together as a team. This method is covered fully in the Tactics and Strategies section (page 141), though you should remind yourself that establishing a productive whitetail drive might require a couple of years' worth of trial and error as you learn the best routes and positions to be used by drivers and standers. But once you figure out a couple of different whitetail drives, you're sitting on gold. As long as the habitat stays the same, a good whitetail drive can produce venison on a yearly basis for decades or more.

DOUG DUREN, A HUNTER FROM WISCONSIN'S DRIFTLESS AREA, WEIGHS IN ON HIS FAVORITE WHITETAIL HUNTING METHOD

"'Mooching' is a term that my friends and family use to describe a form of deer hunting that combines the best of three different deer hunting techniques: stand hunting, deer drives, and still-hunting. The basic idea of a mooch is to take advantage of the terrain, wind direction, and deer travel routes to gently bump—rather than forcibly drive—deer in the direction of your fellow hunters.

"Mooching works best if you have a few hundred acres of hunting ground with varied terrain. The Driftless Area of southwest Wisconsin, with its mixture of hills, woods, bottomland, and farmland, is the perfect area for mooching, but the tactic can be used in many other parts of the country as well.

"A 'mooch day' begins with a plan drawn up while consulting maps and a weather forecast with detailed information about wind direction. Hunters then head out before dawn to established ambush stands that offer good vantage points on multiple deer travel corridors. After a couple of hours of being on stand in classic ambush fashion, one hunter will leave his stand and begin still-hunting. (Wisconsin allows hunters to use electronic devices for communicating, so we coordinate all activities with handheld radios.) As he moves along, the still-hunter is mindful of the wind direction, and he travels in such a way that his odor will blow into likely bedding areas and thereby bump deer in the direction of the hunters who are still waiting at their ambush locations. Meanwhile, the still-hunter may get an opportunity for a shot at a standing deer, or a deer that's trying to slip away unseen through the brush. Eventually, the still-hunter reaches another good vantage point where he can stop and take up an ambush position. He uses his radio to let everyone know that he's completed his mooch and he's ready for the next one to begin. Then the next hunter lets everyone know that he is on the mooch and he begins his predetermined still-hunting route toward the next stand.

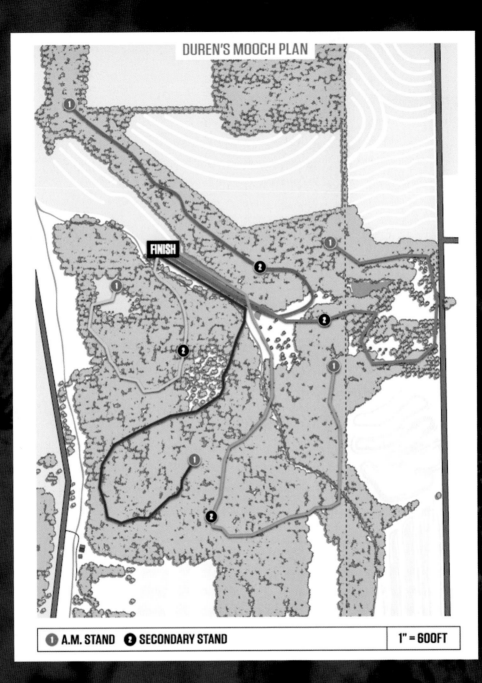

DUREN'S MOOCH PLAN

FINISH

❶ A.M. STAND ❷ SECONDARY STAND

1" = 600FT

"A mooch hunt can go on all day if it's well planned and executed. We conduct mooches with as few as two hunters and as many as twelve, depending on how much area we're trying to hunt. What's important is that the moocher acts like a still-hunter and not like a driver doing a traditional deer drive. Deer tend to just slowly move away from a skilled still-hunter and usually don't leave the area entirely. Rather than deer that are running full-tilt, the hunters on stand get to see deer that are moving at a slow pace and often stopping to look back over their shoulders toward the area they were bumped from. This allows for cleaner standing or walking shots rather than the running shots that are typical of a deer drive. Mooching allows all hunters an equal chance of getting a deer, because everyone gets an equal chance to be a stander in a prime position. And the still-hunters get plenty of action as well. I've had deer that I bumped turn and come back in my direction after a shot was fired.

"In one instance, I bumped two bucks and then moved several hundred yards by the time those deer finally made it to my friend Mike. He shot one of the bucks, and the other one snuck off toward an escape route that was back in my direction. Knowing that at least one of the bucks was still alive, I crept to a location overlooking that escape route and got ready. The five-year-old buck trotted down a hillside and was walking through a thick bottom, quartering into the wind, when he tried to sneak through just 40 yards away. He never knew I was there, and I dropped him right in his tracks."

THE GRAY GHOST

Named after Dr. Elliot Coues, a surgeon and renowned naturalist, the Coues deer is a desert-dwelling subspecies of the whitetail deer that ranges from the mountains of northern Mexico up into Arizona and portions of New Mexico. Coues deer are small, with bucks averaging only around 100 pounds, and they are highly elusive. They evade their many predators by hiding in oftentimes thick brush and rarely venturing outside of their narrowly defined home ranges. The main challenge to hunting Coues deer is finding one. But even then, they have an incredible knack for disappearing into thin air. Any hunter who chooses to chase these shy deer will understand why they are commonly referred to as "gray ghosts."

Arizona has the bulk of the Coues deer hunting opportunities in the United States. Although all Coues tags must be applied for through Arizona's annual lottery, leftover tags are usually available in the more remote parts of the state, particularly near the Mexican border. The southwest corner of New Mexico also harbors Coues deer, though not as many as Arizona. By far the greatest populations of these deer can be found south of the border in Mexico. There, with the help of an outfitter, you can experience a Coues hunt without the hassle of tag applications. And because you'll be hunting private land in Mexico, hunting pressure is virtually nonexistent.

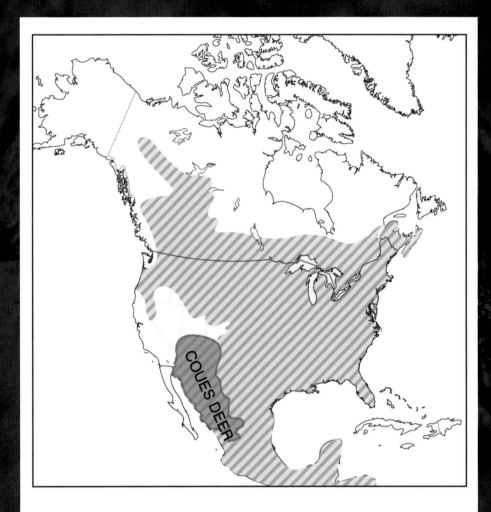

COUES DEER: DISTRIBUTION

BUTCHERING

BIG GAME: IN THE FIELD

The work of hunting does not end with a kill. In some respects, it's only just begun. You owe it to the animal, and to yourself, to make sure that the carcass is handled as carefully as possible to ensure quality meat.

Regardless of whether the animal will be skinned and processed in the field or at home, it needs to be gutted immediately.

GUTTING

Big game should be gutted as soon as possible, preferably within an hour of the animal's death. All big game animals are gutted in essentially the same way, though there are obvious differences in the matter of scale. The sequence of the following steps is not entirely rigid, and there are many shortcuts that can speed the process along. The following step-by-step procedure is meant to give you a full understanding of the work involved. Once you gain some proficiency, you will develop your own favorite way of going about it.

A TIP FOR HANDLING LARGE ANIMALS

When handling large animals or working on uneven terrain, you can use lengths of cord to rig the animal into whatever position you want. Here, an elk hunter in Kentucky uses a piece of paracord to keep a bull's back leg out of the way during the skinning job.

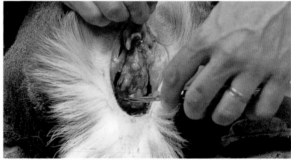

1. Start by positioning the animal on its back, with the spine as straight as possible and the legs pointing toward the sky.

2. Cut through the skin around the animal's anus, leaving the anus connected only to the colon. Use the tip of your knife to free the con- nective tissues that hold the animal's colon in place. Get in there as far as possible. The colon should be lying inside the pelvis like the end of a hose, totally freed up.

3. Starting at the top of the anus incision, slice upward through the hide to a point just past

the animal's pelvis. Do *not* cut through the abdominal wall. Slice down through the muscle until you hit the pelvic bone. On males, cut down on each side of the pelvic ridge. On females, you can make just one slice down to the bone. Note: If you're going to be dragging the animal any appreciable distance, you can omit this step. By leaving this area intact, it's easier to keep the meat clean during transportation. The downside is that the animal does not cool as quickly, and this is a part of the carcass that's vulnerable to spoilage in warm weather.

4. Go up to the point of the animal's brisket and start an incision through the hide. Run this incision all the way down the animal's underside until it meets the opening you created in order to expose the pelvis. Be careful not to nick the muscle beneath the hide, as you might puncture the internal organs as well. (If you're in a state that requires you to leave an animal's evidence of sex naturally attached to the carcass, see the sidebar on page 303.)

5. At this point you're ready to cut through the abdominal wall. The safest place to enter the abdomen is at the very bottom of the rib cage. Make a very shallow and careful cut through the abdominal muscles, just enough to insert your middle and index fingers. With your fingers facing up, lift the abdominal muscles up and away from the stomach and slice through the lining along the same incision that you made through the hide. End the cut at the lower end of the abdomen, where the belly terminates at the pelvic area between the two rear legs.

6. Reach one hand inside the animal's pelvis and press the bladder and intestines away from the pelvic bone as you use your other hand to split the pelvic bone with a saw or small hatchet. On males, cut through the bone on each side of the ridge. On females, cut down the middle. Once the bone is cut, forcibly push

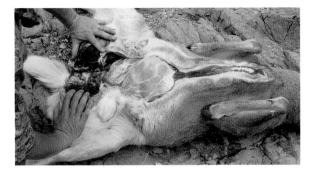

the rear legs apart. You should now have a clear gateway through which the colon and lower intestine will pass when you pull the guts away from the animal.

7. Go back to the point of the sternum where you began your incision through the abdominal wall. From there, use a bone saw, hatchet, or heavy knife to split the sternum all the way to the base of the neck. Then forcibly separate the two halves of the rib cage.

8. Reach into the front of the chest cavity and sever the windpipe. Also slice through the diaphragm, freeing it from the walls of the rib cage on both sides of the animal all the way down to the spine.

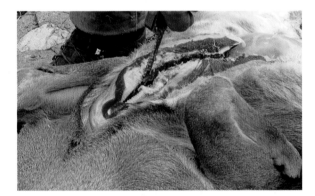

9. Using two hands, reach up to where you severed the windpipe and get a good grip on the package of organs at the top end of the animal. Pulling slowly and firmly, you should be able to walk backward and drag the entire load of guts out of the animal. Keep a knife handy, as you might need to reach in and slice

free the diaphragm or connective tissue around the pelvis if the innards get hung up while you're trying to pull them free.

10. Go through the gut pile and remove the heart, kidneys, and liver.

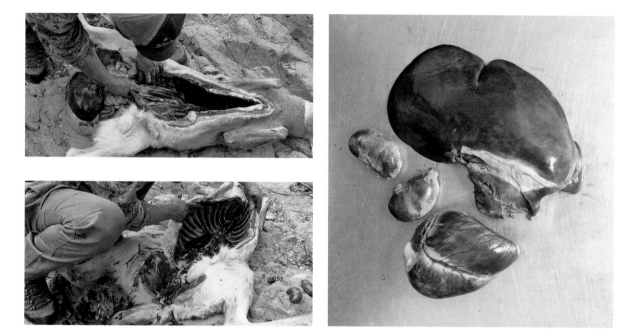

must be left naturally attached to the meat. Acceptable evidence of sex usually includes the vulva or mammary glands on females and the testicles on males. To leave the evidence of sex on a bull or buck:

1. After freeing the anus and colon, find the uppermost end of the penis sheath and start skinning and detaching it, hide and all, with the penis inside. You'll be cutting on both sides of the sheath. (It's like you're skinning off a two-inch wide strip of hide from the center of the animal's belly. When you go to open the animal for gutting, you can use this incision as the starting point for the abdominal gutting incision.)

2. It is important to note that within the animal's hide the penis is free from the testicles. So as you continue detaching the penis, nearing the scrotum, the testicles will appear and naturally fall to each side. The testicles are not attached to each other.

3. If you have a hunting partner, have him or her hold the testicles out of the way as you continue detaching the penis from the carcass.

4. Continue skinning the penis all the way to the anus (yes, it does originate there). At this point you can either cut off the penis at the anus or leave it attached and it will come out with the guts. Both methods are acceptable.

5. At this point the testicles are loosely attached to the hide. Gently peel the testicles free from the hide. They should now be attached solely to the corresponding rear quarter by the narrow tube of the vas deferens.

6. Continue with the gutting procedure, being careful not to disturb the placement and fixture of the testes.

To leave the evidence of sex attached to a cow or doe:

1. After cutting the hide from the loosened anus forward to the neck, come back to the location of the udders and mammary gland. As females with late-born offspring might still have milk in the mammary gland, be prepared for some to flow out as you work. (It was common for Plains Indians to lap up the milk that leaked from the mammary glands of female buffalo during the butchering practice.)

2. Skin the hide, along with the teats, away from the mammary gland. The gland is connected to the meat only by light connective tissue, so work carefully.

3. The gland is rather large, so trim away everything but a chunk measuring about 3 by 3 inches. The quarter can now be removed from the carcass with the mammary attached.

4. Alternatively, you can leave the vulva attached simply by cutting around it and leaving a long tab of skin that connects it to the rear ham. It should look as if you neglected to skin a 5-inch piece of hide away from the rear ham. The only downside of this option is that this patch of skin tends to get a lot of hair on the meat during handling. Wrapping a plastic bag around the tab of hide and securing it with a rubber band or zip tie can mitigate this.

FIELD SKINNING: Hanging Method

As long as you've got a place to hang the carcass and the muscle power necessary to lift it, the hanging method is a clean and simple way to skin your big game animals. Unless you're saving the cape or hide for taxidermy purposes, use the following procedure.

1. Hang the animal by the neck or the base of the antlers, with the noose tucked up tightly behind the ears. (You can also hang an animal upside down, by the gambrels. Everything is pretty much the same; it's just a matter of personal preference.)

2. Make your skinning cuts. Start by cutting through the hide around each ankle. (Some hunters prefer to remove the feet at the ankles for ease of handling; if so, do it at this point. You can use a bone saw for this, though a knife is perfectly adequate once you learn how to find the proper joint and sever the tendon, a skill that comes from practice and experimentation.) Then, on each leg, run an incision through the hide that starts at the ankle and follows the inside of the leg all the way until it joins the gutting incision.

3. Extend the gutting incision from the sternum all the way up to the base of the chin. Then cut through the hide all the way around the animal's neck, passing just behind the base of the skull.

4. Start at the cut around the neck and begin skinning the hide away from the meat as you work downward. Once you've exposed the meat of the neck, you should have enough hide to get a good grip. Pull with one hand, slice with the other.

5. Pull the hide free of the front legs and continue working downward. If you pull outward on the hide with one hand and punch downward to free it from the connective tissue, this part of the job should require very little knife work.

6. Work the hide free of the back legs. Then sever the tailbone at its base. With a few more tugs, the hide should fall away to the ground.

7. You can now remove the legs, backstraps, tenderloins, ribs, and neck meat, either in the hanging position or by working on a flat surface. Whichever way you prefer, the process is nearly the same. Refer to the sequences outlined in the section on breaking down a carcass, which begins on page 318.

A HANDFUL OF FIELD DRESSING TIPS

1. Validate your tag prior to field dressing the animal. This is a law in many states; even where it's not a law, it's still a good idea. Do it now and you don't need to worry about forgetting to do so later.

2. Lay out all needed tools and game bags before starting. This way you won't be searching through your jacket or backpack with bloody hands while trying to locate your bone saw.

3. It's better to touch up the edge of your knife periodically during the field dressing process rather than letting it become hopelessly dull before you sharpen it.

4. Wearing latex gloves makes for easy cleanup after the sometimes bloody process of gutting an animal. It also protects your hands from the drying effects of blood and may help prevent the transmission of parasites.

5. If you plan on leaving a gutted carcass overnight in order to butcher it in the morning, make sure to skin the lower legs, or shanks, if the temperature will drop below freezing. Once frozen, they are extremely difficult to skin.

6. On the inside of the hocks of deer, you'll find the tarsal gland. All deer will urinate on these glands in order to disperse the odor onto the ground, but the glands of rutting whitetail and mule deer bucks become especially odiferous. The gland itself has no adverse affect on the animal's meat—so long as the oily substance doesn't come in direct contact with the flesh. To prevent the spread of the musky odor, it's wise to remove the patch of hair prior to field dressing and skinning. Then you should thoroughly wash your knife and hands with water or snow before continuing the field dressing job.

7. Generously trim around bullet holes, discarding any meat that looks clotted or damaged as well as meat containing bone fragments. There is no sense in packing out meat that will be thrown in the trash at home.

8. If the path of the bullet traveled through the entrails or stomach, make sure to rinse the body cavity with water or snow. A light rinse is best, as too much water is bad for the meat. If the bullet traveled in front of the diaphragm, there should be no need for rinsing if you've done a proper gutting job.

9. Tenderloins dry out quickly; on a whitetail deer, they can dry up to near nothingness in a day if left untended. Since tenderloins do not require aging to tenderize them, pull them out soon after gutting the animal and then either eat them or freeze them. The same goes for the heart and liver, which do not benefit from aging or drying.

10. Always carry an extra gallon-sized freezer bag and garbage bag. The freezer bag is good for tenderloins and organs, while the garbage bag does well as a make-shift tarp for laying meat out on during the butchering process or lining a backpack with to keep it clean. But do not store meat in plastic until it has thoroughly cooled.

11. If you're not going to quarter an animal immediately, always prop open the chest cavity and pelvic area so that the animal's body heat can quickly escape.

12. To ward off any scavenging birds that might be lingering around, such as crows, magpies, or gray jays, cover exposed meat with green brush or pine boughs. You definitely don't want a bird leaving its chalky white calling cards on tomorrow's dinner.

FIELD SKINNING: On the Ground

The hanging method is often out of the question for backcountry hunters due to either a lack of suitable trees or an animal that is too heavy to budge, let alone hoist into the air. This method uses many of the same techniques as the hanging method, but the animal is ob-

viously positioned very differently and there's a much greater risk of getting the meat dirty.

1. For on-the-ground skinning, you're going to work the animal in two stages: right half, left half. Start by cutting through the hide around each ankle on one side of the animal. (In this case, we're working on the left side first.) Then, on each leg, run an incision through the hide that starts at the ankle and follows the inside of the leg all the way until it joins the gutting incision.

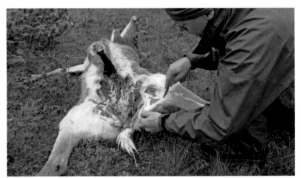

2. Extend the gutting incision from the sternum all the way up to the base of the chin. Then cut through the hide all the way around the animal's neck, passing just behind the base of the skull. (For additional views, refer to the images in the section on the hanging method.)

3. Position the animal so that the left side is facing up, and finish skinning the left legs. By peeling and slicing, remove the hide as though you're pulling back the covers on a bed. Keep skinning until you reach the backbone and the upper half is completely skinned out.

4. At this point, you can remove the front leg, rear leg, backstrap, neck meat, and ribs from the left side of the animal. You can also remove both the left and right tenderloins. (Make sure to store the meat in a clean place while you continue your work.) Refer to the sequences outlined in the section on breaking down a carcass, which begins on page 318.

5. Stretch out the freed portion of the hide like a tarp and roll the animal over, so that the skinned-out left side is lying on the hide and the unskinned right side is facing upward. Repeat the process while working on the right side.

Skinning Big Game for Taxidermy and Tanning

When dealing with horned or antlered game, start by gutting the animal and then clean the surroundings of blood and grime so that the animal's cape (that portion of the hide that you want to salvage for taxidermy purposes) stays as clean as possible. Make a circumscribing cut around the torso of the animal. This cut should be in line with the bottom of the animal's sternum. (A common mistake is to make this cut too far up the body, or closer to the neck, which leaves the taxidermist insufficient hide for a shoulder mount.) Second, make another circumscribing cut around the animal's middle leg joint (similar to our elbow) on both legs. From there, make a cut following the back of the leg up to the armpit and then straight back to join the first cut. Now make a cut following the spine of the animal all the way up the neck and stop about 2 to 3 inches from the base of the antlers or horns. If you are packing the whole head out, you can stop cutting hide at this point. Skin the hide away from the upper torso and neck up to the back of the jaw; sever the head from the spine at the first vertebrae and neatly bundle the hide and head as one package.

If you are fully caping the animal's head (i.e., removing the skull), start at the end of your cut and make two separate incisions going to each antler or horn base. Your cuts will resemble a Y. Be very careful not to cut the hide as you skin around the base of the antler or horn, as the hide is strongly connected here and difficult to work with. A good trick is to get a small piece started with your knife and then pull the hide with your fingers or work it free using a regular screwdriver or the flat driver bit on a multi-tool. As you continue skinning the head, take extra care around the eyes and glands. These areas have recesses where the hide is folded and tucked; haste will result in an unwanted hole. Keep skinning until you reach the gum line. With some careful slicing, the cape should now freely slide off the skull. Removing excess flesh from the cape will lighten your load and help prevent spoilage. Capes should be taken to a taxidermist as soon as possible. If the taxidermist or tannery is more than two days away, freezing the cape is a good option. Do not salt the cape unless it has been thoroughly fleshed from shoulders to nose.

To skin a black bear for tanning or rug making, continue the gutting incision all the way to where the jaw begins. Then make cuts along the underside of each leg, starting at the center of the paw and running up to the gutting incision. Do this for both the front and hind legs. Then simply skin the hide away from the

Two hunters in British Columbia skin a black bear that will make a fine rug. Notice the placement of the skinning cuts.

Here half of the bear is skinned. Notice how the hide is laid out to receive quarters of the meat as they are removed from the carcass.

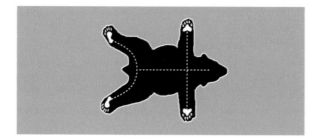

animal. Cut the head off at the back of the skull, so that the whole skin-on head stays with the hide. Sever the tailbone at the base and leave the bone-in tail connected to the hide. The most difficult part of the job is severing the paws from the legs at the wrists without damaging the hide. Do not attempt to skin your bear's paws unless you've been trained by someone with considerable experience. Skinning the head is a tad easier, but it's best left to a professional unless an expert has shown you how to do it.

TIPS FOR HANDLING MEAT IN THE FIELD

When caring for backcountry meat, keep three words in mind: *cool*, *clean*, and *dry*. Maintaining these conditions in adverse circumstances can be challenging, but it's usually possible if you're adaptable and you use your imagination.

1. If conditions allow, meaning the insects aren't getting all over your meat, allow the bone-in quarters and large boneless pieces of meat to air-dry for a while after you remove them from the carcass. They build up a dry crust, or rind, that offers protection to the meat

and allows for a cleaner, neater pack-out job. The rind forms especially quickly in dry, breezy conditions.

2. If bugs or dirt are an issue, put the meat into breathable game bags as soon as you cut it away from the carcass. There are a number of excellent game bags on the market, including those made by Alaska Game Bags, T.A.G., and Caribou Gear.

3. Hang the full game bags in a shaded area where they can get some breeze. Be conscious of where the sun is in the sky. Always try to hang your meat on the north-facing side of a tree. In treeless areas, the north-facing side of a rock or ridge will always be cooler than the south-facing side.

4. You want to allow airflow between the quarters and large pieces, so don't stack them to-

of any water. Pile more brush on top of the meat and cover with a tarp if there's a chance of rain or snow.

6. It's important to keep bears, coyotes, and other scavengers at bay whenever you are absent from your stash of meat. Make your prized meat hard to get to by hoisting it into a tree or otherwise getting it out of reach. Leave the innards that you don't want where they are easy to get at, in order to divert the attention of unwanted visitors. Leave clothing you've worn draped over the meat or hanging nearby; hang a trash bag or tarp so that it flaps in the breeze; urinate on trees or shrubs around the meat, or directly on the ground nearby. All of these methods will help give scavengers and predators some pause before they move in to maul your cache.

gether. If you need to use tarps or plastic sheeting to protect them from rain or snow, put down a buffer of brush to keep the plastic from making direct contact with the meat. If you need to line your pack with plastic in order to keep it clean while transporting meat, then make sure to remove the meat as soon as you arrive at your destination. When storing game bags full of meat on the ground, place them on a framework of limbs, antlers, or rocks so that air can circulate freely beneath the bags.

5. On float trips, the water is often much cooler than the air during the daytime. Think about resting the meat in the hull of a raft or canoe at night, where it's cooled by the water beneath. If the floor of the boat is wet or leaky, lay down a pile of brush to keep the meat clear

AGING GAME MEAT

Meat is aged for two reasons: to tenderize it and to enhance flavor. When possible, this should be done with the hide on and the bone in. The hide protects the meat and prevents excessive drying. The bone keeps the muscles elongated, which helps prevent contraction and subsequent toughness.

Aging meat properly requires a period of seven to fourteen days, depending on the condition of the animal. Ideal temperatures for aging are between 34° and 37°. This allows the natural enzymes in the meat to break down some of the complex proteins. Younger animals do not need to be aged as long; for yearlings, a period of twenty-four hours will often suffice.

Some wild game processors will hang meat for you, though they often charge fees of $10–$30 per day. Ideally we'd all have our own walk-in cooler, but unfortunately that's not the case. However, you can do your own aging with standard household equipment. Whether you're hanging your meat in an outdoor closet, shed, garage, or basement, or from a backyard tree, keep a thermometer nearby to properly gauge the temperature. When temps rise much above 50° for an extended part of the day, you'll have to find a different way to age the meat or just start the butchering process. Keeping a fan running to circulate the air will help keep temps down, as will hanging the meat on the north side of a building. If you have a shed small enough to be cooled by a window AC unit, try that during the heat of the day.

Another option is to put the meat in a standard refrigerator that's cranked down to its coldest setting. Put some kind of wire rack on the shelves (racks used for cooling baking goods work well) and place the quarters and large pieces of meat directly on top. Don't be afraid of some drying, but do watch for spoilage. Give the meat the poke-and-smell test every day. If it meat takes on a bad odor or starts to look like something you wouldn't want to eat, trim away the trouble spots, process the animal quickly, and get it into a freezer.

Note: Because of the volatile nature of bear and wild pork fat, you should never age bear or wild hog meat. Butcher it as soon as possible.

RENDERING WILD LARD

When butchering black bears (or wild pigs, if you get a fatty one), it's very important that you trim away all fat before freezing the meat. The fat will gradually spoil in the freezer and create off flavors or downright inedible meat. Rather than discarding the fat, you should consider rendering it into oil. As long as the animal hasn't been feeding on fish or carrion, the oil will usually be delicious and can be used for any application suitable for lard. It's a simple process.

1. Cube the fat into 1-inch chunks.

2. Put a heavy-bottomed pot over a low burner and add ¼ inch of cooking oil. Add a single layer of the fat pieces.

3. Once the initial fat pieces start to release oil (you'll know because the oil in the bottom gets deeper), add another layer. Keep doing this until you've got a couple of inches of oil in the bottom. Now it's safe to add in the rest of the fat, but don't fill the pot to more than 75 percent full.

4. Let it render on low heat until the oil ceases to sputter and the fat pieces are clear and floating on the top. (This can take several hours.) They should look like cracklings, depleted of oil.

5. Skim away the cracklings and any residue that has collected at the surface. Continue cooking until all sputtering and boiling has stopped.

6. Let the oil cool, then pour it through a fine wire strainer into glass canning jars. Discard the bottom ½ inch or so of oil in the pot if it looks cloudy or contains bits of cooked meat or gristle.

7. Cap the jars. The rendered oil keeps indefinitely in a freezer. You can also store it in a refrigerator.

BONUS PARTS, OR HOW TO SHOW MAXIMUM RESPECT FOR YOUR PREY

1. While not nearly as meaty as cow's head, venison head can still provide a memorable and surprisingly tasty meal. The jowl meat is flavorful and rich, and reminds one of pulled pork when slow-cooked. Skinning the head is simple.

2. The heart should be cored, the way you'd core a bell pepper. Slice away the fatty rim at the thick end of the heart.

3. Cut around the heavy veins and connective membranes found at the base of the liver. For most applications, you'll want to cut the liver into slices just under ¼ inch thick.

4. Peel the outer membrane away from the kidneys. These organs are best cubed for breakfast scrambles with eggs, potatoes, and herbs.

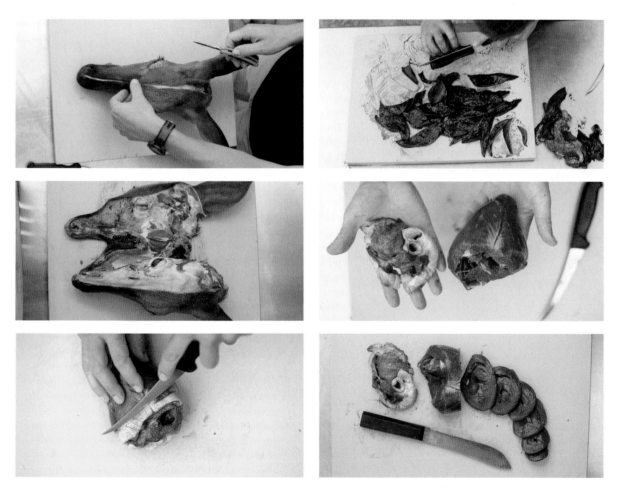

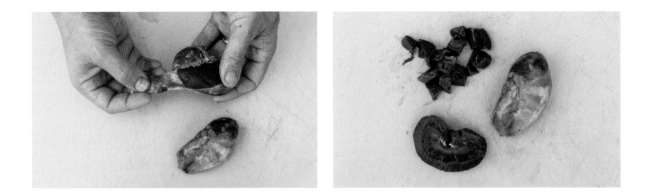

BREAKING DOWN A BIG GAME ANIMAL

The following is a standard method for breaking down a big game carcass into recipe-ready cuts. Though some of the cuts highlighted here are not entirely suitable for bear meat, they are perfect for all horned and antlered game as well as wild pigs. When using these methods to break down a carcass for easy transport in the field, it's usually best to leave the legs intact until they've reached their final place of processing. Most of this work can be done using a thin, stout boning knife with either a 6- or 8-inch blade. Keep it sharp!

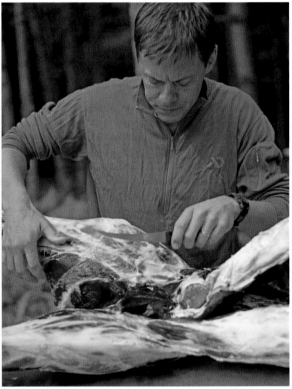

1. Remove the back leg by cutting in from the inside and popping the rear ball joint at the head of the femur. After popping the joint, keep your knife close to the pelvis so that as much meat as possible comes away with the leg.

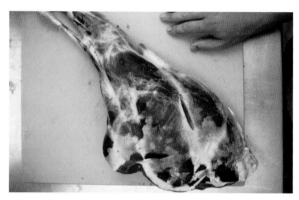

The bottom right piece, sometimes called the ball roast, is much more suitable as a roast. The shank, that portion of each leg from the knee to the ankle (still on the bone in this photo), can be boned out for burger meat. Or, better yet, save it for osso buco. You can either cut it into discs now or freeze the whole shank and cut it before cooking. Generally, it is better to freeze shanks whole because this limits the exposed surface area that might be susceptible to freezer burn.

When cutting muscle groups from the back leg into steaks, cut the muscle in a cross-grain direction.

The leg can now be broken into its primary muscles. These muscles are distinct; by opening the seams with a knife, you can literally feel the divisions.

In the photo at right, the top piece (above the femur) is an excellent choice for steaks; the bottom left piece is also good for steaks.

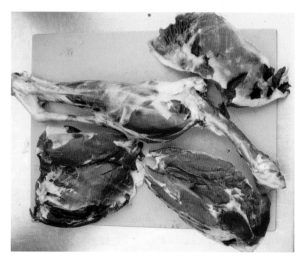

BONING HAMS FOR BRINING AND SMOKING

Below is a black bear ham being boned out for use as a boneless smoked ham. Rather than breaking the leg down along muscle lines, the leg is opened up on the inside of the leg by tracing the length of the bone with a slender-bladed knife. Then the leg bones are carefully lifted and sliced away. The ham can be brined, then re-formed into its original shape and tied with kitchen twine or bound with roast netting.

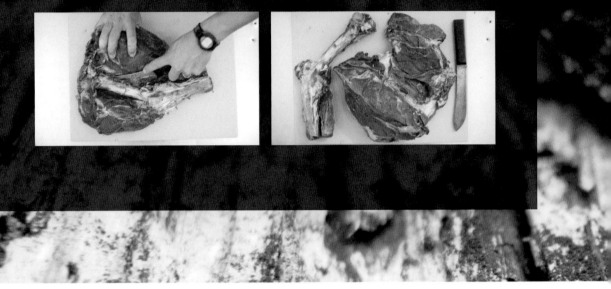

2. Remove the front shoulders by passing your knife between the shoulder blade and the rib cage. There are no ball joints here, just connective tissue.

The shoulders can be handled in a variety of ways, depending on your needs. You can bone them for use as burger or sausage meat, which requires little finesse.

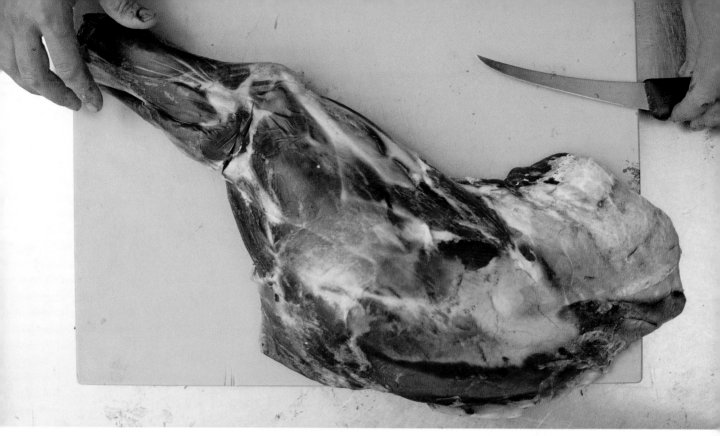

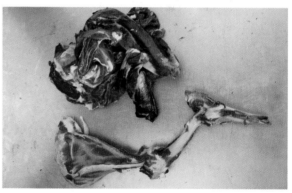

Another way to handle the shoulders is to saw them into large bone-in chunks for making braised shoulder roasts, which are delicious and exceptionally easy to prepare. (See recipe on page 336.) Remember to save the shanks! Pictured on page 338 is a shank that's been sawed into pieces for osso buco. (See recipe on that page.)

3. Cut away the paunch on each side. Trim off excess fat, then cube and save for grinder meat.

4. Remove both tenderloins. This can be done mostly with your fingers, by gently peeling away the tenderloin once each end is cut free. Very little knife work is involved. If eating tenderloins fresh (they are best grilled or pan-fried in butter and served rare) you can peel away the fat and silver skin now. If you freeze tenderloins for later use, peel away the fat but leave the silver skin in place; it helps to protect the meat in the freezer.

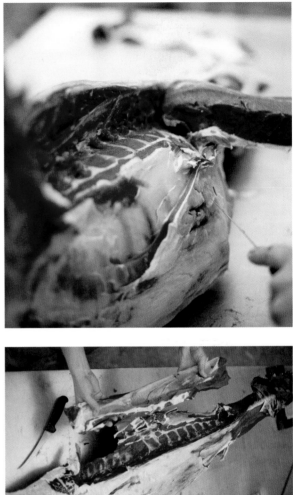

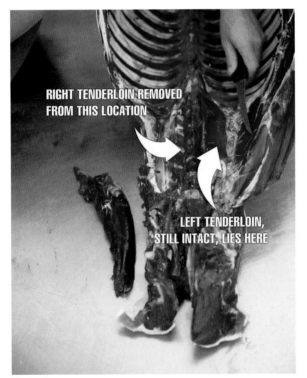

5. Peel the outer layer of silver skin and fat away from either side of the spine along the saddle, exposing the loins, or backstraps. Then, working from front to back, remove each loin by slicing it free from the backbone and upper ribs. Treat these much like the tenderloins. If eating fresh, peel away the fat and slice off the silver skin before cooking. If freezing, peel away any fat but leave the silver skin in place until you're ready to thaw and cook the loins. It's good to freeze the loin in serving-size portions. (About 8 or 10 inches of venison loin will feed two hungry people; with elk loin, half that will suffice.) You can also slice the loin into 1-inch discs and cook them as is, or flatten them out with a meat mallet to ½- or ¼-inch thickness and use the oh-so-tender meat for a variety of preparations.

6. Remove the neck. This can be done with a knife by popping the vertebrae joints, or with a bone saw. The neck can be boned out and cubed for burger meat. However, whole neck roasts are an excellent way to handle this cut. Cook deer necks in one piece. A moose neck might provide six or more bone-in neck roasts as big as dinner plates when you crosscut it into chunks. (See recipe on page 336.)

sausage making, or they can be sawed into bone-in hunks for making preparations similar to the way you'd cook beef or pork short ribs. First, remove the brisket bone. You can usually cut along the seam to get it started, then snap the joints and finish the removal with a knife. Then saw the rack in half and cut into serving-sized pieces.

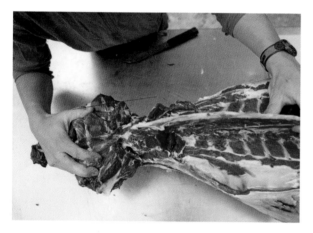

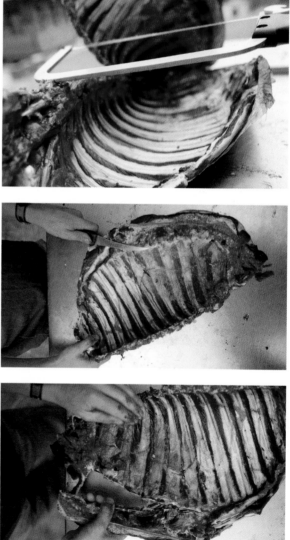

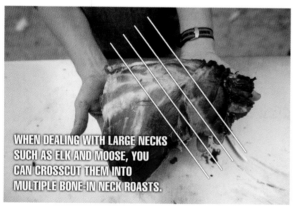

WHEN DEALING WITH LARGE NECKS SUCH AS ELK AND MOOSE, YOU CAN CROSSCUT THEM INTO MULTIPLE BONE-IN NECK ROASTS.

7. Saw away the rib slabs. (This can also be done with a small hatchet or even a boning knife if you can find the small joints where the ribs join up to the vertebrae.)

The rib slabs can be boned for burger and

When butchering whitetail deer, you'll find that there are several common cuts, including flank, hanger, brisket, and tongue, that are too small to use for anything besides making burger. On larger animals, though, these cuts are well worth going after. Elk, moose, and buffalo all have enough of a brisket to make pastrami, and their flanks and hangers are generous enough to be used as fajita meat. The tongues, too, are worth salvaging. They can be boiled, or brined and smoked to make a delicious treat.

GRINDING BURGER

When making ground meat from the flesh of horned and antlered game, it's a good idea to add some pork fat or beef fat. (You can omit the fat, but you'll need to add beaten eggs as a binder to make burger patties and meatballs; even then, the ground meat will be a tad crumbly.) Tastes vary, with hunters preferring everything from 5 percent fat to 20 percent fat. For all-around use, a meat-to-fat ratio of 10:1 is ideal, with pork fatback being one of the best kinds of fat for the purpose.

1. Trim the game meat of tendons, silver skin, and fat. Some butchers suggest removing absolutely all silver skin and tendons, but this leads to a greatly diminished volume of finished product. For instance, it pretty much rules out the use of rib meat. Instead, use your best judgment and trim away heavy concentrations of silver skin and tendons without getting so carried away that you're tossing out 50 percent of the animal.

2. Cut the trimmed venison into 1-inch cubes. Cut the pork or beef fat into 1-inch cubes. Mix the cubes of meat and fat together. Keep the meat and fat very cold while you work; it's wise to place meat in a freezer or in a cooler filled with ice when you need to take a break from your work for cleaning, eating, et cetera.

3. Run the meat and fat through a grinder using a coarse die plate with ⅜-inch (9.5 mm) holes.

4. Thoroughly mix the ground meat to get the fat evenly distributed.

5. Run the meat through the grinder a second time, this time using a medium die plate with ³⁄₁₆-inch (4.5 mm) holes.

BUFFALO FAT

The fat on antlered game such as deer and elk should be trimmed away during the butchering process. Unlike beef fat and pork fat, it is waxy and often has an off flavor that only gets worse in the freezer. The fat from buffalo, on the other hand, is quite good and adds significantly to the flavor and substance of the meat. When grinding buffalo meat, in fact, it's a good idea to cut the lean meat with the buffalo's own fat. The fat of bears and wild pigs can be used for making lard. (See the sidebar on page 316.)

FREEZING BIG GAME MEAT

There are two acceptable methods to use when wrapping whole-muscle red meat for the freezer: vacuum-sealed bags and double-wrapping with plastic wrap and waxed freezer paper. Both will keep meat for well over a year if you do it right. For the vacuum-sealed bags, follow the directions provided by the manufacturer of whatever vacuum sealer you have access to. Once the bags are sealed and frozen, handle them gently. Banging and rubbing the bags together can cause holes to form in the plastic, which will destroy the seal and, eventually, the contents of the bag. If you have space, it's a good idea to lay down layers of newsprint between layers of vacuum-sealed bags in your freezer in order to protect the integrity of the bags.

For double-wrapping, wrap the cut tightly in a plastic wrap. Be careful to squeeze out any air bubbles. Use plenty of wrap, as a couple of layers is better than one. Next cut an ample-sized piece of waxed freezer paper and wrap this tightly around the plastic-wrapped meat. Tuck the ends, like wrapping a Christmas present, and tape it off with a 2-inch strip of masking tape or freezer tape.

The double-wrapping method works well for freezing ground meat as well, but the best way is to use tube-shaped polyethylene ground meat bags that can be purchased from most wild game processing supply houses. These are easy to fill, they stack nicely in the freezer, and they protect ground meat for extended periods of freezer storage.

COOKING BIG GAME

SMOKED HAM

This smoked ham recipe is best suited for black bear and wild pig hams, though it also works fairly well with venison. To make it, you're gonna need about 3½ days. I like to remove the femur from the back leg and brine the meat flat, injecting the brine into the large muscle groups at least once a day to make sure they're saturated. Before smoking, I tie or net the roast into a nice round bundle. If you happen to have a whole week, though, you can brine and smoke the whole leg, bone-in, which makes for an eye-popping presentation. Either way, your friends are going to love the sweet, smoky, peppery flavor of a homemade ham.

- 4 cups brown sugar
- 3 cups kosher salt
- 3 ounces curing salt (often sold as pink salt #1) (optional)
- 1 wild pig or black bear leg, femur and skin removed, 6–10 pounds (keep all the fat on with wild pigs, but with fall-killed black bears, trim away excess fat and leave just a thin layer)
- 1 package unflavored gelatin
- ½ cup freshly ground black pepper

TRICHINOSIS

Wild hog and bear meat often contains the larval form of *Trichinella spiralis*; when ingested by humans, these larvae can cause the disease trichinosis.

It's very important that you cook all bear and wild pig meat to an internal temperature of at least 160°.

For the brine, heat 2 gallons of water and dissolve the brown sugar, kosher salt, and curing salt in the water. Stir with a whisk to dissolve completely. Let cool to room temperature and then chill in the fridge before using.

Lay the leg out flat in a baking dish. Pour the brine over the meat and make sure the leg is completely submerged. Store covered in the fridge for 3 days. Once each day, using a syringe, inject the large muscle groups with brine.

After 3 days, remove the meat from the brine and rinse well. Pat the leg dry with paper towels and set it on a rack to dry. It's going to be tacky because of all the sugar, but it shouldn't be wet.

Lay the leg flat with the open side facing up. Sprinkle the powdered gelatin all over it. This will help to fill in any gaps in the meat. Bind the meat together by running the leg through a net funnel; if you don't have a net funnel, tie securely with butcher's twine, spacing the rows of twine about 1 inch apart. (If the leg is really large, you can make two hams.)

Rub the black pepper all over the ham. You want it to be really well coated so every slice gets a little bit.

Start the smoker. While it's heating up, soak about 2 quarts of hickory or applewood chips in water for at least 20 minutes. When the smoker has reached 100°, set up one pan of wood chips (I like to use the pan that comes with the smoker, but you can use aluminum pie tins if you don't have one). When the smoker is at 150°, add the ham and put a pan of water under it so it can drip into it. The water adds moisture and prevents the meat from drying out.

For the initial smoking period, keep the smoker between 150° and 200°. After a couple of hours you can let the heat climb to 250°, but don't go beyond that. Feed enough wood chips to the smoker so that you're maintaining constant smoke. Smokers vary, and so does the ambient heat. Do what you can to keep a steady temperature, but results will vary based on equipment, season, and geographic location. When in doubt, follow the instructions on your smoker if it doesn't match what is written here.

Smoke until an instant-read thermometer inserted into the thickest part of the meat reads 160°. (It's very important that you test in different spots to be sure the meat is safe to eat—see the note on trichinosis in wild hog and bear meat on page 331.) The overall time will be 3–5 hours, but it's not done until it reaches 160°.

Remove the ham from the smoker. Serve hot or cold, thinly sliced, with coarse mustard.

NECK ROAST BBQ

This is a great dish to make with a whole venison neck, or a 4- to 6-pound piece of elk or moose neck. Since the neck is a heavily used muscle, it takes a lot of cooking to tenderize the meat. I have great luck using a slow cooker. After 6–8 hours, the meat can be pulled right off the bone. The spine ends up looking as clean as a museum specimen, and the meat is perfect for BBQ sandwiches.

SERVES: 8–10 (2 QUARTS OF SHREDDED MEAT)

- 4- to 6-pound neck, bone-in (use a whole venison neck or a 4- to 6-pound piece of elk or moose neck)
- Kosher salt
- Freshly ground black pepper
- 3 tablespoons vegetable oil
- 2–3 quarts game stock or enriched stock (see below)
- ½–1 cup BBQ Sauce (page 335) or store-bought BBQ sauce
- Hamburger buns

ENRICHED STOCK

If you don't have time to make your own stock from scratch, put store-bought vegetable or chicken stock in a large pot on the stove, add an onion (peeled and cut in half), and some extra bones from the freezer (chicken wings, venison shank, etc.). Bring just to a boil, then lower to a simmer. Skim off and discard any scum on the surface. Add a bay leaf, a sprig of thyme, or parsley stems if you have them. Then keep at a low simmer for several hours. Skim off and discard the fat on the surface. Strain out the solids. Use the stock immediately, or cool and freeze.

Bring the neck to room temperature. Season liberally with salt and pepper all over.

Heat a large sauté pan or roasting pan over medium-high heat. Add the oil. When the oil shimmers, swirl the pan to coat well. Sear the neck until it's browned on all sides.

Put the browned neck in a 6-quart slow cooker. Add enough stock just to cover the neck. Cover, set the slow cooker on low, and cook for a minimum of 6–8 hours, until fork tender. (Alternatively, use a 6- to 8-quart Dutch oven, and cook in a 300° oven for 6–8 hours.) Keep checking to be sure it's covered with liquid at all times. You'll know it's done when it flakes into really nice pieces.

Remove the meat from the liquid and start shredding. (Don't throw away the extra cooking liquid—use it like stock.) The meat should shred like pulled pork. Toss with BBQ sauce and serve in soft hamburger buns with sliced pickles and potato chips on the side. A couple of spoonfuls of coleslaw on top of the meat is a great addition.

Alternatively, you can store the meat in the fridge for up to 1 week or in the freezer for up to 1 month.

Leftover shredded meat without the BBQ sauce can be tossed into a simple tomato sauce (page 346) to make a convenient and tasty ragù for pasta dishes.

BBQ SAUCE

This recipe comes from my buddy Chef Matt Weingarten, who tailored the sauce for the flavors of wild game. As you'll see, making your own BBQ sauce is simple and can be well worth the effort.

YIELD: MAKES 2 CUPS

- 3 tablespoons vegetable oil
- 1 large onion, cut into ½-inch dice
- 4 cloves garlic, minced
- 1 cup ketchup
- ¼ cup molasses
- 1 chipotle pepper in adobo sauce, chopped

- ¼ cup apple cider vinegar
- 1 teaspoon dry mustard
- 1 teaspoon ground juniper berries
- ½ teaspoon cumin
- ¼ teaspoon allspice
- 2 shakes Worcestershire sauce

In a 6-quart pot, heat the oil and cook the onions until translucent. Add the garlic and cook for another minute. Add the remaining ingredients. Bring to a boil over medium heat, then reduce the heat to low. Simmer for about 20 minutes, until the sauce flavors have come together. Cool and store in the refrigerator.

BONE-IN BLADE ROAST WITH ROOT VEGETABLES

Years ago, my brother Danny perfected this recipe while working with moose shoulder. I've since used it for everything from whitetail to black bear. As you'll see, it proves that there's no need to grind all your big game shoulders into burger meat. Handled properly, shoulder cuts can be the tastiest, most elegant portion of your kill. For this dish, I braise the roast for 3 hours with lots of garlic and finish it up with some sweet root vegetables. You won't believe how good it is. The texture will remind you of pulled pork, which is commonly made from pig shoulder.

- 1 blade roast, bone-in, 3–4 pounds (from deer, elk, caribou, or moose shoulder)
- Kosher salt
- Freshly ground pepper
- 2 tablespoons vegetable oil
- 2 tablespoons unsalted butter
- 1 onion, cut into ¼-inch dice
- 12 cloves garlic
- 2 quarts game stock (or enriched stock; see page 334)
- ¼ cup dry white or red wine
- 2–3 sprigs fresh thyme or oregano
- 1 bay leaf
- 2 sweet potatoes, peeled and sliced into half moons about ½ inch thick
- 6 ounces whole baby carrots, or 2 large carrots, peeled and cut into 2-inch pieces
- 2 stalks celery, cut into ½-inch dice
- 1 pound russet potatoes (1–2 potatoes), cut into ½-inch dice

Preheat oven to 300°. Season the roast liberally with salt and pepper on all sides.

Heat a heavy-bottomed 6- to 8-quart Dutch oven over medium-high heat. Add the oil. When the oil begins to shimmer, add the butter; it will bubble up. When the bubbles subside, add the roast and sear until dark brown. Flip the roast and sear the other side.

Remove the roast to a plate. Drain any excess fat from the bottom of the pan. Add the onion and cook until translucent and beginning to brown, about 5 minutes. Add the garlic and cook for 2–3 minutes, letting them get a little color on them. Next, loosen the brown bits on the bottom of the pot with a splash of stock, water, or wine. Use a wooden spoon to scrape up the bits; they'll add tons of flavor to your sauce.

Return the meat to the pot and add the rest of the stock and the wine; it should reach about three-quarters of the way up the sides of the roast. Toss in the thyme and bay leaf. Bring the pot to a boil, then cover and transfer to the oven. Cook in the oven for 2½ hours, checking occasionally to be sure that there is still enough liquid; add more if not. If the top of the roast becomes dry, flip it over and continue cooking.

After 2½ hours, check the roast. The meat should be close to tender. Add the sweet potatoes, carrots, celery, and potatoes and cook until the vegetables are soft and the meat is fork tender, 15–20 minutes more.

Remove meat from the liquid. Slice into large pieces and divide among dinner plates. Use a slotted spoon to scoop up the vegetables from the liquid and serve them on the side. Top the meat with a little of the cooking liquid. (Don't throw away the extra cooking liquid—it's like liquid gold! Save it for soup, pasta sauce, or stock.) Delicious with pieces of buttered baguette.

BRAISED SHANKS (OSSO BUCO)

This recipe turns the lowly shank into a fine-dining creation. You can use the shanks from any big game animal with equally great results. When I'm butchering, I simply wrap my shanks in plastic wrap and freezer paper and then freeze them whole. When I'm ready to cook this dish, I unwrap the shanks and slice them into 2½-inch-thick discs while they're still frozen. You can use a standard hacksaw and blade for this job, which is easy and clean. When they are still partially frozen, I tie them around the middle with butcher's twine, which helps keep them together while cooking. While this dish is technically just a simple braise, it ends up being quite fancy. It's perfect for when you want to impress the in-laws or any other special guests.

- Two shanks (about 5 pounds total) cut into 2- to 3-inch-thick cylinders, tied around the middle with butcher's twine
- Kosher salt
- Freshly ground black pepper
- Flour for dredging
- 3 tablespoons extra-virgin olive oil
- 2 medium red onions, thinly sliced
- 2 carrots, peeled and cut into ⅓-inch rounds
- 1 rib celery, sliced into ⅓-inch pieces
- 4 cloves garlic, sliced thinly

- 2 tablespoons tomato paste
- 1 cup dry red or white wine
- 2 quarts vegetable stock (or water)
- Leaves from 2 sprigs fresh thyme
- 1 sprig fresh rosemary, chopped
- Leaves from 2 sprigs fresh sage, rolled and chopped thin
- 1 recipe Polenta (recipe below, or substitute store-bought and reheat according to the package instructions)
- ¼ cup chopped flat-leaf parsley
- Freshly grated Parmigiano Reggiano

POLENTA

- 4 cups water
- Pinch kosher salt
- 1 cup polenta or yellow cornmeal

- ½ cup grated Parmigiano Reggiano
- 2 tablespoons butter
- Milk as needed

Heat an 8- to 10-quart Dutch oven over medium-high heat. Season the shank discs well with salt and pepper. Lightly dredge the discs in flour. Add the oil to the pot and swirl to coat. When the oil starts to shimmer, sear the shank discs in batches (avoid overcrowding the pan, which will steam the meat). When the meat is well browned on all sides, remove to a plate. Be careful not to burn the bits on the bottom of the pan, as it will impart a bitter flavor.

Add the onions, carrots, and celery and cook until the onions are browned. Add the garlic and cook for 30 seconds until fragrant. Push the vegetables to one side of the pot. Add the tomato paste to the empty side of the pot and let it begin to caramelize a little. Once it darkens, stir the tomato paste into the vegetables. Add the wine to the pot and scrape up any brown bits on the bottom of the pan. Allow the wine to reduce slightly.

Return the meat to the pot. Add enough stock to just cover the meat. Bring to a boil, then reduce the heat to low. Skim off and discard any scum that accumulates on the surface. Stir in the thyme, rosemary, and sage. Cover the pot and cook at a bare simmer until the meat is fork tender, 3½–4 hours. Check halfway through to make sure there is still enough liquid covering the meat; add more if needed.

About 30 minutes before the meat is done, make the polenta. In a 4- to 6-quart pot, bring the water to a boil. Add the salt. Whisking constantly to avoid lumps, slowly add the polenta in a thin stream. Reduce the heat to medium-low and continue to stir for 15–20 minutes until the polenta becomes thick and large bubbles form (kind of like a volcano). Remove from the heat and stir in the grated cheese and the butter. Set aside, covered. Add milk if needed to loosen up the polenta when you serve it.

When the shanks are fork tender, remove them from the oven and carefully remove the strings with kitchen shears.

Divide the polenta among the dinner plates. Top each puddle of polenta with a shank piece. Spoon the sauce and the vegetables over the meat. Sprinkle with parsley to garnish. Serve immediately with grated cheese.

FIELD MENU: BEAR MEAT FRIED IN BEAR OIL

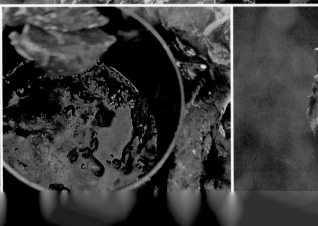

MICHIGAN-STYLE (FRIED, THAT IS) HUNTER'S HEART

When I was growing up, we always ate the heart of a deer soon after killing it. My mom cooked it very simply: sliced thin, dredged in seasoned flour, and then fried in a skillet. My dad always complained if we put ketchup on venison loin, but he didn't mind if we dipped our slices of heart in it. Since then I've had wild game hearts cooked in dozens of ways, but this is still my favorite. It's easy, it's deeply midwestern, it tastes perfect, and it's a great way to introduce otherwise squeamish eaters to a somewhat adventurous food item. Try it, and this recipe is likely to become a ritual of your own.

SERVES: DEER AND ANTELOPE HEARTS SERVE 1 OR 2, MOOSE OR ELK HEARTS SERVE 5 OR 6

- 1 game heart, with upper valves and cartilage removed, sliced into ⅓-inch discs (see butchering note on page 317)
- Kosher salt
- Freshly ground pepper
- Flour for dredging
- 2 tablespoons vegetable oil

Season the heart slices with salt and pepper. Dredge in flour, then shake off the excess. Heat a cast-iron frying pan or other heavy skillet over medium-high heat. Add the oil. When the oil shimmers, add the heart pieces. Brown them on both sides. This will go quickly.

Serve hot with ketchup on the side. There's nothing better in the world.

MARINATING HEART

Deer heart takes to a marinade quite nicely. I like to marinate it and grill the slices. Here's a simple recipe you might want to try. Slice the deer heart ½ inch thick. Combine in a resealable bag 1 cup extra-virgin olive oil, 2 tablespoons steak seasoning, and ⅓ cup white vinegar. Add the heart, turn to coat well, and seal the bag. Marinate for 1 hour in the fridge. Remove the heart from the marinade and let it come to room temperature. Grill over high heat, about 3 minutes per side. Char is good, but don't overcook it, as it cooks fast! The smoky char combined with the vinegary marinade and the buttery heart—it's like paradise on a grill!

LIVER AND ONIONS

For many people, liver and onions is a throwback recipe that reminds them of their grandparents. For me, it's still a relevant dish that should have a place in every hunter's kitchen. After all, you'll find a liver in every animal you kill, and there's no sense in wasting such a delicious and easy-to-use ingredient. I slice my livers into thin strips, about $\frac{3}{16}$ inch thick, and then soak the slices in a solution of water and lemon juice. This removes some of the blood and mellows out any pungent flavors. (Soaking is optional for animals up to about $1\frac{1}{2}$ years of age.) The end result is earthy and tender, and goes perfectly with the sweet taste of the caramelized onions. My mom liked to cook hers in bacon grease. I haven't found any good reason to do it differently.

- 1 deer liver, sliced into ³⁄₁₆-inch-thick pieces
- Juice of 1 lemon
- Kosher salt

- Freshly ground black pepper
- 3 tablespoons bacon grease
- 1 red onion, sliced into rings
- Splash of bourbon, to taste (optional)

Put the liver in a medium-large bowl and barely cover it with water. Add the lemon juice. Let it soak for a few hours in the refrigerator.

Remove the liver slices from the water, dry them, and weigh out 1 pound of sliced liver for this recipe. (Use the whole sliced liver if you're feeding a crowd, and just up the onions in the recipe. If not, save the liver for use later that day—it spoils quickly, so it's hard to save much longer than that.) Season the slices liberally with salt and pepper.

Heat a large sauté pan or cast-iron frying pan and add the bacon grease. Swirl to coat the pan. Add the onion and season with salt and pepper; add the bourbon if using. Sauté over medium heat until onions are translucent, about 3 minutes. Turn the heat up to medium-high and cook the onions until they are deep golden brown, 5–8 minutes. Remove the onions from the pan and set aside.

Add the liver to the pan. (If needed, add a little more bacon grease or vegetable oil.) Cook the slices for 2 to 3 minutes on each side. You want to cook them until the liquid starts to run clear, but not longer. They should still be pinkish inside.

Serve the liver with the onions.

VENISON (OR ANTELOPE, ELK, MOOSE, CARIBOU, ETC.) PARMESAN

This recipe came to me when I needed to feed a crowd and wanted to have all the cooking done before everyone arrived. While most folks know this classic dish as a preparation for chicken or veal, it works brilliantly with pretty much any big game animal as long as you select quality steaks from the loins or back legs and tenderize them vigorously with a mallet. You can use your own homemade tomato sauce or one from the store. I like this simple tomato sauce because it's easy to make, freezes well, and tastes great. This feeds 8–10 people and doubles nicely if you need to feed more.

- 8 steaks, cut from the back leg or loin, ¾ inch thick (about 3–4 ounces each)
- Flour for dredging
- 2 eggs
- 1½ cups freshly grated Parmigiano Reggiano, divided
- 2 cups fresh bread crumbs (see below)
- Extra-virgin olive oil
- Kosher salt
- Freshly ground black pepper
- 2 cups tomato sauce (see recipe below, or use your favorite tomato sauce)
- 12 fresh basil leaves, rolled like a cigar and sliced into thin strips (see below)
- 2 cups shredded mozzarella

TOMATO SAUCE

Heat a large skillet over medium-high heat. Add ¼ cup extra-virgin olive oil and ½ red onion, chopped. Sauté over medium-high heat until the onion is translucent. Add 4 cloves of garlic, chopped, and sauté for 30 more seconds. Add one 28-ounce can of crushed tomatoes (San Marzano tomatoes have the best flavor) and a little salt and pepper. Simmer for 20 minutes. Taste, adjust seasoning, add a sprig of basil, and remove from the heat. Use immediately, cool and freeze, or cool and keep in the fridge for up to a week.

FRESH BREAD CRUMBS

Fresh bread crumbs are so much more delicious, they're worth making every time you have a fresh loaf of bread in the house that's gone a little stale. I like to use baguettes, but sourdough works, too. Just remove the crusts, cut the bread into ½-inch pieces, throw them into your food processor, and pulse until you have bread crumbs. It's that simple. Store the bread crumbs in resealable bags in the freezer for when you need them.

HOW TO THINLY SLICE BASIL

First pick the largest leaves. Stack them up like dollar bills, then roll them like a cigar so you end up with a long roll of leaves. Slice the long roll crosswise with a sharp knife into thin slices. When they unfurl, you'll have little thin slices of basil. Pretty cool.

Taking one piece at a time, lay a steak between two pieces of plastic wrap and use a meat mallet (or a fist-sized rock) to pound the hell out of it until it's ¼ inch thick. Seriously, smash it—you want it to be tender. Smash it to the point that when you lift the meat up, you can see light through it. Then repeat with the remaining steaks. (If the plastic starts to shred on you, sprinkle a little water directly on the meat, then cover it with plastic. This will keep the plastic moving instead of sticking to the meat.) Set the meat aside.

To set up a breading station, use three pie plates or rimmed plates. Fill one pie plate with flour. Crack the eggs into a small bowl, add a little water, beat lightly with a fork, and add this mixture to the second pie plate. Fill the third pie plate with 1 cup of the grated Parmigiano and the bread crumbs; toss with your fingers to combine.

Preheat a cast-iron skillet or other heavy skillet over medium heat. Add about ½ inch of oil.

Season the pounded steaks well with a good amount of salt and pepper on both sides. One at a time, dredge each through the flour, the egg wash, and then the bread crumbs. After each step, make sure to shake off any excess breading materials.

Test the preheated oil by adding a small piece of bread to the oil. If it starts to sizzle, you know it's hot. Carefully lay a couple of the breaded steaks in the skillet (don't overcrowd the pan) and sear them for about 2 minutes per side, until golden brown. Remove to a baking sheet lined with paper towels to drain. Season each steak lightly with salt as it comes out of the oil. Repeat with the remaining steaks.

Preheat the oven to 375°.

Lightly oil the bottom of a 9-by-13-inch baking dish. Ladle about ¾ cup of tomato sauce onto the bottom of the baking dish. Lay the steaks side by side in the baking dish, fitting them as tightly as you can. Top the steaks with ½ cup tomato sauce, a third of the basil, and ¼ cup grated Parmigiano. Begin again with another layer of steaks, the remaining ¾ cup tomato sauce, and another third of the basil. Top with the shredded mozzarella and the remaining grated Parmigiano.

Cover the dish with foil and bake 25 minutes, until hot and bubbly. Remove the foil and bake for another 10–15 minutes, until the cheese starts to brown.

Remove from the oven and let rest for 5 minutes. Garnish with the rest of the basil and serve immediately with extra grated Parmigiano at the table.

GRILLED STEAKS

I f you're a big game hunter, you should know how to grill steak. First off, it's important to know that wild red meat can cook faster than beef because it's leaner. In order to get consistently juicy and tender steaks, you should try using a meat thermometer until you develop a knack for judging a steak's doneness based on other cues. Here are three of my favorite ways to do wild game steaks. The first is just a simple salt-and-pepper seasoning. The second uses a Cajun-style rub that gives the meat a nice kick. The third is for marinated steaks, which are a bit more time-consuming but totally worth the effort. If you've got a lot of meat in the freezer, it's fun to cook a couple of steaks using each method and then let your friends and family choose their favorite.

SERVES: 4

SALT-AND-PEPPER SEASONING

- 4 sirloin steaks, cut ¾–1 inch thick
- Kosher salt

- Freshly ground black pepper
- Vegetable oil for brushing

CAJUN RUB

- 4 sirloin steaks, cut ¾–1 inch thick
- Kosher salt
- Freshly cracked black pepper

- 1 recipe Cajun Dry Rub (see below)
- Vegetable oil for brushing

SPICY ORANGE MARINADE

- 4 sirloin steaks, cut ¾–1 inch thick
- 1 recipe Spicy Orange Steak Marinade
  (see below)

- Vegetable oil for brushing
- Kosher salt
- Freshly ground black pepper

CAJUN DRY RUB

Mix in a small bowl 5 tablespoons paprika, 1 tablespoon garlic powder, 1 tablespoon onion powder, 1 tablespoon kosher salt, 2 tablespoons freshly ground black pepper, 2 teaspoons cayenne pepper, and 1 teaspoon red pepper flakes.

SPICY ORANGE STEAK MARINADE

Combine in a blender 1 teaspoon orange zest, ½ cup orange juice, 4 tablespoons olive oil, 6 cloves garlic, 2 tablespoons red pepper flakes, 2 tablespoons fresh oregano leaves (or 1 teaspoon dried oregano), 2 teaspoons kosher salt, and 2 teaspoons freshly ground black pepper. Blend until smooth.

Prepare your grill. Bring the steaks to room temperature.

SALT-AND-PEPPER PREPARATION

Season the steaks liberally on both sides with salt and pepper.

CAJUN RUB PREPARATION

Season the steaks with salt and pepper. Rub the steaks liberally with the Cajun Dry Rub. You can let them sit in the fridge up to an hour like this or cook them right away.

MARINADE PREPARATION

Place the steaks in a baking dish or a resealable bag. Add the marinade. Marinate in the refrigerator for at least 1 hour and up to 12 hours. Remove the steaks from the marinade, letting the excess drip off. Season the steaks lightly with salt and pepper.

TO GRILL

With a basting brush, brush both sides of the steaks lightly with the vegetable oil and then place the steaks on the grill. As with all grilling, let the grill do the work. Don't move the steaks at all until they release easily from the grill, about 4 minutes. Flip the steaks and grill on the second side for 3–4 minutes. Use an instant-read thermometer to tell you when they're done: insert the thermometer horizontally into the steaks from the shorter side. Remove the steaks from the grill at 125° for medium rare and 130 for medium. Set aside to rest for 10 minutes before serving.

GRILLED WHOLE LOIN

f you like carpaccio, then you'll love this dish. It's one of my favorite ways to cook up a whole loin. I grill it, keeping it very rare, then let it rest for a while before slicing it super thin. Before serving, I drizzle the slices with olive oil, lemon juice, and sea salt. Or better yet, I make up a batch of gremolata using lemon zest, parsley, and garlic. Especially good with elk loin, this dish is a refreshing crowd pleaser.

- 2- to 3-pound section of loin, cleaned and trimmed, silver skin removed
- Kosher salt
- Freshly ground black pepper
- Vegetable oil
- Gremolata (optional; recipe below)
- Extra-virgin olive oil
- 1 lemon, cut into wedges
- Sea salt

GREMOLATA

This is a great combination of ingredients to put on just about anything. Classically used as a garnish on Osso Buco (page 338), you can put it on fries, grilled steaks, or thin slices of grilled whole loin. Grate the zest of 2 lemons and 2 peeled cloves of garlic on a Microplane. Combine in a bowl with ⅓ cup finely chopped flat-leaf parsley. Add 2 teaspoons sea salt and freshly ground black pepper and toss together.

Prepare the grill for indirect heat.

Season the meat liberally with salt and pepper. Brush the meat lightly with vegetable oil. Let any excess oil drip off. Put the meat on the hot side of the grill and sear on all sides. Rotate the loin while you sear, turning it only when it releases easily from the grill—let the grill do the work. Close the lid in between turns to keep the grill hot while you're cooking. Once the entire loin has been seared and the color shifts to a deep mahogany brown, check the internal temperature of the meat. You'll want to pull it off the grill really rare, about 117° (125° for medium rare). If it's still not there, move the loin to the indirect-heat side of the grill for 6–8 minutes, depending on the heat of your grill. Then check the temperature again.

Let the meat rest for about 20 minutes. Slice the meat as thinly as possible. Lay the meat slices out on a plate, top with the gremolata (if using), drizzle with extra-virgin olive oil, and squeeze the lemon wedges over the meat. Season with sea salt and pepper. Serve at room temperature.

SWEET AND SPICY JERKY

I t'd be interesting to know how many pounds of game meat get turned into jerky every year in the United States. It has to be an astounding number. After all, there's nothing better than chewing on last year's deer while you hunt for this year's. While there's certainly no shortage of great preblended jerky-making kits on the market, it is fun and rewarding to make your own. This is a favorite recipe of mine, developed by the folks at Weston Products. It has a much more complex flavor profile than any jerky blend you can find at a sporting goods store. When slicing the meat, take the time to do it right. If your slices are of uniform thickness, they'll finish drying at the same time and you won't have to hover over the dehydrator while you remove individual pieces as they get done.

- 1 cup soy sauce

- ¼ cup orange juice

- Zest of 1 orange

- 1½ tablespoons honey

- 3 cloves garlic, finely minced

- 2 shallots, finely minced

- 1 jalapeño, finely minced

- 1 tablespoon brown sugar

- 1 tablespoon freshly ground black pepper

- 1 tablespoon red pepper flakes

- 1 tablespoon ground ginger

- 1 teaspoon onion powder

- 1 teaspoon cumin

- 1 teaspoon cayenne

- ½ teaspoon ground cloves

- 2 pounds lean meat from horned or antlered game (deer, elk, caribou, moose, etc.), sliced into ⅜-inch strips (freezing the meat for a couple of hours makes the slicing easier and helps to get slices of even thickness)

A NOTE ON DRYING JERKY IN YOUR OVEN

I like to use a dehydrator—it's the most efficient way to control the heat and rate at which the jerky dries out. But if you don't have one, you can use an oven set at very low heat—say about 170°. Crack the door of the oven, and let it go for several hours at least. (It usually takes somewhere between 4 and 7 hours.) Watch it carefully throughout the process—you want it to cook evenly and not get overdone.

Combine all of the ingredients except for the meat in a medium bowl. Whisk to combine well. Add the strips of game meat to the marinade, being sure to cover it all completely. Marinate in the refrigerator at least 12 hours and up to 48 hours; the longer it's in the marinade, the better.

Remove the meat from the marinade and drain. Pat it dry. Lay out the meat on dehydrator trays, with space between the slices. Set the dehydrator to 145°–155° and dry the jerky for 1½–2½ hours or until completely dry. (Dehydrators may vary.) You want the meat to still have some flexibility. The pieces shouldn't crack in two when you bend them; rather, they should break to reveal a network of thin white lines.

FRESH SAUSAGE (THREE STYLES)

ausage making is my favorite category of wild game cookery, as it turns low-grade cuts of meat into high-grade food. My favorite sausages are fresh—meaning not cured or dried—and stuffed into hog middle casings. I like to view fresh sausages as a sort of blank slate, since you can flavor them in so many different ways. This recipe makes a basic sausage mixture to which you can add whatever flavorings you like. I've got three styles here: a classic Italian sausage, a bratwurst-style sausage, and one that uses Vietnamese-inspired ingredients for a slightly more original taste.

For all of these sausages I use a mixture of 80 percent lean game meat and 20 percent pork fatback. This makes a sausage that is lean without being dry. Some guys use up to 40 percent fat, but that's excessive and entirely unnecessary. Other guys go leaner, but then you risk having a strangely textured and dry sausage that doesn't hold together well. For the following sausages, I prefer natural hog casings with diameters between 32 and 35 millimeters.

BASIC MEAT MIXTURE

- 8 pounds lean game meat (deer, elk, caribou, etc.), cut into 1-inch cubes
- 2 pounds pork fatback, cut into ½-inch cubes

ITALIAN SEASONING

- 4 tablespoons fennel seeds
- 3 tablespoons kosher salt
- 3 tablespoons minced garlic
- ½–1½ cups iced red wine
- ¼ cup plus 2 tablespoons finely chopped flat-leaf parsley
- 1 heaping tablespoon freshly ground black pepper
- 3–4 tablespoons red pepper flakes (optional; makes a spicy sausage)

BRATWURST SEASONING

- 2 tablespoons ground white pepper
- 3 tablespoons kosher salt
- 1 tablespoon ground ginger
- 1 tablespoon freshly grated nutmeg
- ½–1½ cups ice water
- 2 teaspoons ground cloves

VIETNAMESE-STYLE SEASONING

- ½ cup grated fresh ginger
- ½ cup lime juice
- 6 tablespoons fish sauce
- 1 medium carrot, finely grated
- 4 serrano peppers or other hot fresh chiles, minced (about 3 tablespoons)
- 5 tablespoons minced garlic
- 2 tablespoons sugar
- 2 teaspoons kosher salt
- ½–1½ cups ice water
- 1 cup finely chopped fresh cilantro (add after grinding)
- ½ cup finely chopped basil or mint (add after grinding)
- ½ bunch scallions, thinly sliced (add after grinding)

When I make sausage or grind meat, I work out of the freezer in order to make sure that everything is super cold. Another option is to work out of a cooler filled with ice. The meat is easier to work with when it's on the verge of freezing, and it's much safer. If your meat is so cold that your hands get an arthritic ache when mixing it, you're doing it right.

1. Combine the meat and fat from the basic recipe. Then add whichever style seasoning you choose to the cubed meat mixture. Toss to combine.

2. With a bowl placed at the output of the grinder, run the combined mixture of meat, fat, and seasonings through a ¼-inch grinder plate.

3. For a coarser sausage, pass the blend through that same plate again. For a finer-grained sausage (recommended for tougher meat) pass the sausage mixture through a ³⁄₁₆-inch grinder plate.

4. If making the Vietnamese-style sausage, add the chopped herbs and scallions and mix well.

5. Remove a golf-ball-sized sample of the mixture and refrigerate the rest. In a hot skillet, cook up the sample to be sure you like the seasoning. Adjust the seasoning of the larger batch as needed. At this point, the sausage mixture can be used (or wrapped and frozen) as bulk sausage. Or you can proceed to stuff the sausages into casings.

STUFFING SAUSAGES

1. Plan on using about 20 feet of 32–35 millimeter natural hog casings for 10 pounds of sausage. Start by soaking the hog casings in lukewarm water, then set them to soak in clean water at room temperature for 20 to 30 minutes. When the casing is pliable and clean, rinse the inside of the casing by fitting an end over the faucet in your

sink and running water through the entire length of the casing.

2. Fill the hopper of your sausage stuffer with meat, and fit the tube with a length of the washed and rinsed casing. Tie the end of the casing in a simple granny knot, so that the knot is tight against the end of the tube of casing.

3. Working slowly, stuff the sausage into the casings. Be careful to avoid overstuffing the casings, and don't allow air to build up inside the casings. When you are finished with a length of casing, tie off the end with a granny knot.

4. Twist the sausage into links measuring 5–6 inches long. There are several ways to do this, but the following is easy and works quite well. For the first sausage, measure the desired length of your link and press with a finger to form a crease. Spin this link about eight times. Then measure ahead another 5–6 inches and press a crease there. Spin this link about eight times. Then move ahead to the next sausage.

5. When done twisting links, cut the center of each twist. Refrigerate or freeze immediately.

TO COOK

Preheat your grill for direct heat on medium-high. (If using charcoal, make a slightly cooler section of the grill so that you can remove the sausages from the heat if they are cooking too quickly.)

Lightly brush the sausages with oil and set them on the grill. Grill them gently, reducing the heat if necessary; high heat will cause the casings to burst. Cook them all the way through, until they reach 150° internally.

Serve immediately with crusty bread and grilled veggies on the side. Invite some friends over; these sausages go great with beer.

SUMMER SAUSAGE

There are three main reasons I love summer sausage. First, it's virtually indestructible. You can bring it along on backpack hunts and camping trips without having to worry about it going bad or getting crushed inside your backpack or cooler. Second, I love it because it's flavored heavily enough to hide the off flavors of rutty old bucks or black bears that have gotten themselves involved with less-than-ideal food sources. Third, I love it because it tastes so damn good. My two brothers and I have experimented with many summer sausage preparations over the years, and this is the best I've come up with. It's based loosely on Michael Ruhlman's method as described in his book *Charcuterie*. I'll pack one of these sausages when I'm on overnight hunts, and I'll eat it on pita bread along with mustard. It's one of the best and simplest sandwiches you'll ever taste on the hunt.

I make this sausage in 10-pound batches, but you could halve the recipe if you wanted to make just 5 pounds. I like to go with a 2-day ferment, so carve out a little extra time if you want your sausages to reach perfection.

- 8 pounds game meat, cut into 1-inch cubes
- 2 pounds pork fatback, cut into ½-inch cubes
- 6 tablespoons kosher salt
- 4 tablespoons dextrose
- 2 teaspoons curing salt (often sold as pink salt #1)
- 1½ tablespoons mustard seeds
- 1 tablespoon dry mustard
- 2 teaspoons garlic powder
- 2 teaspoons freshly ground black pepper
- 2 teaspoons ground ginger
- 1 cup Fermento
- 1 cup water
- Four 2½-by-18-inch collagen casings

While keeping everything ice cold (see methods for fresh sausage), combine the game meat, pork fat, and all of the other ingredients except for the Fermento, water, and casings in a large bowl. Mix to combine with your hands. Work in small batches if you need to, and don't be afraid to throw the meat back in the fridge or freezer, or into a cooler with ice, to get chilled again. Using the ¼-inch plate on your grinder, grind the meat mixture into the bowl set over ice. Change out the grinder plate to the ³⁄₁₆-inch plate and pass the mixture through the grinder again.

Meanwhile, dissolve the Fermento in the water and stir with a spoon. Add to the ground meat mixture and again mix with your hands (or throw the meat mixture in the bowl of a standing mixer and mix on low) until it's all incorporated.

Press a piece of plastic wrap over the surface of the meat, making sure there are no air bubbles. Then wrap the bowl with a second layer of plastic wrap and set it in the fridge for 2 days to ferment.

Make a little test patty and cook it up in a sauté pan to be sure you got the seasonings right. Adjust them if you didn't. Then, using a sausage stuffer, stuff the sausage into the casings. Let the stuffed casings rest in the fridge to dry out for 1–2 hours.

While the stuffed sausages are resting, soak a panful of applewood chips for 20 minutes. Preheat the smoker to 112°–130°.

Set the pan of chips in the smoker. Lay or hang the sausages in the smoker. Smoke for about 60 minutes at this temperature, then raise the temperature to 180°. Smoke until the internal temperature reaches 150°, which will probably take 2–3 hours, depending on your particular smoker and the ambient temperature. Keep refilling the pan of applewood chips as they get low.

When the sausages are done, let them hang at room temperature for 1 hour to cool, then wrap well and refrigerate. They can be frozen for several months.

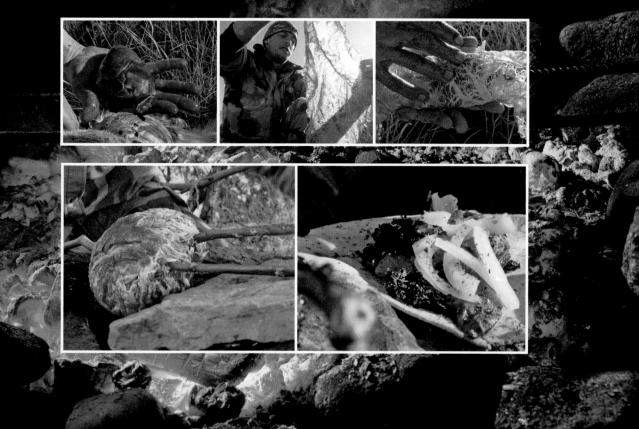

FIELD MENU: FIRE-ROASTED VENISON HEART WRAPPED IN CAUL FAT

GAME BURGERS

I might seem strange to find something as simple as a burger recipe in a cookbook, but in my opinion burgers deserve every sentence that's ever been written about them. They are just that good. In fact, I've probably eaten more pounds of wild game as burgers than any single other preparation. Back in college, when we lived off whitetails, I probably ate my weight in venison burgers every year.

For my general all-purpose ground meat, I go with a ratio of 90 percent lean game meat and 10 percent pork fatback. You can go fancy by putting all kinds of stuff in these burgers, but I never do. I like them prepared in the classic style.

SERVES: 6

- 2 pounds ground meat (90 percent lean game meat and 10 percent pork fat)
- Kosher salt
- Freshly ground black pepper
- Vegetable oil
- Sliced cheddar cheese (optional)
- Kaiser rolls, toasted on the grill
- Lettuce leaves
- Tomato slices

Prepare your grill for direct heat.

Form the ground meat into six patties ¾ to 1 inch thick. Season each patty on the outside with salt and pepper on both sides. Drizzle lightly with oil.

Set the patties on the grill and close the lid. Grill for 4 minutes on the first side; time it. Don't touch the burger once you set it on the grill, or it will fall apart. When you lift the lid, it will release easily. Flip the burger and cook on the second side about 3 minutes more for medium rare, 4–5 minutes for medium, or until it's done to your liking. You can also use a meat thermometer: 120° for rare, 130° for medium, and 140° for well done. Remove the patties from the grill and serve immediately.

If making cheeseburgers, top the patties with cheese after you flip them; the cheese will melt while the bottom cooks.

Serve the patties on toasted kaiser rolls with lettuce and tomato; add mustard and ketchup if you like. And start telling stories about that deer you killed and butchered all by yourself. . . .

MEAT LOAF

A lot of hunters complain that they use up all their roasts and steaks too quickly and then get stuck with a mountain of ground meat. When I hear this, I start singing the praises of meat loaf. Granted, the name of the dish sounds a little folksy and oafish, but you can do some innovative things with meat loaf that make it seem worthy of a higher-minded title. This recipe is based on my standard ground meat mixture of 90 percent lean game meat and 10 percent pork fatback, bound with bread crumbs, oatmeal, egg, and milk and then flavored with an all-star cast of ingredients ranging from pine nuts to provolone. It's fancy, but not overly so. Perfect for almost any occasion.

- 3 tablespoons extra-virgin olive oil, or 2 tablespoons bacon grease
- 1 medium onion, finely chopped
- Kosher salt
- Freshly ground black pepper
- 5 cloves garlic, minced
- 10 ounces baby spinach
- ¼ teaspoon red pepper flakes
- ¼ teaspoon freshly grated nutmeg
- ½ cup fresh bread crumbs (see page 346 to make your own)
- ¼ cup oatmeal
- ¼ cup finely chopped flat-leaf parsley
- 3 tablespoons finely chopped chives
- Leaves from 3 sprigs thyme
- ½ cup milk
- 1½ pounds ground meat (90 percent lean game meat and 10 percent pork fat)
- 2 eggs
- Butter for greasing the pan
- 3 ounces provolone or fontina cheese, cut into sticks about ⅓ inch by ⅓ inch by 3 inches
- 3 tablespoons pine nuts, toasted
- ¼ cup seedy mustard
- 1 teaspoon honey

Preheat oven to 350°.

In a large sauté pan, heat the oil over medium-high heat. Add the onion and cook until browned, about 6 minutes. Season it with 1 teaspoon salt and ¼ teaspoon black pepper. Add the garlic and cook for 1 minute more. Remove half the onion-garlic mixture and set that aside to cool. Then add the spinach and red pepper flakes to the half remaining in the pan and toss with tongs until the spinach is wilted. Stir in the nutmeg. Set aside to cool.

Place the bread crumbs, oatmeal, parsley, chives, and thyme in a small bowl. Pour the milk over the top. Let it sit while you mix the meat.

In a large bowl, combine the ground meat, cooled onion-garlic mixture, and the eggs. Season well with salt and black pepper. Add the soaked bread crumb mixture and combine well. You could use a spoon for mixing, but it's easier to just use your hands.

Once the mixture is combined, lay a 1-inch layer of the meat loaf mixture on the bottom of a 1½ pound or 2-pound loaf pan. Pat it down so it reaches the corners, and allow it to come up the sides a bit. You will fill this cavity with the filling.

Next, lay the cooled spinach mixture over the meat layer, leaving a ½-inch border of meat around the spinach. Top the spinach with the cheese sticks lengthwise in the pan, forming a stripe in the center that runs the length of the pan. Sprinkle the pine nuts over the cheese stripe. Top with the remaining meat mixture and pat down. You want to be sure the top of the meat mixture meets the bottom meat mixture along the sides.

Pat the top of the loaf so it's flat and even. Mix the mustard with the honey, then coat the top of the loaf with this mixture. Bake for 1 hour or until an instant-read thermometer reads 150° when inserted in the center.

FIELD MENU: ROASTED RACK OF DALL SHEEP RIBS

WILD GAME MINCEMEAT PIE WITH BEAR LARD CRUST

My grandparents lived about four hours away when I was a kid, so they were never able to attend Grandparents' Day at our elementary school. Thankfully, my parents were friends with an older couple named Vivian and Barney Kokuma, who faithfully dropped by to play the role. What I remember most about Vivian was that she loved to make mincemeat pies. Her preferred meat was venison neck. My dad would pass a couple of necks along to her every year, and she'd return the favor by bringing over a finished pie. It's actually an ancient preparation dating back to medieval times, though by now it's been forgotten long enough to qualify once again as fresh and exciting. I especially like to make it by using rendered black bear lard in the crust, which makes this dish even more potent as a conversation starter.

- 1 cup cooked neck meat, minced (left over from Neck Roast, page 333, or Blade Roast, page 336)
- 1½ cups chopped tart apples
- ½ cup finely chopped beef or pork fat
- ⅓ cup seedless raisins
- ⅓ cup currants
- ½ cup game stock (or enriched stock; see page 334) or store-bought chicken or vegetable stock
- ¼ cup chopped dried apricots (optional)
- 2 tablespoons apple jelly
- 1 tablespoon blackstrap molasses
- ¾ cup packed light brown sugar

- 1 teaspoon ground cinnamon
- ½ teaspoon ground cloves
- ¼ teaspoon ground ginger
- ¼ teaspoon nutmeg or mace
- ¼ teaspoon allspice
- Kosher salt
- Freshly ground black pepper
- 1 recipe Double-Crust Dough with Bear Fat (see recipe on page 369), or substitute store-bought or homemade pie dough
- 2 tablespoons cider brandy
- Egg wash (1 egg beaten with 1 tablespoon water)

Preheat oven to 375°.

Combine the meat, apples, fat, raisins, currants, stock, apricots, jelly, molasses, brown sugar, and spices in a medium saucepan over low heat. Add salt and pepper to taste. Simmer for 1 hour, stirring often. Remove from the heat and allow to cool.

Meanwhile, take your pie crusts out of the fridge and let them sit until they reach room temperature, 10–30 minutes.

When the mincemeat mixture is cool, stir in the brandy and taste. Adjust the seasoning if necessary. Set aside while you roll out the crust.

Take one disc of dough, unwrap it, and put it on a well-floured cutting board or countertop. Flour your rolling pin and tap the surface of the dough methodically to flatten and soften it a little. Begin to roll out the disc from the center out. The dough should not stick too tightly to the work surface; you should be able to easily lift it away at all times. If the dough does begin to stick, add more flour to the work surface. Roll the dough out to a circle that's about ¼ inch thick and 11–13 inches in diameter. Brush off any extra flour with a pastry brush and transfer the dough to the bottom of a 9-inch pie dish, allowing the dough to hang over the sides. Add the mincemeat filling in an even layer.

Roll out the top crust in the same manner as the bottom. Lay the top crust over the bottom crust and the mincemeat. Press the layers of pie crust together with your fingers. Trim any excess with kitchen shears and crimp as desired. Use a pastry brush to brush the top crust lightly with egg wash. Using a sharp paring knife, make three slits in the center of the pie.

Bake the pie until the crust is golden brown, 40–45 minutes. Allow to cool on a wire rack for 10–15 minutes before serving.

DOUBLE-CRUST DOUGH WITH BEAR FAT

- 4½ cups sifted all-purpose flour
- 2 teaspoons table salt
- 1 teaspoon sugar
- 12 ounces well-chilled bear lard (see note on how to render on page 316), or substitute pork lard
- ½ cup cold milk, or substitute ice water

Add the flour, salt, and sugar to the bowl of a food processor. Close the lid and pulse a few times to mix. Cut the chilled bear lard into small pieces. If it gets warm while you are cutting it, throw it in the freezer for a few minutes and then continue. Open the lid of the processor and distribute the bear lard evenly in the flour. Return the lid to the processor and pulse until the mixture looks pebbly. You want to still see chunks of bear lard in the flour. Pour the cold milk through the chute and pulse until a dough starts to form. Don't overmix.

Turn the dough out onto a floured board and pat the dough together—don't knead. Divide the dough into halves, flatten into discs, and wrap well in plastic wrap. Refrigerate for 1 hour before using.

WILD GAME MEATBALLS

Back in the 1800s, when Swedish immigrants were settling areas of the West and Midwest, they surely had no idea that their Old World meatball recipes would someday become standard appetizer fare at events ranging from art openings to football parties. But there's a perfectly good reason it happened: Swedish meatballs kick ass. It's hard to screw them up, everyone loves them, and you can keep a batch of them on a hot plate for hours on end and they only taste better as time goes by. What's more, it's perfectly acceptable to eat them with toothpicks. What more could a person ask for?

- 1 cup panko or other dry bread crumbs
- 1¼ cups cream, divided
- 1½ pounds ground game meat (80 percent lean meat, 20 percent pork fatback)
- ¼ cup grated onion
- 1 clove garlic, minced
- ¼ teaspoon ground allspice
- ¼ teaspoon ground white pepper
- Kosher salt

- 1 egg, beaten
- 5 tablespoons unsalted butter, divided
- 3 tablespoons flour
- 2 cups beef broth
- 1 bay leaf
- 1 sprig thyme
- Freshly ground black pepper
- Lingonberry jam (or substitute red currant jelly)

TIP: MAKING THIS DISH FOR A PARTY

When making this for a party, stop before adding the final ¼ cup cream to the thickened gravy. I hold everything covered at room temp (no more than 2 hours) until my guests arrive. Then I heat up the sauce, mix in the cream, and continue as described in the recipe.

In a medium bowl, combine the panko and 1 cup cream. Stir and set aside to soak.

In a large bowl, combine the ground meat, onion, garlic, allspice, white pepper, 1½ teaspoons salt, and egg and mix with your hands. Add the soaked bread crumbs along with the soaking liquid if there's any left.

With wet hands, form small meatballs about 1 inch in diameter and lay out on parchment-lined baking sheets.

Heat a large skillet over medium-high heat and melt 2½ tablespoons of the butter. Add the meatballs in batches, being careful not to crowd the pan. Cook, turning occasionally, 8–10 minutes per batch, until browned and cooked through. Remove the cooked meatballs to a plate and cook the remaining meatballs. Set the meatballs aside.

Add the remaining 2½ tablespoons butter to the pan and melt. Add the flour and stir to form a roux. Add the beef broth, bay leaf, and thyme and whisk over medium-high heat until it thickens. Reduce the heat and whisk in the remaining ¼ cup cream. Season with salt and pepper to taste.

Return the meatballs to the pan (do this in batches if you need to) and coat with the sauce. Warm through. Transfer to a serving platter.

Serve with lingonberry jam on the side and toothpicks.

GAME MEAT AND COCOA (YES, COCOA) CHILI

Chili is one of those dishes that's great to reheat in a Dutch oven suspended over a fire pit. Before heading out on a hunt, we used to fill empty milk cartons with the stuff and then staple the tops shut and freeze them. The frozen chili would help keep the contents of our cooler cold. When it was time to eat it, we'd simply peel the carton away from the frozen chili and put the icy block into a pot. Then we'd use the carton to light the fire that would heat the chili. This particular recipe is as inventive and unconventional as our old chili-cooking method. It comes from my friend Chef Matt Weingarten, who's an expert at adapting his restaurant dishes that use wild game for cooks working at home. Whenever I serve this, people say, "Oh my God, that's amazing." I think you'll agree.

- 2 pounds game meat (from the shoulder or leg), cut into ¾-inch cubes
- Kosher salt
- Freshly ground black pepper
- 4 dried ancho chile peppers (or 2 tablespoons ancho chile powder)
- 3 tablespoons vegetable oil
- 2 medium onions, cut into ¼-inch dice
- 10 cloves garlic, minced
- 1 jalapeño, minced
- ¼ cup unsweetened cocoa powder
- 2 tablespoons sugar
- 1 tablespoon ground cinnamon
- 1½ tablespoons ground cumin
- ½ teaspoon ground allspice
- 1 teaspoon ground juniper berry
- 1 teaspoon ground coriander
- 2 cans (15 oz each) chopped tomatoes
- 2 chipotle chiles in adobo, minced
- 1 quart game stock (or enriched stock; see page 334)
- 1 bunch cilantro
- 4 sprigs fresh oregano
- 4 cans (15 oz each) kidney beans, drained and rinsed
- Hot sauce, chopped scallions, grated cheese, cilantro sprigs, and sour cream for serving

Season the meat with salt and pepper. Set aside and allow to come to room temperature.

Toast the whole ancho chiles. (If using chile powder, skip this step and incorporate the chile powder when you add the other spices.) In a 6- to 8-quart heavy-bottomed stock pot, heat the whole ancho chiles over medium-high heat, turning occasionally, until they become very aromatic and dark brown all over. Remove to a bowl. When cool, remove the stems and finely chop the chiles, seeds and all. Set aside.

Add the oil to the pot. When it shimmers, sear the game meat in batches, never crowding the pot, until browned on all sides. Remove the meat to a plate.

Reduce the heat to medium-low and add the onions, garlic, and jalapeño. Cook until tender, about 5 minutes. Add the chopped anchos to the pot along with the cocoa powder, sugar, and spices. Stir to incorporate.

Add the meat back to the pot, along with any juices that may have collected on the plate. Stir to incorporate and cook for 5 minutes. Add the tomatoes, chipotles, and a splash of game stock. Using a wooden spoon, scrape up any brown bits that may be stuck to the bottom of the pan. Add the remaining game stock plus 1 cup water (or as much as needed to cover the meat). Raise the heat and bring to a boil.

Reduce the heat to low. Skim off and discard any scum that has accumulated on the surface of the chili. Tie the cilantro and oregano sprigs into a bundle with butcher's twine and add the herb bundle to the pot. Partially cover the pot and simmer for 2½ hours on low heat or until the meat is tender and the sauce is thick.

About 30 minutes before the chili is done, add the kidney beans and heat through.

When the meat is tender (it won't spring back when crushed on a spoon with a fork), remove the herb bundle. Adjust the seasoning with salt and freshly ground pepper as needed. I like to add a huge dash of hot sauce at the end.

Serve around the fire pit with chopped scallions, grated cheese, more cilantro, and sour cream.

FIELD MENU: JAVELINA MEAT COOKED IN STOMACH

BIG SKY ROASTED HEAD

This recipe was inspired by the classic western novel *The Big Sky*, by A. B. Guthrie. It calls for a skinned-out deer's head to be buried beneath the coals of a fire, which is fun, rugged, and surprisingly effective. The meat comes off the bone easily, and it's super succulent. You can eat it with nothing but salt, but it's even better when you use it to build a taco. I like mine made with corn tortillas, crumbled cheese, green salsa, cilantro, and scallions. It makes a perfect hunter's snack, and your friends will never forget it.

- 1 deer head, skinned out
- Kosher salt
- Freshly ground black pepper
- For serving: small corn tortillas,

crumbled queso fresco or fresh goat cheese, green salsa, thinly sliced scallions, cilantro sprigs, and lime wedges

Build a big fire and let it burn vigorously for a good 45–60 minutes in order to build up a strong bed of coals. Really let it rip. You can use about any wood, but a dense hardwood will produce hotter, longer-lasting coals. An ideal choice would be mesquite, but oak is also great. While the fire is burning, you can prep your head.

Salt and pepper the head heavily and triple- or quadruple-wrap it in foil. Take a burlap or game bag and soak it in a creek or with a hose until it's fully saturated with water. Wrap your foil-covered head tightly in the wet burlap or game bag to make a neat package.

When a good crop of coals has collected, use a spade to scrape out a trench in the center of your fire, deep enough and large enough around for your venison head. Put about a gallon of coals in the hole. Cover it with 3 inches of dirt. Then set the head in the trench. Cover the head with another 3 inches of dirt and build the fire back on top of the head. Cooking time may vary from fire to fire, but in general 3–4 hours is a pretty good amount of time to let it cook.

Pull the roasted head out with the spade and put it on a stone to cool down. If you're concerned, insert an instant-read thermometer through the foil into the flesh in the head (aiming for the brain is a good idea). It should be at least 160°; 170°–180° is ideal. Unwrap the burlap and the foil. Don't remove the meat from the head until it has rested 10–20 minutes.

Meanwhile, wrap the corn tortillas in foil and warm on the dying embers.

Begin shredding the meat. There's all kinds of good stuff on the head, particularly the tongue and the jowl meat, which tastes a bit like pulled pork. And it's easy to remove with a knife and fork. Season the meat with salt and pepper and a squeeze of lime juice. And then get your fixings ready.

Assemble the tacos, crack open some beers, and check out the stars. You've earned it.

BONE-IN BBQ RIBS

've been troubled by the subject of wild game ribs my whole life. Boning them out for burgers takes a lot of work and yields only a small amount of meat, yet cooking them whole often results in dishes that are unchewably tough. But then this recipe came along and solved my rib problems once and for all. The rib meat is cooked on the bone, and it turns out as tender and flavorful as the finest pork ribs. It's turned what used to be a problematic cut of meat into one of my all-time favorite wild game preparations. Once you try it, you might never again bone out a rib cage.

SERVES: 2–4

DRY RUB

- 1½ tablespoons sweet paprika
- 1½ tablespoons smoked paprika
- 4 teaspoons kosher salt
- 2 teaspoons coarsely ground black pepper
- 2 teaspoons red pepper flakes
- 2 teaspoons dark brown sugar
- 1 teaspoon garlic powder
- 1 teaspoon onion powder
- 1 teaspoon dried oregano
- 1 teaspoon ground cumin
- ½ teaspoon celery seed (optional)
- 3½ pounds big game ribs (two full racks, each rack split in half lengthwise down the middle and cut into portions of 2–3 ribs)

MOP

- 1 cup cider vinegar
- ¼ cup yellow mustard
- 1 teaspoon kosher salt

In a small bowl combine all of the dry rub ingredients. (You can double or quadruple this mixture and keep it on hand for any worthy occasion.) Rub the ribs all over with the dry rub.

Pop the ribs into a pressure cooker. Add water to cover and cook for 20 minutes with 10 pounds of pressure. (If you don't have a pressure cooker, I'm afraid this takes a bit longer. You'll have to braise them on the stove for at least 2 hours, though it may take longer.)

Preheat your grill on high.

In a small bowl, combine all the mop ingredients with a whisk. (Again, this can be doubled or quadrupled as needed and used for anything you feel like mopping that goes on a grill.)

When the ribs are done, remove them from the pressure cooker. Set the ribs over direct heat on the grill to caramelize them and get some char. Close the lid to keep the heat high. As they get closer to done, mop liberally with the cider vinegar mop.

Remove from the grill when the sauce is adhering nicely and they have the perfect amount of char. Serve with pickles and raw onions.

FIELD MENU: MOOSE STEAKS TOPPED WITH BONE MARROW

ACKNOWLEDGMENTS

Many biologists and big game hunters gave freely of their knowledge in order to make this book as good as could be. It's impossible to list them all, but special thanks to Robert Abernethy, Ed Arnett, Chad Baart, Mark Boardman, Ronny Boehme, Arnis Burvikovs, Ryan Callaghan, Bill Carman, Darr Colburn, Chris Denham, Doug Duren, Chris Eberhart, Jerod Fink, Rick French, Joseph Furia, Floyd Green, Martins Grendze, Brody Henderson, Scott Justice, Ethan Kohn, Cody Lujan, James Miller, Paul Neess, Cody Nelson, Janis Putelis, Jr., Martins Putelis, Steve Reid, Danny Rinella, Matt Rinella, Gabe Runyon, Jay Scott, Janis Staks, Peteris Staks, Sam Terrell, Tom Toman, and Remi Warren.

At some point or another, at least a dozen or so of my colleagues from Zero Point Zero Production were engaged in the creation of this book. Thanks to Dan Doty for his contributions on camping and wilderness safety, as well as his work in outlining, organizing, writing, and overseeing graphics production. Thanks to Jared Andrukanis for general oversight; Helen Cho for cheering us on and spreading the word; Chris Collins, Lydia Tenaglia, and Lou Festa for finding good people and giving them a great place to work; and Joe Caterini for making all of this possible in the first place. Huge thanks also to stylist/producer Krista Ruane and her crew, Ericka Martins and Ashley Berman, for bringing the recipes to life and making them look so beautiful.

And thanks to Sportsman Channel for the support and continued partnership.

Thanks to Marc Gerald, at The Agency

Group, for helping to shape the concept of this book and then explain it to the right people. Thanks to Cindy Spiegel and everyone at Spiegel & Grau and Random House, including Annie Chagnot, Carole Lowenstein, Benjamin Dreyer, Tom Perry, and Christopher Zucker.

Finally, I'd like to acknowledge the work of Peter Sucheski, John Hafner, Brittany Brothers, and Janis Putelis. Peter's illustrations can be found throughout this book. Thanks to him for enduring endless requests for revisions as we tried to make everything look just right. Thanks to John Hafner for the splendid food photography and also for generously opening up his archives of wildlife photography for our use. Brittany Brothers took on the role of archivist and photo editor throughout this project. Not only did she apply her technical expertise to the use of imagery, she brought to the project a consistent and refreshing sense of style and taste. And to Janis Putelis, who worked on all aspects of this project from start to finish, including research, writing, and photography. There's hardly a page within this book that has not benefitted from his touch as both a hunter and writer.

INDEX

Page numbers in italics refer to illustrations.